CINDERELLA

INSIDE THE RISE OF MID-MAJOR COLLEGE BASKETBALL

MICHAEL LITOS

SOURCEBOOKS, INC.
NAPERVILLE, ILLINOIS

Published by Sourcebooks, Inc.
P.O. Box 4410, Naperville, Illinois 60567-4410
(630) 961-3900
Fax: (630) 961-2168
www.sourcebooks.com

Printed and bound in the United States of America.
BVG 10 9 8 7 6 5 4 3 2 1

To George and Jenny Litos, my teachers. I've always said that if more parents were like them, the world would be a better place; and to Kathleen, whose beauty inspires me every day. My life is wonderful because of you.

CONTENTS

Foreword

by Jay Bilas

In my judgment, there is no better or more compelling game than college basketball. While I believe it to be the best and most exciting game, complete with buzzer-beating jumpers and colorful personalities, it is also the best administered. The NCAA postseason tournament provides the most compelling, gripping month of the year in sports, and every college basketball team in the country has a fair shot to make noise in the "win or go home" format. It's called "March Madness" for a reason. Unlike college football, college basketball is not ruled by polls and computers, and has the fairest manner to determine a champion. Amazingly, it usually does so in dramatic fashion.

This past season, the incredible run to the Final Four by George Mason was perhaps the biggest story in NCAA Tournament history. It also demonstrated that you don't have to have the best facilities, television package, or team to do well in the NCAA Tournament. However, George Mason's improbable journey to the Final Four did not mean that there has been a sea change in college basketball. While it may be more probable for a team like George Mason to break through, it is still extraordinarily difficult. Remember, one could make a credible argument that a few major conference schools had better resumes than George Mason, and should have received a bid into the field of sixty-five before the Patriots. That is how fine the line has become in college basketball.

That said, there is an unmistakable divide in the world of college basketball; while there has always been a gap between the two distinct groups in the game, over the last thirty years that divide seems to have widened. The popular terms being used today are "majors" (the "haves") and the "mid-majors" (the "have nots"). The topic is widely debated and discussed, gaining momentum each spring as the college basketball season nears the tournament.

Though the term *mid major* is used extensively, I know of no proper definition for the widely accepted and ubiquitous moniker. Unfortunately, some coaches and administrators bristle when the term mid-major is used in reference to their program, as if it is meant to be damaging or demeaning, or implying they are operating a minor league franchise. Nothing could be further from the truth. If postseason play has shown anything, it is that mid-majors can compete on the court.

When I'm asked to define a mid major, I adopt the same view taken by the United States Supreme Court with regard to defining obscenity: I can't define a mid major, but I know one when I see one. Being a mid major has nothing to do with whether a team, player, or coach is capable. It has only to do with one thing: money. mid majors do not have the same resources at hand as their major brethren.

Basketball is a game of resources. The programs that have the most resources consistently field the most competitive programs. Significant basketball resources include more than just a larger alumni base contributing more dollars to the university. A program's facilities, fan support/attendance, a quality league of competitive partners, and most importantly, television exposure are important and related factors. Many of the majors have all of those resources, and they are thus much tougher competition. There is no salary cap or revenue sharing in college basketball, which provides for a greater disparity in resources than almost any other game.

This disadvantage makes it more difficult to recruit, to retain coaches, to get exposure, and to schedule quality opponents. Still, the coaches, players, and administrations seem to have the same expectations. Without reasonable debate, mid-majors simply have it much tougher, especially in the following four areas.

1. Recruiting: Some coaches can lose with talent, but no coach can win without it. Mid-majors have to canvass a larger landscape than the majors, and they cannot afford to be as selective. If a mid major finds a "diamond in the rough" and recruits that kid harder and earlier than everyone else, the kid will almost always still bolt to a major when his talent surfaces for all to see, leaving the mid major in the dust. A mid-major coach can do everything right and in the end lose a recruit, at the last minute, to a BCS conference coach with a suddenly-available scholarship. In many cases, mid-majors have to stay with kids that think they are major talents and wait until the realization hits the kid that he will not realistically get a major scholarship. In today's game, however, it has become even more difficult for the mid-majors to "outwork" the majors in recruiting because of all the rules intended to "level the playing field." The rules set forth by the NCAA, designed to limit recruiting and the access a coach can have to a player, give an advantage to the majors right out of the gate.

2. Retaining Coaches: mid-majors have a very difficult time in retaining successful coaches. A coach that reaches the NCAA Tournament from a mid-major conference is not unlike anyone else looking to further their career. The opportunity for more money, more stability, more resources, and a better chance to compete at the highest level usually presents itself, and the coach usually takes it. You cannot blame him for this. Because success in basketball is the quickest and least expensive road to increasing the profile of an institution, expectations are high for many mid-major basketball programs. Success breeds unreasonable expectations from administrators and fans, and many coaches feel that it is better to trade upon that success quickly by taking a higher profile and higher paying job.

3. Television Exposure: In my judgment, television exposure, not whether a team can really play, is the most significant difference between the majors and the mid-majors. Television exposure affects everything from scheduling, to recruiting, to perceptions of accomplishment. Television equals money, and money equals power in the college game. Mid-majors rarely get on national television, and they

cobble together the best regional and local deals they can muster. The issue for mid-majors is that television is about ratings, and the public wants to see recognized, traditional powers play against each other. Television wants to deliver that to the public in order to get the highest rating. Competitive balance and equal opportunity mean little and have little to do with the matchups you see on television every week. While regular season games in the Mid-American Conference, the Colonial Athletic Association, or West Coast Conference can be just as compelling, well-played, and hard-fought as regular season games in the ACC, Big East, or Big 10, the smaller conference games are relegated to local television at best, or off of television altogether. Because it is harder to get on television, it is harder to recruit the top players out of high school. Players go where the exposure is.

4. Scheduling: There are precious few opportunities for the little guy to get a fair fight against a major, unless it is in an early season exempt tournament or in the NCAA Tournament. Of course, that plays right into the hands of the majors and makes them even more powerful. Few majors will schedule an away or neutral game against a mid major that is capable of winning. Syracuse provides the perfect example from the 2004-2005 season. The Orange participated in the Coaches versus Cancer Classic, where Northern Colorado and Princeton were given the opportunity, in the Carrier Dome, to play the fifth-ranked team in the country. After defeating Memphis and winning that tournament, the Orange played ten nonconference games. Nine were at home, and the lone road game was at Siena, a fellow New York school.

Since the home team wins in college basketball close to 70 percent of the time, where you play a game is very important. Recent alterations in the way the RPI is calculated provides a stronger incentive to go on the road and win, which is a start. Inclusion into the NCAA Tournament field is dependent upon who you play and who you beat. Therefore, if you cannot get a winnable game against the big shots, you have very little chance of being invited to the NCAA Tournament as an at-large team.

The cry of the mid-majors goes something like this:

MM School: "How can we compete for a spot in the NCAA Tournament when nobody will play us? If we beat the big shots, they won't play us anymore, and we will not be able to get on television. Without television, we cannot recruit, we cannot retain coaches, and we cannot generate revenue. Our conference games are real battles, but we get punished when we lose, while the majors just suffered a 'tough loss.' How is that fair?"

Fans, Administrators, and Media: "Well, just go out on the road and play the majors on their home courts!"

MM School: "It isn't that simple. We have to have some home games, too, you know! We have to make some money off of ticket sales, and our kids have to be in town to go to school, so how can we trot around the country taking on all comers? Plus, the coach has to find some wins to keep his job, so going into the lion's den game after game is counterproductive. It is really tough being a mid major."

The plain and simple fact is that the system that governs college basketball, while designed to be as fair as possible, cannot produce a level playing field for all of the different programs on the college basketball landscape. Yet a level playing field is yearned for by some observers of college basketball, as if all of these differing institutions should be the same on the field of play. That is unrealistic. There is no reasonable person who would suggest that Eastern Kentucky University should be expected to compete favorably on a "level playing field" against the University of Kentucky with regard to admissions or medical research, yet some believe that the field should be leveled so that EKU can compete favorably over time with Kentucky on the hardwood. Eastern Kentucky may be able to beat Kentucky on a neutral floor, but such a win would be an upset of near epic proportions. It is the exception, rather than the rule.

The system in place makes it much tougher to be a mid major, but the system is not unfair. We may be able to do some things to make it more fair, but there is no way to level the playing field to accommodate every single program that has chosen to play Division I basketball.

Interestingly, the playing field may be leveling itself somewhat, albeit slightly, due to the influence and effect that the NBA has had upon the college game. Because of the lure of the NBA, many of the top college and high school prospects have left school early to turn pro. That has disproportionately affected the majors. As a result, the mid-majors have benefited by having older, more experienced teams playing against the younger, less experienced talent of the majors. Several mid-majors have been more competitive over the last few years, but the public only seems to notice how good some mid-majors are by way of the NCAA Tournament, where the games are played on a neutral court with neutral officials. During the regular season, when the mid-majors are essentially in a national television blackout, the public cannot gain an appreciation for just how good some of these teams are because they are watching the majors play over and over again. As a result of the NBA, we are seeing more mid-majors compete favorably with the majors in the NCAA Tournament.

I've spent a lot of time around mid-major programs over the last fifteen years, and I know how accomplished, dedicated, and hardworking these players and coaches are. I understand that they fight just as hard on the floor to win as the majors, yet have a much slimmer margin for error. A major from a big-time conference can afford to lose conference games and bow out in the early stages of its conference tournament. A team like Davidson in 2005 can go undefeated in the Southern Conference, yet lose in the semifinal of its conference tournament, and go to the NIT instead of the NCAA Tournament. Mid-major basketball today is much like the college game was thirty years ago...if you don't win your conference tournament, you stay home. Now THAT is pressure.

I've heard some say that an expansion of the NCAA Tournament field would be an appropriate solution to level the playing field. I do not agree. While there will always be heartbreaking stories of teams that fail to qualify for the NCAA Tournament, which has now become the Holy Grail of college basketball, we are always talking about, at best, the thirty-fourth, thirty-fifth, and thirty-sixth best teams in the country. Any line drawn between those teams is remarkably thin and, quite frankly, only a matter pf perspective. You can make arguments for and against any of the clump of teams that sit atop "the bubble" come tournament selection time.

What it comes down to is that everyone knows the rules going in, and every team in America has the same shot at its league's automatic bid. Every league in the country can determine on its own how to award that automatic bid, whether to the regular season champion or a postseason tournament champion. Most leagues choose to stage a tournament. The common factor for a team wanting to make the tournament is simple: Win the games you're supposed to win. This also solves another argument I frequently read that I also disagree with: requiring an at-large team to have at least a .500 conference record. With talent spread out across more than 300 Division 1A teams, who can draw a real difference between, say, an 8-10 Georgia Tech team and a 10-8 Iowa team? Allowing teams to play their way into the tournament is as fair as it can get.

The main issue that needs to be recognized and acted upon is that mid-majors can absolutely compete on the floor. They need to be provided with more opportunities to play against the majors.

As I mentioned, there have been recent changes in the RPI computations to reward road victories more heavily, adding incentive to play away from home. This may help mid-majors, but still does not provide incentives to majors to travel. For example, last December CAA member UNC Wilmington traveled up the road to face eventual national champion North Carolina in Chapel Hill. UNCW would go on to finish tied for second in the CAA, so they were a good team that had the ability to test the Tar Heels. A loss for North Carolina, no matter where the game was played, would only negatively affect the Heels by perception. It would be considered a "bad loss" by most, even though UNCW is a quality team.

Conventional wisdom says that the Tar Heels "should" win the game at home. Conversely, if it were played in Wilmington at Trask

Coliseum, the game sells out and the frenzied crowd will only add to an already decided home court advantage. Plus, the game likely doesn't make national television, so just the score and perhaps a couple of highlights would be seen by the masses. North Carolina is essentially in a no-win situation. Because of that, most coaches would rather not play the game at all—no credit for a win; beat up by fans and media for a loss.

Perhaps the answer lies within adding incentives for majors to play mid-majors on the road or on neutral courts, without punishing the major for a loss. Maybe it's allowing the majors to add a couple of games to their schedules as long as those games are against mid-major teams. Whatever the case, there are ways to provide more occasions for the mid-majors to prove they can play and this, in my estimation, is how the landscape can best be leveled. Opportunity is all that any team or coach can ask. The NCAA Tournament provides that opportunity, but it is difficult to get there for any team, let alone a mid major.

The mid-majors are not any better now than they were twenty years ago. Teams of that level have always been able to play, and have always had good players. The difference now is that the majors are more subject to cycles. Star players leaving early for the NBA have made things much tougher for major schools to maintain continuity, and it is much more difficult now than in past years. Mid-major basketball has always been cyclical. There are always capable teams, but not always the same teams from year to year. Now, the major schools are finding out exactly how things have been for the mid-majors all these years. Let them play.

George Mason has made the Final Four seem like a more attainable goal for every mid major. The truth is, however, that parity is still the basketball equivalent of Mt. Everest, and people still need to be realistic. The best way to make sure that the mid-majors get treated fairly in the NCAA Tournament selection process is to ensure that the system provides as many opportunities as possible for mid-majors to play quality games. There will never be a level playing field, but with more opportunity to play, it will be easier to evaluate which teams really can play.

PROLOGUE

Thus in the beginning the world was so made that certain signs come before certain events. –Cicero

By now you know what happened. The George Mason Patriots of the Colonial Athletic Association redefined the way in which sports fans, particularly college basketball fans, view mid-major college basketball. After season upon season using the Cinderella metaphor for a win or two by a small-conference school in the NCAA basketball tournament, CBS and the NCAA found a school—and a conference—on which the glass slipper truly fit.

George Mason, a controversial choice to even make the field and the first CAA at-large participant since 1986, defeated Michigan State, defending champion North Carolina, Wichita State, and #1 seed Connecticut to reach college basketball's summit, the Final Four. Along the way the Patriots found themselves media darlings, making the cover of *Sports Illustrated* and breaking office pool brackets. Throughout March Madness they were *the* story.

But the story is so much more than four improbable victories and three weeks. Old Dominion would play in New York in the NIT semifinals. Hofstra, led by its personable and quotable head coach, burst onto the national scene. The 2005-2006 college basketball season would alter the course of mid-major college basketball. It was defined by this school and this conference.

"We were the only league who had a team in the semifinals of the pre-season NIT, post season NIT, and NCAA," said Tom Yeager, commissioner of the CAA. "It's significant because the next close call in a similar situation, it's now known [that a mid major] is every bit as good."

Standing in the lobby of the Westin Hotel in Indianapolis, Tom O'Connor, director of athletics at George Mason, worked the crowd. Fans and alumni from the Fairfax school had traveled a long way, and he wanted to make sure they knew he appreciated the effort.

It had been an exhausting three weeks for O'Connor. He survived the aftermath of one of his players punching a rival in a CAA tournament semifinal loss, agreeing with his coach's decision to suspend that player. He had weathered the controversy of his team being selected for an at-large berth because, in the eyes of conspiracy theorists, he was on the NCAA selection committee. O'Connor traveled where he was needed and he conducted every requested interview. He was clearly running on fumes.

I had been alongside O'Connor for much of the ride, and after yet another round of handshakes I asked him bluntly if he was having any fun.

"A little," he said, giving me a smile and nod that said it all: his team, from the league Billy Packer said should not have been in the tournament in the first place, would challenge the Florida Gators in twenty-four hours for the right to play for the national championship.

Looking back, the magic for George Mason and the CAA may have begun on Saturday, February 18, 2006, when CAA commissioner Tom Yeager's bags did not arrive in Wichita for George Mason's game against the Wichita State Shockers in ESPNs Bracket Busters matchup.

Yeager had been attending NCAA meetings in San Antonio, and heavy storms wreaked havoc with flight schedules. So, while it wasn't surprising that Yeager had arrived at the Hilton hotel ahead of his luggage, there was still the issue of his wardrobe.

Yeager had made himself comfortable on the flight by wearing a pair of clog-like shoes, carrying his jacket, and opting out of a tie. As you can imagine, the commissioner of a conference cannot attend important basketball games on national television in such casual dress. Most of the national media were dubbing this game an at-large bid qualifier—the team that won would likely lock up an at-large bid to the NCAA tournament should it lose in its conference tournament. The loser was likely on the outside looking in, given the same scenario.

Yeager was stuck. His only option for a tie was displayed in the hotel lobby gift shop—not exactly renowned for sartorial splendor. Running late, Yeager purchased the best quick option—a truly hideous burnt orange number, with slanting tan and green stripes, exactly the kind of tie you'd expect to find in a hotel gift shop—or a yard sale.

Three hours later George Mason senior guard Tony Skinn would hit a three-pointer with twelve seconds to play to give the Patriots the key road victory that day. Yeager jokingly told Mason coach Jim Larranaga that surely his lucky tie had something to do with it.

As further evidence, that same February day Michigan, a bubble team, was losing to Michigan State. Colorado, another bubble team, was losing to 110+ RPI Kansas State. The legend began to grow.

By the time George Mason had rallied from a 16-2 deficit against defending champion North Carolina—after dominating Final Four participant Michigan State—the lucky tie had morphed into the Magic Tie, and Larranaga's players began rubbing it prior to games. The tie faithfully remained around Yeager's neck through the Washington, D.C., regional finals, where Mason defeated Wichita State (again) and Connecticut.

It went with him all the way to Indianapolis.

———

As teams advance in the NCAA tournament, every game becomes bigger and bigger, and not in the basketball sense. The event becomes more of a television show and less of a basketball contest. The arenas are bigger; there are more fans, more media, and more distractions. Everything is just bigger. The game, though, never changes: forty minutes on a 94-foot court with baskets ten feet off the floor.

And that was the brilliance of Jim Larranaga's strategy on how to prepare his team to attack the monster known as the NCAA tournament. He implored his team to have fun. He smiled everywhere he went. In interviews, he would quote Confucius and William Jennings Bryan. He became the guy everybody wanted to talk to because he actually walked about two feet off the floor. Jim Larranaga became the cheesy coach figure and he didn't mind a bit—he was going to enjoy every moment, and he wanted his team to do so also.

"One of the things about being in an environment like this, there's so much around us," he said. "Even though we know it, we're not distracted by it. We're having so much fun, it's not like we're in a situation where we're nervous and have no fear. As long as we can continue to do that, anything is possible."

If his guys were having fun, Larranaga reasoned, they may not notice how big everything had become. They enjoyed it, embraced it, basked in it, and ultimately succeeded in it.

They played baseball at practice. Larranaga coined corny slogans such as "We are the color of kryptonite" to North Carolina's Supermen. He danced. He altered his conference's name to the Connecticut Assassins Association prior to his team's Elite Eight matchup against the #1 Huskies. Every single one of them cracked up his players.

Their run was about more than basketball victories. The smiles were genuine. It showed what senior leadership, great coaching, and an unwillingness to accept norms can do in any situation. It turned the basketball world on its ear.

It was also the culmination of a season's worth of building. This team was no flash in the pan. George Mason had lost three games since the first of the year entering the NCAA tournament. It had played a full season prior to the events that shaped the run.

The fairy tale would not be complete without turmoil. Skinn, the team's floor leader, punched Hofstra's Loren Stokes below the belt late in Mason's semifinal loss to the Pride. After seeing tape of the incident, Larranaga knew he had no choice but to suspend the senior guard for the team's next game. Considering that game could be an NCAA tournament game or an NIT game, the unwavering and quick decision drew raves from around the country.

Here was a dark irony, for Hofstra had beaten George Mason twice in the two weeks leading up to the NCAA selections. While Skinn had hit the shot to defeat Wichita State, it was also Skinn who hit Stokes and potentially put the Patriots out. It was Hofstra who was inexplicably left out of the field of sixty-four. And it was Jim Calhoun and Connecticut who, at the beginning of the season, suspended point guard Marcus Williams for only one semester for stealing a laptop computer, that George Mason defeated to get to Indianapolis. The disparity in punishments of Williams and Skinn was notable, if not for how the country viewed the coaches and the programs.

———

Larranaga, however, would not say that the CAA season was fun. Those twenty conference games—among them, a heartbreaking buzzer-beating loss at Old Dominion, a massive comeback victory at VCU, and a controversial CAA tournament semifinal loss to Hofstra—would prepare them for the rigor of the NCAA tournament.

Nobody on the outside knew how good this league was, though they had an inkling.

In early December the Drexel Dragons were tied late in their game with Duke in the preseason NIT. Duke had just beaten Seton Hall by 53 points and had its way with Davidson. They had looked invincible until that night. ESPN's Dick Vitale, as the game waned and the score remained close, openly wondered how the media could've forecast Drexel as the seventh-place team in the CAA. Vitale wanted to see the other six.

Vitale was right. Drexel didn't finish seventh. The Dragons finished eighth.

There were signs.

———

Truth is indeed stranger than fiction. Nobody, including myself (having seen nearly fifty games in fourteen cities in person, plus television and the conference tournament), could have predicted what would come next for the CAA. What began, ironically, with George Mason beating Cal-Irvine and then losing to Wake Forest in overtime—and proceeded through a controversial CAA tournament semifinal loss—turned into the country's biggest sports story. For once, it was a good story.

But the magical, unprecedented, Cinderella run to the Final Four meant far more than basketball success, and it was notable for more than that team and that conference.

The 2005-2006 season in the CAA stands as the hallmark for mid-major college basketball and what the teams, schools, and conferences fight for every day. The hardships and heartbreaks of this season define that existence, as do the watershed victories and inevitable fallout that occurred in the weeks following the season.

Some would argue that George Mason's run to the Final Four and the Missouri Valley Conference placing two teams in the Sweet 16 was an anomaly; a freak occurrence. However, many would argue the opposite, saying the 2005-2006 college basketball season served as the start of a revolution. Mid-majors had arrived. George Mason's purpose was much like the man after whom the school is named.

This book is not a story about a player, a coach, a team, or even a conference.

This is a college basketball story.

Introduction

"I am ashamed to think how easily we capitulate to badges and names, to large societies and dead institutions." –Ralph Waldo Emerson

I remember the very moment I knew this book would become a reality. In the spring of 2004, I was relaxing on a sailboat in the Caribbean Sea. I had left all my worries back home in Virginia for this specific vacation, including a demanding corporate job and the everyday stress that dominate the events of my life.

I left them all at home, save one.

You see, when this trip was planned, I had no hand in the details. A friend's brother who was an experienced sailor cooked up this trip, and I immediately signed on as a passenger. All I knew is that I would board a 42-foot catamaran and sail the southern Caribbean islands with three others, and our only decisions would be when to eat and on what island we'd next moor. That was good enough to get my check. Everything else was mere window dressing.

It was when I realized that the week of this long-awaited, much-anticipated vacation would coincide with the Colonial Athletic Association basketball tournament that my jaw dropped. As an avid college basketball fan, especially a fan of mid-majors and my local team, the VCU Rams, this was disastrous.

VCU had earned the CAA regular season title with a 14-4 record and I had had a blast following the Rams. The sense of community in following a mid major is very real. The success of the team you follow is tighter, if only because its true fans and die-hards travel with a mid major.

Still, the success meant little in the grand scheme of college basketball. The CAA was, and still is, a mid-major conference. Mid-majors don't have the luxury of playing their conference tournaments for better seeding in the NCAA Tournament. No, the Rams, led by second-year coach Jeff Capel and CAA player of the year Domonic Jones, would have to win the CAA postseason tournament in order to hear Greg Gumball call their name, signifying they had made the NCAA field of sixty-four. An entire season of success would ride on those four days in early March.

So when George Mason University center Jai Lewis fired up an air ball at the horn—which followed Jesse Pellot-Rosa, a freshman walk-on for VCU, making the second of two free throws to give VCU a 55-54 lead—Rams fans everywhere celebrated. There was a simultaneous and collective cheer, and exhale.

That is, everyone except me. I was floating at the foot of the Pitons off the coast of St. Lucia. I had no idea. I wouldn't for three more days until we hit an Internet café in Bequia.

The more I agonized about what I did not know, the more I thought about what I did know. There is luxury to following BCS conference schools. VCU had finished the regular season in first place in the CAA but were guaranteed nothing. If they were Duke, who had won the ACC regular season that year with a similar 13-3 record, then the conference tournament would be more of a coronation than a four-day grind-a-thon that would make or break a successful season.

In the CAA, whose last at-large bid came in 1986, it meant everything.

Further, I realized VCU faced issue after issue for a mid-major program. VCU had a young, successful coach in Jeff Capel, whom everyone knew would eventually be snapped up by a larger program that could offer him much more money. I knew the administration at VCU and their struggles with revenue generation and managing the balance of successful yet underfunded nonrevenue sports like tennis and baseball. I understood that exposure on television and other media outlets hampered everything from recruiting to ticket sales.

That's when I realized the VCU basketball program was the poster child for the struggles of any "mid-major" basketball program. Right then, I knew the idea for the book was born, in part because I knew I wasn't alone.

The topic of mid-majors and their place in the NCAA landscape is discussed, passionately, daily on sports radio and nightly on ESPN. Coaches are asked about it and talk about it. Administrators openly lament the hurdles. Everyone has an opinion, yet nobody has a solution or relevant data to support any position. During football season it is the dreaded BCS; in basketball season it is the teams that make the Big Dance and the dreaded "bubble." There are newspaper articles and talk show guests, yet there has never been a definitive work on a very real issue.

So five weeks after Pellot-Rosa made that clinching free throw, I found myself sitting in the office of Dr. Richard Sander, Director of Athletics for Virginia Commonwealth University. I would bounce off of him my initial ideas for the project that eventually became *Cinderella,* and I requested (and received) access to his staff and to the basketball team so I could write a book about the struggles of mid-major athletic programs.

The makeup of the book from that first meeting with Dr. Sander took many twists and turns as I processed the best way to illustrate the story. However, the issues eventually presented themselves clearly. I noticed that while football and the BCS pop up often when discussing the issues in collegiate athletics, nowhere is the plight of the mid-major collegiate sports program more apparent and more hotly debated than in the selection of teams to the NCAA's annual postseason basketball tournament. When you consider CBS is paying the NCAA $6 billion over eleven years for television programming rights to March Madness, the importance of winning a conference tournament and thus earning an automatic berth into "The Big Dance" becomes staggering.

For mid-major college basketball programs, the stakes of an NCAA Tournament bid are far greater than on-court wins and losses. In addition to the duress of winning basketball games, these programs daily battle revenue, exposure, recruiting, and future growth pressures.

This would be the story.

Cinderella documents the wins and losses—on and off the court—of the 2005-2006 Colonial Athletic Association basketball season, buffeted by information surrounding the Missouri Valley and other mid-major conferences.

The year-in-the-life approach is replete with compelling storylines and serves as a springboard for a national, in-depth look at the issues surrounding mid-major NCAA sports programs.

The dichotomy of the action on the floor and the ramifications off of it truly embodies March Madness.

With the events of the 2005-2006 season concluded, I can safely say this: While I knew going into the project this could be a special season for the CAA, I had no idea. Actually, I feel better knowing that nobody did.

The first time I sat down with Old Dominion Coach Blaine Taylor, we were talking about the issue of scheduling as a mid major and he summed up the frustration with a terse and accurate statement:

"Some of these middle-of-the-pack teams from the big conferences are phonies. All we want is the opportunity."

Foreshadowing indeed.

CINDERELLA

CHAPTER ONE

MADNESS

"Madness need not be all breakdown. It may also be break-through. It is potential liberation and renewal." –R.D. Laing

S tanding on the floor of the Richmond Coliseum, nearing midnight and well after his team's hard fought victory over UNC-Wilmington in the 2005 CAA semifinals, Virginia Commonwealth University Head Coach Jeff Capel's mind was amazingly clear.

"Tomorrow is the longest day," he said, shaking his head with a half smile. "Soooooo long."

On a good day, the Richmond Coliseum appears its age. The venerable building was built in 1971 and stands as an homage to the circular, multipurpose venues that became popular during that era of sports stadium construction. What makes it worse is the entire building, inside and out, was painted brown. It annually hosts concerts and graduations, minor league hockey, and the circus. The CAA does everything it can to spruce up the place, adding colorful sponsorship signage and bright banners championing the history of the league.

At this moment, however, the building was showing its age. It was almost empty, save players, their families, and media members who chose to hang around and finish up the night's work on press row.

There was an odd feeling—a chilly warmth tempered with the smell of age and basketball—that seemed to hang in the air.

Three days of basketball action had filled its walls. There had been stories, but it was the thought of the final chapter that bounced around the staleness.

Jeff Capel, on the other hand, is among the best-dressed coaches in the college game—his sideline sartorial choice is always a sharp suit well put together. In fact, VCU fans came to know the signal for an upset Capel—it was only then that the jacket came off.

Now, nearly an hour after a big victory, Capel's tie was loosened, his jacket folded across his left arm. Beads of sweat glistened on his forehead and shone through the armpits of his shirt. Even after such a rigorous day, one he knew would be only his second longest, Capel held a "together" look. As he took in the scene, the obviously tired coach seemed buoyed by the thoughts of what his team had accomplished.

The previous year, in only his second season as head coach at VCU, Capel had guided the Rams to the regular season championship and a CAA Tournament title, garnering the school's first trip to the NCAA Tournament since 1996, their first season in the CAA. He vividly remembered the agonizing wait for the 7:00 p.m. ESPN tip-off as he considered his schedule for this season's final game day.

"I'll get some breakfast, we'll shoot, and then…"

And then his voice trailed off as he looked over to his players, who were milling about, talking with friends and family members. Capel saw nothing though. His mind's eye was walking through the following day—the whole gut-wrenching twelve hours, if he slept, leading to the CAA championship game against rival and regular season champ Old Dominion. All the work of the past year had brought Capel back to this precipice. One more win and the Rams would return to the NCAA Tournament.

For VCU and the other nine members of the Colonial Athletic Association in 2005, winning the conference championship and securing its automatic bid was the only path into the lucrative NCAA field. The exposure, and quite frankly the money, is a boon to mid-major basketball programs which often struggle to compete in a changing NCAA sports landscape. The automatic berth that is on the line at the CAA Tournament is a Holy Grail for its members. It's unlike the ACC, the conference in which Capel starred at Duke during his playing days, where a tournament berth is more a reward for a well-played season.

Capel understood this, and you could see that fact as he pondered his tasks at hand.

In an instant, the half smile overtook his entire face.

"I'm going to eat pancakes," he blurted spontaneously, thus returning to the conversation. "We haven't lost when my wife makes me pancakes."

For just one moment, after all the preseason practices, film sessions and academics, twenty-eight regular season games, radio and television shows, interviews and public appearances, mentoring of the young men in his charge, and two postseason tournament victories in two nights—not to mention being less than twenty hours to the tip-off of the championship game—Jeff Capel permitted himself the joy of his wife Kanika's homemade pancakes.

That day was now nearly a year in the past. The 2006 CAA Tournament would be different. It would showcase how far this conference had come in just one season. For once, for the first time in twenty years, more than an automatic bid was on the line. Though it was one season removed from Capel's stress, it was an eternity.

In many ways, the 2006 CAA Tournament had set itself up to be the absolute ideal of what a conference postseason tournament should be. Its members were good teams, recognized nationally. It would be played at one site, and six teams could make a legitimate argument that they had the ability to win. It would be highly competitive. Five of the teams were located less than a two hours' drive from the venue. A sixth, UNCW, always traveled well.

The top four teams—UNCW, George Mason, Hofstra, and Old Dominion—could all claim victory based on their talent and regular season success. The top three dominated at some point, and Old Dominion was still Old Dominion. The Monarchs faced some difficulty throughout the season, but in the end this was essentially the same ODU team that had won twenty-eight games the previous season, the one in which they defeated VCU in that championship game Capel awaited so eagerly.

VCU, playing about twenty-five blocks from its home floor, could also win. The Rams were 8-3 in the tournament the past four years, playing in three finals. Though it was not an official home game, everybody knew differently. They were dangerous.

Most importantly, the tournament meant something. The CAA most likely had risen itself above one-bid league status, which meant that more than just the championship game mattered. Then again, who really knew?

Attendance at early-round games would be more than the usual diehards. Early-round play could spell doom for the NCAA hopes of at least Hofstra and UNCW. Old Dominion and VCU certainly had the talent to win: VCU drilled Hofstra and ODU beat UNCW earlier in the regular season.

There would be intensity, but what made things incredibly compelling was that the teams would be fighting for up to three NCAA bids. If things went horribly wrong, the CAA would get only its tournament champion into the NCAA Tournament. If things went incredibly right, the CAA could get three teams into the Big Dance.

Every possession of every game mattered.

What's more, the teams were not playing for seeds, which occurs at the ACC or Big East Tournament. At those events, the basketball game and the basketball atmosphere is more of a so-called event. They lack the sheer intensity that would descend upon the Richmond Coliseum.

So on one hand, you had the one-bid leagues where a championship game was all that mattered. On the other hand, you had the major conferences where, really, none of the games mattered. In the middle, along with the Missouri Valley, sat the CAA.

Drama.

"Our teams are not household names," CAA Commissioner Tom Yeager said, "but that's the neighborhood we're living in. It's good to have the Valley having the year that they've had. The two of us are part and parcel in the same argument."

That argument was more than just the winner of this conference tournament making the Big Dance.

Interestingly, Yeager, who is the only commissioner to ever preside over the conference, announced two days prior to the start of the tournament that it would be staying in Richmond through the 2012 season. Richmond is where the conference offices are located, but that reason was always overplayed in the media. It came down to the fact that only two cities—Richmond and Norfolk—offered bids, and Richmond's was far better.

The CAA has conducted its tournament at the Richmond Coliseum since 1990, which ranks as the second longest tenure in the nation among Division I conferences, behind only the Big East Conference at Madison Square Garden, New York City.

Fans and administrators could debate the merits of financial packages, economic impacts, central locations, entertainment, and hotels surrounding the venue; but it often came down to one thing: It seemed natural.

The drama, of course, also meant issues. They are only natural when staging an event of this magnitude. Patrons of the conference's annual Thursday night banquet, a dinner in which legends from each school were honored and the current season was celebrated—complete with the announcement of the All CAA teams and players of the year—were greeted upon arrival by a throng of guests of the downtown Marriott and four fire trucks.

Instead of the usual banter and small talk that dominates the minutes before a typical banquet, about fifteen minutes before the scheduled start of the CAA awards banquet at the Richmond Marriott, the fire alarm sounded. It required not only banquet rooms but also the entire hotel to be evacuated. About 500 players, administrators, and guests were ushered outside, standing on the downtown sidewalks waiting for the fire department to arrive, which of course they did with lights and sirens blaring.

Winters in Richmond are a mixed bag, a Forrest Gump-esque box of chocolates: You never know what you're going to get. Luckily for the guests, that evening was fairly mild, so the twenty minutes spent outside waiting for the fire department to clear the building was bearable. Even so, the situation disrupted the evening's program and was a harbinger.

The typical milling about occurred on a sidewalk.

This was only half of the story, though the inconvenience was the only story the patrons knew at the time. The alarm, perhaps, was not coincidence.

When Yeager returned to start the banquet, the general manager of the Richmond Coliseum approached and informed him of an FBI alert about a possible terrorist threat at a televised sporting event on the East Coast that weekend. The CAA qualified on all three counts, and Yeager had already received a phone call.

On Thursday afternoon, a few hours before the banquet and as teams were practicing in the frigid Richmond Coliseum, Yeager was walking the halls and heard a loud crash around the corner.

"Of course you know what the first thing was that went through my mind," he said. "It's odd to say that I was relieved it was 'just' a sign, but your heart gets racing in a situation like that."

Before Yeager had taken a bite of his chicken dinner and eighteen hours before the CAA Tournament would actually begin, he'd spoken to the FBI, ducked a falling sign, and weathered a fire drill.

March Madness, indeed.

The nooner between David Henderson's Delaware Fighting Blue Hens and Bruiser Flint's Drexel Dragons began as chilly as the air inside the Richmond Coliseum. Shots were not falling for either team.

It was your typical first-day noon game in any conference tournament. Everybody would have to get a feel for things. Neither team would lead by more than four points in the hotly contested eight-seed versus nine-seed game. With thirty-four seconds to play, Delaware's Sam McMahon, a little-used sophomore guard pressed into action because of foul trouble, drilled a baseline jumper, and Delaware took the lead at 51-49.

After Drexel missed, the Dragons fouled Delaware's Herb Courtney, a 62 percent free throw shooter. When Brian Kersey looked up at the scoreboard, the team fouls for Drexel read "ten," so he signaled for two shots. Courtney bricked the first, and Flint called time-out to allow the Delaware sophomore to think about the second one as well.

At that time, the official scorer and both schools' score keepers alerted Kersey that they all had nine team fouls for Delaware and the scoreboard was in error. Obviously this would have necessitated a one-and-one, and Courtney's miss would have given Drexel a chance at a rebound down two points.

Kersey, one of the best officials working college basketball, knew what had to occur next. The error would be corrected by going to the possession arrow, which favored Delaware. Looming for Kersey was the tough part: telling Flint. The combustible coach, known to have equally large amounts of coaching ability and sideline antics, reacted somewhat appropriately, all things considered. There was screaming, some flailing of the arms, and a disgusted tone all near half court. Flint, however, knew his anger did not have to be directed at Kersey.

None of the scorers had alerted the officials of the mistake until after the first free throw.

With Flint temporarily calmed, the Blue Hens threw the ball inbounds and were fouled. Henry Olawoye, another sophomore who was a 45 percent free throw shooter, bricked the first of two shots. (This *was* the tenth foul.) The second banked in, giving Delaware a 52-49 lead.

Drexel's possession and the game ended with point guard Bashir Mason leaning in to Olawoye, trying to draw a foul, as he shot a three pointer to tie. There was a lot of contact, but no whistle, because Mason initiated all of it. This didn't please Flint and he stormed off the court in a huff. The sequence didn't beat Drexel as much as its 29 percent shooting, nor did sixteen points from Gibran Washington.

The team that three months earlier hung with Duke and UCLA, and Dick Vitale could not believe was picked seventh in the Colonial Athletic Association, had lost, not making it to the middle afternoon on the tournament's first day. The Dragons, seeded eighth, finished the season 15-16, losing eight of its final eleven.

The relief of basketball had provided Yeager and the CAA staff exactly thirty-nine minutes and forty-seven seconds of respite. Flint controlled himself well in the postgame press conference, noting that those kinds of things had been happening to him all year. His conversation with Yeager in the hallway when the reporters had left was more animated.

The new kids on the block, the Northeastern Huskies, followed in their first CAA Tournament game. They were matched up against Dean Keener's James Madison Dukes. Huskies player Jose Juan Barea, the outstanding and flashy point guard from Puerto Rico, had won player of the year, and Shawn James, a wiry 6-foot, 9-inch shot-blocking expert was defensive player of the year.

Head coach Ron Everhart's halftime discussion must have been a doozie. Down two, the Huskies came flying out of the locker room and began getting up and down the floor and scoring at will. The fast pace was preferred by Barea, who was becoming famous for his mad down-floor dashes for layups and passes on three-second offensive possessions.

Northeastern, buffeted by a small yet vociferous crowd, opened the half on a 26-3 run in less than eight minutes and cruised to 74-56.

The nightcap turned into more of a game than anyone imagined. Capel's VCU Rams had beaten William & Mary twice during the regular season, including an eighteen-point whipping in Williamsburg six days prior. The Rams, with superior talent, figured to wipe the floor as the partisan crowd of 6,900 filtered into the coliseum.

The 62-59 victory wasn't sealed until two Nathan Mann threes fell harmlessly away.

Walking through the handshake line, William & Mary assistant Dee Vick, frustrated at the conclusion of an 8-20 season, commented to Capel that "you guys were fucking lucky." The barb incensed Capel and he turned to confront Vick. Both had to be physically restrained.

"It was a youthful, stupid mistake," Capel would say after the game, once he had cooled down. "I was completely wrong."

Though Tribe Coach Tony Shaver would also say that he spoke to Capel and there was no issue between the two head coaches, Vick never apologized.

Still, Capel knew the end result: The name of the game in tournament play is to survive and advance. It doesn't matter how you do it.

The fans that follow UNCW are hearty. They travel in big numbers, they know basketball, and they love their Seahawks. So it was not a news item that more than 3,500 UNCW fans made the four-hour drive to Richmond to cheer on their team, the #1 seed. The fans always stay at the same Embassy Suites located about ten miles west down Broad Street from the coliseum.

Perhaps it is because they have no football team, but UNCW fans have a sense of pride in their program that emanates from their talk and radiates in their support. Most wear teal. They cheer loudly and are smart—they appreciate a good play by the opposition. They are like other fans in that the college students involve themselves in pranks, such as a late night visit to the Drexel fans' bus to wreak havoc. In addition, alums and adults who follow the program have never had an official's call go their way.

It was no surprise that even when the game clock still read 45:02, at roughly 11:15 on a Saturday morning when most people are shaking off breakfast and getting things together for the day, UNCW students filling the Richmond Coliseum raised the first chant: "T-J-Car-ter...T-J-Car-ter..."

The Teal Nation was in full force. End zone bleachers featured teal faces, teal hair, and the requisite teal T-shirts. One student painted the hair portion of his mohawk, of course, teal. Another fan dressed in a teal toga. He was not a student.

UNCW would lead off the day everybody had awaited— Quarterfinal Saturday—eagerly following the action because good teams would play good teams, and an at-large bid possibly loomed. Though the coliseum was still frigid, the emotion of the UNCW fan base warmed it.

It didn't take long for the Seahawks to show their muscle and pull away from overmatched Delaware. The final was 69-56. It was a typical UNCW victory: precision and execution on offense, and rugged discipline on defense.

Delaware had been forced to run its offense a few feet farther than was comfortable. The lack of cohesion made a difference that would show up in its shooting percentage. UNCW forced eleven steals while committing only seven turnovers on its own. Though the Seahawks missed twelve of thirteen attempts from three-point land, it didn't matter.

It never does for UNCW. They play a true team game, so they are able to afford a good player having an off night (as T.J. Carter had on this occasion). They can afford difficulty in one area, such as the three-point shooting. UNCW is not a team to run off a flashy 16-2 run. They prefer a style where they put together several 10-4 runs and the next thing you know they lead by fifteen.

It's called "being Dubbed."

If there was a "Dubbing" of Old Dominion as it warmed up for its quarterfinal matchup against Northeastern, it was that they were going to win the CAA Tournament. Beat writers and coaches all feared the Monarchs. Blaine Taylor's team had rebounded from every known distraction to win six of its last seven games. More importantly, they were playing as well as they had in weeks.

A championship game is exactly what Monarchs Coach Blaine Taylor had been planning for his team since practice began in

October. Taylor is an analytical, educated, and humorous man. He knows how to deal with the media, so he enjoys the interaction more than most. You can tell within the first five minutes of conversing with him that his approach to coaching a basketball team and leading young men is heavy on philosophy, and it is validated via execution. Taylor carries an uncompromising belief of his system and an unwavering sense of confidence in and appreciation of the people who work with him. It takes everybody "rowing in the same direction," Taylor frequently says.

The Monarchs would play at this level most of the game against Northeastern, continually working the offense into areas the team wanted. This allowed ODU to push a lead; but because the team was continually missing free throws, including the front end of all three one-and-ones in the second half, they could not put away the stubborn Huskies.

The game featured a comical moment. Northeastern's Barea drove the lane for a layup with about six minutes to play and felt he was fouled, and fouled hard. There was no whistle. Barea's shoe had been torn off his foot during the play, and while action continued at the other end of the court, Barea kicked his shoe off the court, over the curtain separating the court from the stands, and about six rows into the end zone bleachers.

"I got fouled pretty hard," Barea said. "Then I made like a soccer player. I kicked it really good."

Regardless, Northeastern would not go away. Leading 60-54 with less than five minutes to play, ODU imploded. The missed foul shots caught up with them. The Monarchs began missing shots from the field, which would not be so costly if a few had made free throws, giving them a cushion. ODU missed eight of its final nine field goals.

Northeastern finished those final five minutes on a 17-3 run to win 71-63. The more than four thousand ODU fans sat in stunned silence. This team was supposed to be ranked; it was supposed to challenge an at-large bid, possibly make the Sweet 16. They were supposed to win the CAA regular season going away.

It turned out that the Monarchs would finish fourth and lose to the fifth seed, not making it out of the tournament quarterfinals. Old Dominion, the team that was supposed to bring glory to the Colonial Athletic Association, would have to settle for a potential NIT berth.

"There were some crazy rolls," Blaine Taylor said afterward. In recalling last year's thrilling finals victory over VCU, Taylor added, "A year ago here we made fifteen free throws in a row to close the game. These are the same guys. The tournament format is fickle. And we're one and done."

Oddly, Taylor was the least surprised. He had been telling fans of the basketball team that the previous season, the one in which ODU finished 28-6, was the dream season. They were lucky, because they didn't face the challenges of injuries, they had an easier schedule, they lacked the distractions of personal and program tragedies, and they held no wild expectations.

People wanted to be disappointed in the 21-9 Old Dominion Monarchs of 2005-2006; to say that it wasn't great. The truth of the matter though, the truth that Taylor had been talking about all along, is that the team wasn't great the previous season. They were very good, but not great. Two CAA teams had matched ODU's 15-3 regular season mark this season, and three had surpassed its RPI number.

Tom Pecora asked that morning if Taylor was taking heat for ODU's season. After finding out he had been hearing a little, Pecora shook his head.

"That's ridiculous," Pecora said. "A 21-win season and he's getting a hard time."

Pecora walked away, still shaking his head.

———

The Saturday night session had all of the makings of a glamorous evening. George Mason was set to drill poor little old Georgia State in the opener. After all, the Panthers felt wonderful that they had pulled a minor upset over seventh-seeded Towson the previous night. No matter what happened, they could feel good about their first CAA

Tournament. The second game would be the game everyone awaited—the home team, VCU, against the team playing the best basketball, Hofstra.

There was, however, a pall in the Richmond Coliseum. As fans filtered into the building for the evening session, scores from around
the country dominated the idle chatter.

Bradley and Southern Illinois had both pulled upsets in the
Missouri Valley Tournament. The MVC had become a muddled mess,
where anywhere from three to six teams had made their case for the
NCAA Tournament.

Seton Hall had beaten Cincinnati in the Big East, and Cincinnati
had in turn beaten West Virginia. That would strengthen both of
those teams' credentials for an at-large berth. Indiana had gone to
Ann Arbor and beaten Michigan to accomplish the same thing.

Texas A&M had upset Texas and then had beaten Texas Tech.
Florida State had beaten Duke and then Miami.

The final four games were especially troubling for fans of George
Mason and Hofstra. Traditionally, the 17-13 sixth place team from a
BCS Conference was chosen ahead of the second place 24-7 team
from a mid-major conference. It was an easy thought process to think
there was no reason this would change. After all, the NCAA selection
committee could choose from any number of Missouri Valley teams
to reach its hypothetical "mid-major quota."

Though Hofstra Coach Tom Pecora has said his team needed to defeat
VCU to be in consideration, fans of the Pride were slowly buying into
the notion that even that would not be enough. Likewise, though
George Mason fans felt comfortable thinking they would have an easy
time this evening, they also considered that the Patriots rematch against
Hofstra, assuming both teams won, would be an elimination game.

The tension was obvious for both teams. The nervous chatter,
though good natured, was in fact nervous. It grew in strength and in
numbers, because the more people discussed the at-large bid the more
it became a product of its own self. It was clear and painfully obvious.
The bubble was shrinking.

As people were getting comfortable in their seats and uncomfortable with the games from other conferences, Tony Skinn was called for a charge on George Mason's first possession. Nobody knew it at the time, but the play set the tone for the Patriots' evening, and in reality the entire tournament.

Top seeds normally start slow, especially when playing for the first time in a week. It takes a few minutes to shake the rust and get the game legs warm. There was no real concern, even when Mason fell behind Georgia State 15-4.

By halftime, Mason had clawed back and led 27-25, and the game was shaping up as one of those where the early momentum had passed and the better team pulls away in the second half and wins comfortably. Georgia State and particularly Herman Favors, however, would not allow that to occur. Every time Mason worked itself to a comfortable margin, Favors would hit a three or make a steal. Favors' final trey came with 6:45 to play and pulled the Panthers to 40-38.

Favors hit two free throws with 32.9 seconds to play, tying the game. The crowd rose, applauding the effort of the nine seed but also cheering for them. It was the kind of situation in which favorites find themselves in postseason tournaments: The longer the lesser-talented underdog hangs in the game, the more confidence the team gets, and the more fans begin rallying behind them. By the time George Mason set up for the final shot, the Patriots were playing a road game.

Jim Larranaga's team whipped the ball around the perimeter but could not find an open seam or easy shot. The tough defense forced an off balance jumper from Lamar Butler that missed badly, and two contested tip attempts fell away.

Overtime.

In a season in which his team had lost only once in January and once in February—and had beaten Wichita State on the road in a nationally televised game to move on the radar for an at-large berth—Larranaga's Patriots were fighting for their lives against a team that had won seven games all season. They were on the precipice of disaster, five minutes from the Cinderella Story never getting off the ground. Georgia State had momentum and the crowd. Everybody in the Richmond Coliseum could sense what lay in front of their feet.

Though nobody had an inkling what history had in store for them over the next month, fans understood the significance of the Georgia State Panthers. So could Larranaga, but he wasn't about to begin yelping now. Larranaga's team was experienced, confident, and consistent. They were struggling, but they were the same group who had gotten them this far.

He trusted them, and was rewarded.

Sammy Hernandez, playing in front of his grandmother and sister, visiting Richmond from Puerto Rico, and seeing Hernandez play for the first time, hit a layup and then a three to start the overtime period. Hernandez had made four threes all season to that point.

There was a larger reason to smile and applaud Hernandez. At the age of seven, he found his mother, Gloria DeJesus, dead in her bedroom. Hernandez was raised by his sister and grandmother. He had already lost his father when he was just an infant.

After Hernandez personally asserted control of the game, Mason punched the ball inside to Will Thomas for two straight easy layups and it was over. George Mason had avoided the unthinkable upset, 61-56.

"There are a lot of yellow shirts in here," Tom Pecora noted from the entrance of the tunnel to his team's locker room. Pecora was catching the end of the George Mason game and generally killing time before he had to get down and get serious.

Most of the crowd of nearly seven thousand would be cheering for the local team, the home team in the eyes of many, the VCU Rams.

Pecora didn't worry long. Off the opening tap, Loren Stokes hit Antoine Agudio in stride and Agudio's three pointer swished. Five seconds into the contest the crowd had been silenced and Hofstra had a lead that it would never relinquish.

It would turn out that VCU's ensuing possession would be the only possession that they held the ball until the final minute of the game, with a chance to even tie the game. A turnover on their first possession and another Agudio three put VCU in a 6-0 hole, and it was all uphill from there.

Agudio would continue his shooting clinic in the first half, nailing five three pointers and scoring twenty points in all. Aurimas Kieza had ten of his own. Loren Stokes, whose bum ankle kept him from practice until a light workout the day before, was not really being missed.

Even though the Rams would get the deficit to two twice in the final thirty seconds, Hofstra made its free throws and held VCU at bay. The throng of seven thousand would retreat home unhappy, as VCU lost 72-66.

"We couldn't stay in front of them," Jeff Capel said. "They spread us out and drove. Agudio and Kieza kicked our butts."

Hofstra had driven out the crowd favorite, leaving the CAA with its two best draws watching the games from home. Considering last year's incredible success, there was a tangible pallor in the Richmond Coliseum. Nobody really knew what the effect would be. Last year's finalists were home.

More importantly for Capel, he may have just watched his first recruit, Nick George, play his last game in a VCU uniform. "I don't know," Capel said, and then repeated, when asked about the possibilities of an NIT berth. His mind was certainly on the young man from England sitting to his left.

"He's the guy I talk about," Capel said prior to the start of the tournament. "I've watched him and how hard he's worked. I've seen him have success, failure, and face adversity. He's always fought." Capel continued, "I love the kid," his smile widening with each word. "And I mean the person and the player. He could've gone a lot of places, but he believed in a twenty-seven-year-old coach. He was a part of my vision and he trusted and believed in me."

Nick George fulfilled his coach's promise. Through hard work and spirited play, George would go down as one of the best and most loved players in the history of VCU basketball. George and Capel came of age together in a time when you rarely get to see such a positive and symbiotic relationship.

It was somehow fitting that after the interviews were done, after the cameras had stopped rolling, after the attention had shifted to other people, other teams, and other games, George and Capel walked alone down a back hallway in the Richmond Coliseum, arm in arm.

Semifinal Sunday had as much to do with off-court issues and crisis management as on-court performances; and it was just the warmup. The CAA had seen its two heavy attending teams, VCU and ODU, go out before the semis for the first time since 2000. While the few hundred walk-up tickets could be forgotten, the potential for a mostly empty Richmond Coliseum loomed. The "show" that had been so important and so expertly pulled off the previous year may look entirely different if three thousand attended the finals.

Even though nobody from the CAA offices would openly say yes, the smile that creased lips when asked, "would you trade a half-empty Coliseum for a second bid" was noticeable.

It would be no more of a sore spot than a mosquito bite that was scratched too much.

Tom Yeager was dealing with issues, though. The night before, the VCU and Hofstra mascots and then the cheerleaders had a bit of a dustup that was more comical than painful. Still, it was not a shining moment, and it deflected attention from the court.

Additionally, during the Hofstra/VCU game a small-scale riot ensued.

Two African-American men sitting behind the benches were asked to move from seats they occupied, unticketed, to their true seats. Squatting has become a recognized and understood practice at events such as this. If nobody is using a better seat than yours, the option is there to sit in those seats. It's a gentlemen's agreement among fans. The second half of that gentlemen's agreement, however, is when the real ticket holders show up, you move.

It's expected and everybody knows the ground rules. In this case, however, one man in particular decided to become belligerent. Tom Yeager stated, "Race was brought into the picture rather quickly."

Security and Richmond police were able to control the situation well, but not after clearing out five rows of fans and their folding chairs, including the George Mason team. If there was an incident, innocent people were not going to get caught in the melee.

The police were able to get the men to further discuss the matter in a back tunnel, where the discussions turned loud and lawsuits were threatened. Eventually, the men backed down and fans resumed interest in the basketball game. The following day there was a rumored phone call about a $5,000 payoff "to make the whole thing go away," but in the end the situation just ended.

But this was Sunday, a new day, and Tom Yeager had reason to smile. Though he was without his two big-ticket teams, he had one perfect matchup in George Mason and Hofstra. Both teams were getting just due about at-large bids and bubble aspirations. The winner of the game would further its individual cause, and the cause of the conference—the second bid to the NCAA tournament. The loser would not relinquish a season's worth of quality play. For the CAA, this was a no-lose game.

Nearly.

The other semifinal pitted UNCW, the third CAA wannabe, against upstart Northeastern. Though the Seahawks had only escaped Northeastern 46-44 at home during the regular season, the Huskies would be playing its third game in three days. Fatigue would matter, and UNCW is the last opponent a team wants to play tired. What's more, UNCW carried with it about 2,500 fans. Northeastern might have had 100. There was good reason to believe the CAA final would pit UNCW against the survivor of the night game.

The afternoon unfolded according to plan. UNCW began a slow, precise dismantling of Northeastern. The Seahawks made shots early, established a lead (42-29 at half), and didn't turn the ball over. The lead would reach eighteen by the 7:00 mark and UNCW cruised on home.

It was a scary repeat of the Delaware game, and likely a repeat of about twenty of UNCW's thirty games during the season. It certainly looked like a high percentage of its twenty-four victories. The final score was 69-54, eerily close to the 69-56 decision over Delaware.

UNCW had become the CAA's version of Ivan Drago from the *Rocky* movies. They were the irresistible force. The only issue that could be discussed was off the court, where the Delaware victory had dropped UNCW's RPI to forty-three—exactly ten spots lower than fast-charging Hofstra.

On the first possession of the Hofstra/George Mason semifinal, Hofstra star guard Loren Stokes was inadvertently hit in the eye. Stokes lost a contact lens, and though he adjusted quickly and ran back to the scorer's table, four minutes would run off the clock before another stoppage in play allowed him back onto the court. Unfortunately, the inadvertent sock in the eye served only as a harbinger.

Though Greg Johnson didn't play poorly subbing for Stokes, Hofstra still trailed 11-6 and Jai Lewis was headed to the free throw line to increase the margin. George Mason had made four of its first five shots from the field—not exactly the start Tom Pecora had wanted.

In the locker room prior to the game, Pecora listed his four keys for winning the game:

Championship possessions.
Defend the post with passion.
Our stops will lead to scores.
Attack and handle pressure.

In order to "defend the post with passion," Hofstra had chosen to have Aurimas Kieza front the burly Lewis and utilize weak side help to slow the Patriots' most dangerous weapon, but it wasn't working. Hofstra had managed only one stop in five possessions, negating the third key.

Being part of the Hofstra locker room before a big game is an interesting experience. Time alternates between idle sitting, idle chatter, and intense focus on the game ahead. A nervous energy is not the ideal descriptor, because you don't sense nerves. It is rather a feeling of anxiety, as if this is where the coaching staff wants to be, doing what they want to be doing. The odd down time is part of the total experience.

Someone tells a joke.

Assistant coach Van Macon laments, "I'm up to 242 (pounds)."

Someone tells another joke.

Stu Klein, Tom Pecora's first coach on the junior college level, comments that "nobody works harder at his profession." Out of nowhere, Pecora speaks up: "We're going to have to get some good minutes from Gads." Pecora is referring to freshman big man Chris Gadley, who had shown signs of progress during the year but had seemingly hit the freshman wall.

When the players return to the locker room, it is all business.

"It's mindset, fellas," Pecora starts, his voice rising with every word. "Up tempo helps us. We play a full forty and if it takes us five more, then so be it." Keeping with routine, the players huddle, shout "Team First," and head onto the floor to start the game.

Before walking out, Pecora adjusts his tie. Everyone in the room exchanges hand shakes. This is a family. Then, before heading onto the court, Pecora muses, "It must be March. I'm running out of things to say. If we get past the Sweet 16, I'm in trouble." Pecora didn't have a clue to the dark irony in his seemingly innocent and tension-breaking quip.

Hofstra worked the deficit back to 14-12 before George Mason scored eight of the next ten points to assume a 22-14 lead at the under 8:00 media time-out. Particularly worrisome for Pecora had to be the defense being played on Antoine Agudio. Fresh off of his thirty-four-point performance against VCU, Agudio had four points and missed both of his three-point shots. He was not a part of the Hofstra offense.

The teams would settle into the flow and Mason held a 33-27 half-time lead. When Loren Stokes made back-to-back runners in the lane to cut the deficit 33-31, Larranaga called for time-out.

Above any strategic adjustment, everybody knew how this game was going to finish: close, intense, and down to the final minute. This became evident quickly, as after Mason's Will Thomas converted a layup, Larranaga let loose a rare strong emotion on the sideline, urging on his defense with two loud whistles and clenched fists.

Hofstra would take its first lead of the game on a Carlos Rivera layup and foul shot. The conventional three-point play made it 41-40 in favor of the Pride with 8:38 to play.

The first key Pecora had written on the white board in the locker room read: "Championship Possessions."

On the defensive end, George Mason was being challenged on every shot. Hofstra was boxing out. On the other end, Hofstra ran its offense as efficiently as, well, UNCW. Rivera hit a three pointer, and after another stop Loren Stokes swished a baseline jumper and Hofstra led 51-44, prompting a Larranaga time-out with 2:24 to play.

Both teams would trade free throws over the next minute. Rivera's pair for Hofstra at 1:12 restored the lead to 53-46. Then two Tony Skinn shots turned the tournament on its ear.

Larranaga had inserted little-used junior Tim Burns as a three-point shooter, and Hofstra quickly took note. The overplay on Burns gave Skinn an open look and the senior buried a three to make the score 53-49 with 55.2 seconds to play.

George Mason was down, but not out. Since the advent of the three-point shot, a four-point lead with less than a minute to play became nowhere near insurmountable. Then, as everyone began making the calculations—a steal and another bomb, a missed free throw here and there, what is the foul situation—it happened.

As George Mason was setting up its press, Loren Stokes suddenly crumpled to the floor in front of the George Mason bench, writhing in pain. He held his hands between his legs, much like athletes do when they hurt their wrists. A whistle stopped play.

Stokes continued in agony and everyone and everything stopped. It couldn't have been a wrist; nobody had been moving. It was the simple nanoseconds when Hofstra's Aurimas Kieza was grabbing the basketball and preparing to throw it inbounds.

The bizarre scene became almost surreal. It would be a minute before Hofstra trainer Evan Malings could be allowed onto the floor to check out Stokes. Malings, by rule, had to be waved onto the floor by the officials to check out an injured player. Oddly, all he could do is stand alongside Pecora, ten feet from the still helpless Stokes. Meanwhile, the officiating crew of Bryan Kersey, Mike Eades, and Tim Nestor were desperately trying to figure out the situation.

The officials weren't alone. You could almost hear Malings' footsteps as he was finally allowed to approach Stokes. The buzz in the Richmond Coliseum was created by a collective "what happened" emerging from the crowd. Speculation was rampant, especially among the members of the media.

Matt Smith, who was doing color commentary on the game for Sirius radio and the Richmond ESPN radio affiliate, put down his headphones to check with anyone who might know what happened. Smith was greeted with shrugging shoulders. The incredible moment could only be captured by the irony that everyone knew something monumental had just happened, but nobody knew exactly what it was.

Loren Stokes spent most of the regular season packed in ice with one injury or another. He had hurt his thumb, back, knee, ankle, and elbow. He had fought through various bumps, bruises, pokes, and stitches. He had bounced up and played every single time.

Except now.

The officials consulted the replay video time and time again, but it showed nothing. The ESPN feed showed an isolation of Stokes and Skinn, but it produced only Stokes dropping straight to the floor.

But the players knew. Stokes managed to eke out one word to his coach: "yes."

Tom Pecora asked Stokes if he had been hit below the belt. Though tape proved inconclusive and the game would continue, it was clear that Tony Skinn had delivered an unprovoked punch to the groin of Loren Stokes.

Larranaga didn't see it, but upon questioning Skinn during the delay, Skinn admitted it to his coach.

"Why would you do something like that?" Larranaga asked his senior.

"I didn't want to lose," replied Skinn.

Larranaga put Skinn on the bench. That act alone by the coach confirmed things in the minds of spectators. Although no video confirmed the incident, Larranaga put his senior guard on the bench for the final fifty-five seconds.

Hofstra would continue to make free throws and George Mason would respond by missing harried three-point attempts. It may not have mattered how the game actually ended, because most of the people in the stands had stopped watching the action, and the media continued their assault on the events. The significance of that moment would reverberate for weeks and ultimately change two seasons.

The final was 58-49 and Stokes was in the locker room before the final buzzer. Carlos Rivera was the offensive star for the Pride, scoring twenty-five points and handing out four assists with zero turnovers while playing all forty minutes.

Two impressions from the game would be lasting. First, Hofstra's defense limited George Mason to 17 percent shooting in the second half and only four field goals and sixteen points. Second, nobody knew how badly Stokes had been injured by Skinn's cheap shot. Oddly, it was a Wilmington television station that perfectly caught video evidence of the punch.

As imaginable, everybody said the right thing at the postgame press conference.

Larranaga said he had nothing to comment on "because I didn't see the play."

Pecora was a little more forthcoming, but not by much, saying that Stokes had told him that's precisely what Skinn had done but that he hoped one incident wouldn't mar an otherwise great basketball game.

After the news conference, Larranaga asked his athletics director, Tom O'Connor, to conduct an investigation into the incident. Larranaga, O'Connor, Tom Yeager, and Ron Bertovich huddled quietly but poignantly deep in the tunnel of the Richmond Coliseum to share what they knew.

Larranaga was led into the media work room and shown the footage. He knew an investigation was unnecessary. The video was clear.

Larranaga also knew that some things are more important than basketball, and he recommended that O'Connor skip the investigation and suspend Skinn for the Patriots' next game. Larranaga headed back into the locker room to talk to his team.

Yeager and O'Connor, friends for many years, went the other way. The two ended up sitting alone on the vacated George Mason bench, ten feet from where the incident that may be altering the fates of three teams and the conference had occurred.

"We knew what had to happen," Yeager said the morning after. "We were disappointed and sad at this dumb thing with enormous consequences. There was never any debate about what had to happen. We were just two colleagues and friends talking through a difficult situation."

Yeager also concurred with Larranaga's evaluation. "You cannot espouse to believe in all these values and then put your head in the sand. To Jim's credit, he never wavered, there was no rationalization."

It was a defining moment for a man who made his career coaching mid-major basketball teams. In a season that began with the hammering of Connecticut Coach Jim Calhoun's first semester suspension of point guard Marcus Williams for stealing and selling a laptop computer, Larranaga would do what he knew had to be done.

The suspension meant Skinn would be unavailable for Mason's next game, and with Mason losing in the CAA semis, the Patriots found themselves back squarely on the NCAA bubble. Committees look at such things as "injured" players when evaluating the teams they select.

Skinn's punch and subsequent suspension may have cost George Mason an at-large bid to the NCAA Tournament. Larranaga knew this, and was no less decisive. He had a point to make.

Carlos Rivera was the second player to enter the Hofstra locker room after the tumultuous victory over George Mason. He bolted immediately for the training room in which a slumped, tearful Loren Stokes sat. Rivera put his arms across Stokes's shoulders and mumbled words only teammates appreciate.

Once the team congregated, including Stokes, Tom Pecora slowly but excitedly addressed an obviously spent group of young men.

"In sports, we're fortunate because it's one of the only times this term can be said in a positive manner."

"Tonight," Pecora said, "we were motherfuckers."

Even Stokes managed a smile.

After a quick recap of the game in which Pecora praised his team's resolve and then urged them that "we're here to win a championship," the coach headed down the hallway to the postgame press conference where he knew he would be asked about the Stokes incident.

He was stopped on his way and exchanged more than a brief embrace with George Mason Athletics Director Tom O'Connor.

As Hofstra and UNCW were pulling themselves out of bed on Championship Monday, Yeager was on a conference call with Jon LeCrone, commissioner of the Horizon League. LeCrone served on the NCAA selection committee, and the CAA is his "designated conference." (Each person on the ten-member committee is assigned three conferences at the beginning of the season to monitor closely. They are expected to be experts on their assigned conferences so that when teams are discussed during the at-large evaluation process, in-depth information on every team is assured.)

With Hofstra winning, there was renewed interest in the Pride for an at-large bid. The phone call took a decidedly sharp turn when LeCrone inquired about Hofstra's nonconference schedule.

"Tell me about Indiana's!" snapped Yeager in response, surprising LeCrone. Yeager's ire was valid. When you get down to the last two or three teams, comparing that kind of detail is okay. "But when you're #25 (in the RPI), if you're not asking the question of them (Indiana) then you can't ask it of us."

Yeager had to feel as if he were suddenly arguing uphill. George Mason had the league's strongest resume, but they had just lost and would play the first round of any tournament without their second leading scorer and catalyst. Hofstra had a very weak out of conference schedule and was openly being questioned; and UNCW had two bad losses and the worst RPI and "resume" of the bunch.

The real possibility existed that despite doing everything they could to get their first at-large bid in twenty years, the CAA would once again be a one-bid league. It was an unprecedented season. Four teams had won more than twenty games. George Mason was ranked. Three teams were in the top forty of the RPI.

"We used to talk in terms of the good loss," said Yeager. "There are no more of those. It's all about shedding labels, a branding issue. We may not have the sex appeal of a Kentucky," Yeager continued, "but these guys (George Mason, UNCW, and Hofstra) are not backing into the tournament. They all have closing speed. What the committee looks for is your record in the last ten games, not your record in the first ten games. The only teams these guys have lost to are each other."

Yeager was right, yet the reality existed that it still would end tragically, with one bid. "Why bother?" scenarios crossed everyone's minds. So did the fact that one ill-timed and dumb punch may wreck two teams' at-large hopes. Frustratingly, too, was that none of it was in their control. There would be a full week of games from other conferences, bids to be stolen, resumes to be improved.

———

As the Richmond Coliseum slowly filled up—much more slowly and much less full than the previous year, a noticeable dichotomy from the moments prior to the ODU/VCU game—the media was provided a press release from George Mason University.

It would be Tony Skinn's "official" apology, extended to "Loren

Stokes, Hofstra University, his George Mason teammates, and the Patriot fans."

It read, in part:

I am very sorry and I deeply regret my actions on Sunday. In the heat of a tense game, I lost my head and made a bad decision. I'm not making excuses for my actions and I take full responsibility for what I did.

It was of little consequence to Tom Pecora. He had a championship game looming.

The Hofstra locker room prior to the championship game was no different than an early season contest against Binghamton. Four keys to the game were written on the white board. Tonight, they would read:

Execute off versus very physical D
Most intense/phys team wins
Defend-Reb-Run
Champ effort on every possession

Pecora isn't much for fire and brimstone. He figures his players know the stakes and will react appropriately. Stokes would play, but the sinewy guard would be at best 50 percent. He was still urinating blood from the previous night's punch. Pecora's words were short and direct and he repeated them twice: "Remember 8-20."

Only three years ago, Hofstra had actually finished 8-21 on the season and lost badly to UNCW in the CAA Tournament. In a short time, Hofstra had come a long way.

Sam Albano had witnessed 8-20. The founder and chairman of the Hope Through Hoops Foundation, a nonprofit group based on Long Island, is a long-time friend of Pecora. The Foundation was established in August 2002, in honor of former Marist basketball player Tom Crotty, a victim of the World Trade Center tragedy.

Albano's train was more than two hours late, and he made it into the Hofstra locker room with about fifteen minutes to spare. He and Pecora hugged. Albano would hitch a ride home after the game. He traveled nearly twenty hours to spend two hours with Pecora. Families do that.

Brad Brownell was in no mood to be hospitable. He, too, had a championship to win. His defense was indeed physical, and Hofstra started by missing its first four shots. UNCW, running its precision offense, made three of its first four and led 8-2 as the teams broke for the under 16:00 media time-out.

The tone, however, was set. UNCW would use that and step on the gas pedal. By the 12:00 mark, it was 17-3, and when the whistle blew at 11:11, the score was 22-5 UNCW. The Seahawks were shooting 60 percent while Hofstra missed twelve of its thirteen field goal attempts.

Stokes was nowhere near the player that led Hofstra to this point, but it didn't matter. UNCW was carving up Hofstra and CAA officials were visibly squirming. A bad loss meant two horrible things: the click factor of viewers not tuning in to see the game, and the nonclick factor of NCAA selection committee members tuning in. Neither was ideal.

The 22-7 became 28-9 and then 35-15. The game was getting beyond ugly. Stokes, however, hit a floater in the lane, his first field goal, that triggered an 11-0 run that got Hofstra back into it. The Seahawks made seven of its first eight shots in the second half, and the lead swelled again, this time to a high of twenty-three points at 53-30. Over the next five minutes, however, Hofstra would fly on a 29-9 run to get the game to 62-59.

They also had the ball. With a chance to tie, Antoine Agudio and Carlos Rivera miscommunicated on a cut and Agudio ended up throwing a pass directly into the hands of UNCW's Mitch Laue. On the ensuing possession, T.J. Carter would drain a three to give UNCW a 64-59 lead.

The Seahawks made the free throws down the stretch, and the CAA final would end 78-67. Carter scored the last twelve points for UNCW and was named the tournament's MVP.

Brad Brownell would sum up the championship performance, the fourth in seven years for UNCW, and the week leading up to it perfectly.

"I thought our experience showed," Brownell told the media afterward. "We came into the tournament with a little chip on our shoulder.

Nobody has been talking about us all week. We felt like we had to play our way into the (NCAA) tournament."

UNCW had punched its ticket to the Big Dance as the CAA's automatic qualifier. For the sixth consecutive year, the CAA's top seed had won its postseason tournament.

More than 1,500 fans would file into Trask Coliseum six days later to hear the fate of the Seahawks. For the Teal Nation, as their fans are called, RPIs and at-large bids and records against nonconference opponents didn't matter. Every single one of them knew it was a matter of who, where, and when.

In the locker room after the game, Pecora told his team, "The greatest gift I can give you is the truth. I want better. You have a second life."

The only question was where.

———

The near capacity crowd and frenzied excitement of the 2005 overtime final between ODU and VCU was something to behold. Students lined up outside the door two hours prior to tip-off. The building didn't completely sell out, but it was darn close—the 10,650 total attendance in a building that held 11,600 for basketball was a tournament record.

Though it wasn't technically a home game for VCU, the Richmond Coliseum is about twenty-five blocks from the Rams' campus. Turnout is high because there really is no road trip. VCU Director of Athletics Dr. Richard Sander had made it even more of a home game atmosphere by picking up the tab for VCU students—show a student ID and you were admitted free of charge.

Gold clad VCU fans circled three-quarters of the Coliseum, with the other quarter ODU blue. They arrived early, prepared for the tournament final and the ESPN television audience. The normally dark brown coliseum shone brightly in the light of the television backdrop and the energy of the fans.

It was a bonus that the overtime game lived up to its billing.

Even though it was a full year in the rearview mirror, smiles were everywhere for the CAA administration. The tournament was a financial success, and it had looked very good on television.

It was a show pulled off expertly. Officials could be happy that ODU would be slotted into the CAA's customary twelve or thirteen seed, and ESPN had plenty of footage of a quality event for its mind-numbing repeats of SportsCenter.

Everyone would band together and hope for an upset in the Big Dance. It was a nice little moment.

The 2006 CAA Tournament was quite different. It was played in front of an announced crowd of 4,580 between a team from North Carolina and one from Long Island, New York. There was a considerable churchlike feel to the building.

Neither VCU nor ODU fans would fill the building. Diehards remained and chose sides, but there is a difference in intensity between wanting someone to win and needing someone to win.

Though the coliseum had been spruced up with a smattering of new seat-back colors, it seemed stale. The energy of the crowd wasn't there to distract fans. The game itself wasn't a taut, back-and-forth thriller either.

Media coverage centered on the Skinn punch, but discussions were not on a 28-5 team being a trendy upset pick in brackets as had happened last year with Old Dominion. Discussion centered instead on how many teams the CAA could or would get into the NCAA Tournament.

The results had not changed. The top seed won the tournament. This year, however, the precise result was surrounded by new storylines.

Despite the lack of emotion, crowd, and Cinderella angle, there was a greater feeling of bigness. More than one team was being discussed. The spin was no show, only anticipatory conversation. You got the feeling that the Tony Skinn punch was the day the CAA grew up; perhaps became big.

In a quirky sort of way, that suited Tom Yeager just fine.

CHAPTER TWO

TORRENT

"The waiting is the hardest part." —Tom Petty

It was a very long week for the CAA. Grueling, in fact. Unless the folks who ran the conference could come up with a new angle, new strategy, or new data to prove why its teams should be included in the field of sixty-five, all anyone could do was sit and wait. No more games remained in which to prove themselves.

Hofstra and George Mason had to feel somewhat safe. Both teams sported gaudy records and RPIs in the twenties. No team with an RPI worse than thirty-three had ever been left out of the NCAA Tournament. Although George Mason had the better resume, Hofstra had beaten the Patriots twice in the past ten days.

Hofstra had lost only two games since January 21, at UNCW and then again to UNCW in the CAA finals. George Mason had lost only three times since December 30, 2005, at UNCW, Hofstra, and again to Hofstra in the CAA semifinals.

Tom Pecora and Jim Larranaga would each say that his team—as well as the other team—should be included in the field as an at large.

"If you look at our body of work, we belong in the tournament," Pecora said. "Our RPI is still going to be in the twenties, and I think we're good enough to get in the tournament and win some games. This conference has been outstanding all year and we deserve three bids."

But only UNCW knew it was safe.

Throughout the week that led up to Selection Sunday, CAA administrators, coaches, fans, and players would sweat. Bubble teams were
winning and nontournament teams were playing, and beating, locks.

They would sweat a missed, buzzer-beating open layup from Loyola
Marymount that would have defeated Gonzaga in the West Coast
conference finals. If the shot fell, Loyola Marymount would have
stolen a bid that otherwise would go to a bubble team.

George Washington bowed out in the Atlantic 10 quarterfinals, giving a coveted spot to the winner of that tournament (Xavier).
Maryland would win its first game in the ACC Tournament. Syracuse
would win in the Big East Tournament; ditto Texas A&M in the Big 12.

The farther the week unfurled, the less likely it appeared that the
CAA was getting its at-large bid. Hofstra? George Mason? Neither?
Both!

Craig Littlepaige had as much insight as anyone. The chairman
would see more than one hundred games himself during the year, and
he would buffet his sights envisioning conversations with those he
trusted in the college basketball community. "[Data] is not nearly as
persuasive as someone [who has seen a team] twice in league play or
many times as a result of scouting or preparation."

RPI was Littlepaige's prime example. "For me, RPI means very little.
For another [committee member], it may be the deciding component."

The national media were split. None of their opinions, in truth,
mattered.

While focus remained on the Hofstra and George Mason at-large
conundrum, Tom Yeager, for once, had other things on his mind.
Both VCU and Northeastern were on the bubble in terms of an NIT
berth.

In the end, three hours after a wild NCAA selection show had completed, the NIT pairings were announced. Neither Northeastern nor
VCU were a part of the field. As it would turn out, VCU was the high-

est rated team, in terms of RPI, to be left out of the postseason. Northeastern was second. Yeager was not in a diplomatic mood.

"I see a 15-14 Penn State team ranked 103; I see 15-13 Notre Dame; Charlotte is number 104. All are behind VCU. It makes you wonder 'what's the deal?'"

Blaine Taylor was equally uncomfortable. His Monarchs had won twenty-one games and weathered more adversity than any three teams should be forced to endure. They played well and conducted themselves in a first-class manner throughout the season.

Taylor has put those values into practice since first arriving in Norfolk nearly five years ago. His primary goal, and the aspect that most excited him, was the rebuilding of a once proud program. The x's and o's of coaching were his blood and love, but the higher goals of the program are his passion.

Blaine Taylor is a builder and leader in a niche that rewards builders. Mid-major basketball is all about building a program. "We don't talk a lot about winning and losing," said Taylor. "I'm more abstract in my thinking, more general. I believe the components (of building a program) will rise up. The wins and losses will come. It's a matter of preparation." Taylor added, "Mike Montgomery really helped me. He is very organized and manages well. I like to call him sneaky subtle. A lot of stuff just gets done. I learned a lot from him, some that is visible, and some that is invisible."

Visible to the ODU players, situated directly beside the white board in the locker room in which the team goes over strategy in the Ted Constant Center, their home, is a blank picture frame. Beside that, various sample rings for checking ring size. The championship team picture is invisible, though the players have a daily reminder.

After middling 13-16 and 12-15 seasons in his first two campaigns in Norfolk, Taylor's recruiting savvy began paying dividends. He landed both Alex Loughton (from Australia) and Arnaud Dahi (from the Ivory Coast) and stole Drew Williamson from major schools. ODU's victory total grew to seventeen, against twelve losses, in 2003-2004. Then there was the championship and school-record twenty-eight wins in a season in which Loughton was the conference player of the year as a junior.

"I feel like I'm at an optimum age to come in here with energy and experience, some wins and some championships, some rankings, and some of the things that you aspire to here," Taylor commented during his first news conference. He wasn't wrong.

Taylor was rebuilding the ODU program faster than anyone would have expected, but not without help. Beyond Dahi, Taylor plucked Valdas Vasylius (Lithuania), Janko Mrksic (Canada), and Sam Harris (Australia) to round out an international roster. Taylor has spent time in France and Finland in the search for players as well.

"You build as you go," he said. "It's easy to come into a situation where you have a good team; you must have good students and take care of the components that go with it, such as facilities. I have a simplistic view of management. Take what it is and make it better."

Part of Taylor's decision resided in the fact that Old Dominion pledged $54 million to build the Ted Constant Center, which opened in October 2002 and is the newest and most grand facility in the CAA.

"You try to effect change where needed, and I'm very happy that the administration has been responsive and committed. There was hunger here. People wanted to have a good program. Everyone, especially the athletic director and president, has been responsive and cooperative. Once those components are in place, things start to swell. Winning is the aftermath. We have a strong belief in everything we do. Core values and our standing on campus are very important."

Taylor immediately set his plan into motion, and it was paying off. Season ticket sales had increased by 300 percent since Taylor arrived. He also understood that the downstream effects, such as increased revenue inside the arena, were important factors. This was all part of the building process and it was taking shape, if not a year earlier than he thought.

"College basketball is the most efficient vehicle for revenue generation on the college campus," Taylor said. "You only pay for thirteen scholarships and play lots of games."

This is an especially important element for a mid-major school. In the reporting year July 1, 2003, through July 30, 2004, ODU posted men's basketball revenues of about $537,000. Its expenses crept toward $1.2 million. Taylor could do the math. In a very short time, he flipped that model.

It had to be bothersome to Taylor that people were actually disappointed in ODU's 21-9 season. It was further made difficult when Taylor found out that he would be playing a road game in the NIT, traveling to Colorado to play the Buffaloes.

Taylor told the *Norfolk Virginian Pilot,* "I would have thought the selection committee would have regionalized things a little bit. Here to Colorado certainly isn't regional by nature."

That's the fate of a preseason heavyweight when it doesn't meet expectations. The talk is about the Sweet 16 and the reality becomes an NIT road game. The margin in mid-major basketball is razor thin.

The NCAA Selection Show has become one of the most anticipated properties that sports programming can muster. Considering the amount of money on the line and the incredible growth and interest in the NCAA Tournament, it can reasonably be argued that this sixty minutes is more popular than, well, *60 Minutes.* The Selection Show has become a Sunday 6:00 p.m. staple.

The dynamics of the announcement of the teams that make the NCAA Tournament are interesting in their own right. Greg Gumball hosts, with his two analysts—Seth Davis and Clark Kellogg—sitting alongside. However, everyone at CBS knows why people tune in: They want to know who is making the tournament, and who plays whom. The show moves at a metered pace: the unveiling of a bracket, some quick commentary, followed by a commercial.

For coaches and players, who typically sit together to watch the telecast at the coach's house or an on-campus meeting room with family and supporters, it is rather like a doctor providing your diagnosis. Your fate is already sealed; it is a matter of finding out that fate. For the thirty-one conference champions and roughly twenty-eight of the thirty-four at-large teams, they know they are in. They await only their seeding and opponent. The mood at these get-togethers is more of a celebration. Without the burden of selection looming, they are free to speculate on opponents and seeds, which leads to exciting and festive conversation.

The feeling for those final teams on the vaunted bubble, however, brings a different vibe. Palpable nervous energy runs through the room. Some tell pithy jokes to fake laughs. Everyone tries to be calm in a situation that is anything but calm. Players huddle in small groups; coaches sit with their families. The food is never eaten.

Everyone believes they should be in the tournament, but they also know the sometimes strange choices made by the selection committee. They don't want to talk too much; nobody wants to tempt The Fates to rule against them. Thus, everyone mills about the room until 6:00 p.m., when Gumball, playing the role of drill sergeant, calls everyone to attention.

The celebration for the CAA came quickly. By 6:10 that evening, UNCW would know its fate. The Seahawks would draw a nine seed, the highest for the conference since 1987 when Navy was seeded eighth. They would play in Greensboro, about a four-hour drive from campus, against George Washington of the Atlantic 10. The winner drew #1 seed Duke.

By 6:20, nerves had turned to anger. Two bubble teams, Bradley and Texas A&M, had found their way into the field.

The next ten minutes won't soon be forgotten by the people that follow the CAA. Disbelief replaced anger after first Utah State, then Air Force, were shown to have made the field as at-large teams. Neither team had been on anyone's serious radar for a week, nor been close to the credentials of Hofstra or George Mason. Yet they were both in, and the available spots for bubble teams had all but disappeared.

Then, Seton Hall, widely considered the ninth option from the Big East, was called. Disbelief was fast becoming shock. As people were getting their wits about them and coming to terms with what was unfolding in front of their eyes, the sixth versus eleventh matchup was unveiled: Michigan State versus George Mason. In a rare moment in which a television commentator is able to accurately and succinctly sum up the collective thoughts of viewers, CBS's Seth Davis did just that: "I'm stupefied," he said quickly, just as the network was cutting to commercial. No two seconds were more priceless or more fitting than those.

The collective exhale from the George Mason gathering while CBS was in a commercial break produced hurricane-force winds. After the exhale, jubilation came. High fives, hugs, and beatless dances broke out in the room. It was especially poignant for Tony Skinn, whose wide smile was more of relief than joy. His team, the one he had shot into the tournament with his dagger at Wichita State, had made the NCAA's Big Dance.

It was different, though, for Tom Yeager. In fact, there was a moment of conflicting and fast-moving emotions for everyone associated with the CAA during the commercial break. The groundswell moved from amazement and took a decidedly positive turn and then hovered into a sense of disbelief. For the first time in twenty years, the CAA had a team selected to play in the NCAA tournament via the at-large berth.

While Yeager could savor that fact, he still had a metallic taste in his mouth. At least two teams—Utah State and Air Force—clearly did not deserve a bid before Hofstra; there were arguments about two others.

Little did anyone know that the unveiling of the brackets was only the beginning of the fun. When CBS cut to Jim Nantz and Billy Packer for analysis, the duo had harsh words for the selections and attacked, many say unfairly, Craig Littlepaige.

The duo denounced the bids of MVC teams and CAA teams in the place of major conference schools such as Florida State, Michigan, and Maryland. In the end, Nantz cut Littlepaige off, not giving him the opportunity and courtesy to congratulate all sixty-five teams.

Nantz and Packer continued their assault during the week leading up to the games. No matter where they turned up, the question about Selection Sunday was asked; and they would continue to banter and berate.

Nantz would go on "Mike and the Mad Dog Show" on New York's WFAN radio and talk about even his alma mater, Houston, deserving to be in the field instead of Hofstra or George Mason. What Nantz either had forgotten or never knew was that Houston had lost, at home, to VCU earlier in the season. (VCU finished sixth in the CAA, losing twice to George Mason and once to Hofstra.)

While attempting to remain diplomatic, Craig Littlepaige let slip in an interview with the Associated Press a comment that summed up the frustration:

I think Billy made the comment that he hadn't seen the Missouri Valley Conference play, but he felt comfortable enough to talk about their lower level of performance not only this year but over time. It seems to be counterintuitive, if you will, that he'd make a comment like that.

It wouldn't help the cause of Nantz and Packer that the first three games on the Thursday of the NCAA Tournament featured mid-majors against majors. Wichita State, the same Wichita State team that had been beaten at home by George Mason and was a quarterfinal loser in the MVC Tournament, drubbed the Big East's Seton Hall 86-66.

Wisconsin-Milwaukee (Horizon) also won, beating Oklahoma 82-74, and Pacific took Boston College to double overtime before tiring and losing. Two of three games ended with the mid major beating the major, and the third went to double overtime. The clock had not made it to 3:30 on the first Thursday, and mid-major schools had proven their point.

————

Tom Yeager remained conflicted, even after being told he had two teams in the Big Dance. Though it had defeated George Mason twice in the past ten days, the Hofstra Pride had been left out of the NCAA Tournament. It would be seeded third in the NIT.

"What is normally sheer joy—chasing the at-large bid—has been something less than that in the last twenty-four hours," Yeager said on the Monday morning after the announcement. "It's supposed to be good, but I have feeling of disappointment."

Yeager wasn't alone. Missouri State, the Missouri Valley team with the best RPI in the conference going in to Selection Sunday (#21), had also been left out.

"I was on a conference call last night with Doug Elgin (commissioner of the MVC) and some writers and he's in the same scenario," said Yeager. "Both of us were kind of saying 'huh?' We shared identical emotions. Thrilled. Bittersweet."

Yeager continued, "Air Force is the one that puzzles me. I hear Hofstra's Achilles heel was its schedule strength. Right above them is Marquette. Texas A&M is bad. Air Force is below Hofstra! So you had Air Force twenty spots below Hofstra in the RPI, both have similar credentials and may be weaker than Hofstra. They are clearly weaker than Missouri State. Yet one made the cut and these two didn't. That's what you get out of the 'tough team' criteria."

In a dejected manner, Yeager said, "I don't know. In your worst years maybe one of the big conferences swoops in and gets a bid unexpected. You don't expect to fall to Utah State and Air Force."

The process for the 2005 NCAA Tournament saw sixty-two ballots cast by the selection committee before agreement was reached on the sixty-four at-large teams. The first ballot is cast on the Thursday evening prior to Selection Sunday, and any team that makes eight of the ten ballots is automatically placed on the big board for consideration. A second list created on Friday of "other teams nominated" is also tracked. Though the committee tries to get the final brackets in the hands of CBS by 5:00 p.m., it was 5:34 before anyone from the network got a look at the field.

Yeager also knew, considering that George Mason Athletics Director Tom O'Connor was on the selection committee and George Mason Coach Jim Larranaga coached with Craig Littlepaige under Terry Holland at Virginia, conspiracy theorists would have a field day.

"I have a universal respect for basketball committees. A number of them are very good friends," Yeager said. "One of the things I learned [while serving as head of the NCAA infractions committee] is that until you're one of the people in the room, all of these conspiracy theories can be very far off base. I don't want to substitute some things that may not have come into play. In fairness to everybody there, Doug Elgin is asking the same thing. Whether we agree with it or not is immaterial because it is what it is."

Somehow, you got the feeling that sometimes there is little justice in the world. ("It's been an interesting twenty-four hours. Bed and sleep were two different things," said Yeager.) It had been twenty years since Yeager, the only commissioner the CAA had ever known, had been able to celebrate an at-large bid to the NCAA Tournament.

Instead of popping champagne and toasting the incredible success of the season, Yeager had spent twenty-four hours explaining, equivocating, and trying like hell to figure out why it was so unpleasant. Yeager was being asked questions to which he didn't have the answers.

He was being robbed of a moment he felt due—overdue. He certainly didn't picture the moments after the elusive at-large bid to be this way. To Yeager, that stunk.

None of this was particularly soothing for Tom Pecora. He still had nobody who could explain the Air Force inclusion to him. Nor did it make any sense in the world that his Hofstra could be passed over in favor of George Mason. He would say the right things to the media and take the high road, but privately he fumed.

"You can't tell me we don't belong," said Pecora on the night of the selections. "You just can't. By any measure we had the credentials. Somebody needs to explain it to me."

It all mattered. Though the buy games and scheduling philosophies of Florida State had backfired—and despite the irony that mid-majors were fighting among themselves about inclusion and exclusion—the reality existed that the CAA had missed out on another NCAA Tournament credit. More importantly, that credit equaled more than $1 million over five years. That would be critical money to funnel to the member schools.

After all, in the reporting year of July 2003 to July 2004, George Mason claimed men's basketball revenues of roughly $1.039 million. Its expenses were $100,000 more than that. Old Dominion, even with the new Ted Constant Center, claimed basketball revenues of just over $500,000 against expenses twice that number. Neither of those teams made the NCAA Tournament.

In comparison, the previous year, 2002-2003, Louisville *did* make the tournament and claimed revenue of $14.6 million, according to figures compiled by the Department of Education for the 2002-2003 school year. The average revenue figure for the sixty-four teams that made the NCAA Tournament that season was slightly greater than $4 million.

Granted, much of the revenue disparity comes from greater ticket sales and alumni donations and buy games, but it is also another data point for the cycle discussed in an earlier chapter. You need money to put yourself on the purchasing end of the buy game contract. For example, 2006 Atlantic 10 champion Xavier paid five schools a total of $290,000 to play in Cincinnati. That money had to come from somewhere.

More money for the conference means more money can be given to schools, and it means more flexibility for television and exposure. The absence of the need for buy games, because NCAA Tournament money is included, is a key igniter.

Expense flexibility is a key as well. Mid-majors are typically watching every dime, working on trade, and battling support for lesser sports. To wit, in the same 2002-2003 year, Illinois-Chicago spent about $125,000 on its basketball program, whereas Syracuse wrote checks for an astounding $8.4 million.

So despite any economic theory put forth, the financial disparity between majors and mid-majors becomes simple: Those teams generating the most money will carry the most influence. It sounds rather like big business. Like big business, there was a bottom line: The CAA had two teams in the NCAA Tournament.

CHAPTER THREE

PREAMBLE

—

"Dancing and building are the two primary and essential arts."
—Havelock Ellis

There is a thin line that separates creativity from desperation. In many cases for college basketball coaches, the departure of genius and futility is determined solely by whether a particular act or decision is successful. It could be the lineup change when a star player is injured. Perhaps it's the decision to schedule a November road game at Cameron Indoor Stadium against Duke instead of facing the regional rival. Whatever the case, coaching college basketball in the twenty-first century has become a profession of risk. It is scored increasingly on the bottom line—wins and losses—and that simple reality blurs the line between the crafty vagabond and the luckless desperado.

Sometimes, though, success is born from both.

One important, hazy, and frustrating challenge for a mid-major coach is in his quest to schedule the approximately ten games each season that will round out his team's opponents—the nonconference schedule.

"For me, it's the number one pain," says Jeff Capel, who was getting ready to begin his final campaign before being hired to replace Kelvin Sampson at Oklahoma. "If fans knew how tough it is…"

Capel's voice trails off and he shakes his head and laughs. "You have nine or ten nonconference games and basically late November and December to play them."

You look around Jeff Capel's office and you see order. The kind of order that lets you know he's thought deeply about this. It's also the kind of order that borders on overorganization. There are stacks of paper and videos; the white board is neatly erased; and there's just enough space from his desk to the round table to use as a research facility.

When you look just a little more closely, however, the frustration is evident. The edge to his voice tells the truth when he discusses scheduling: He's made the calls and heard the excuses.

Capel pauses for another moment as he considers the intricacies of who he wants to play, who will take his calls, and who will fit in terms of how he wants to bring his team along prior to the grueling CAA conference season. His mind then thinks logistics.

"You need (corresponding open) dates for starters. We also try to be cognizant of needing attractive match-ups for fans."

This basic issue is often overlooked when scheduling. The logistics issue Capel refers to is only exacerbated when factoring in holidays, exam schedules, and other obligations. (Most coaches try to keep their players' legs fresh early in the season, as well as spend some time interacting within their community.) Outside of any creative methodology, such as conference versus conference challenges or exempt tournaments quickly becoming the exclusive domains of the power conferences, you must simply have open dates that align with a prospective opponent's open dates.

Blaine Taylor agrees with Capel.

"It is the most misunderstood thing among fans," he says. "It takes two to tango. Our lot in life is that as we've gotten better, people don't want to risk losing to you. I wish people wouldn't think it's a strange notion that we could beat them, but you can't tell people their business. I can't be critical of them. I do wish it were an easier environment."

That environment and its intricacies is precisely what makes scheduling a basketball game for a mid major daunting. Heading into a season, a coach needs to balance several factors in gearing up his team for conference play. While Roy Williams and Lute Olsen garner most of the headlines for their team's preparation, it is even more important for a mid-major coach.

Remember, the regular season in a mid-major conference is unlike that of the ACC or Big East, where a .500 conference record likely gets you into the NCAA Tournament, assuming you have taken care of business (read: won) with the out-of-conference games. It's a vicious cycle for the mid-major team trying to get noticed. The major school is shooting for a 9-1 nonconference schedule, thinking that combined with its 8-8 conference season they are at 17-9 entering the conference tournament. When you factor in strength of schedule, based in part on strength of the conference, they can make a credible case. So the major coach can throw a toughie in there, such as Arizona's trip to Charlottesville and loss to Virginia in December 2004. The rest of the games, however, should be easy wins—home games, for sure. This is where the mid-majors get left out, because often they stand a legitimate chance of beating the major school.

In 2004-2005, NC State and Iowa accomplished better, both going 7-9 in the regular season and making the NCAA Tournament as at-large selections. Since 1997, in fact, the following eight teams from the BCS Big Six have made the NCAA Tournament as an at-large team with a losing record in conference play.

1997-Virginia (18-12, 7-9); 9 seed
1998-Florida State (17-13, 6-10); 12 seed
1998-Clemson (18-13, 7-9); 6 seed
1999-Purdue (19-12, 7-9); 10 seed
2001-Penn State (19-11, 7-9); 7 seed
2003-Alabama (17-11, 7-9); 10 seed
2004-2005-Iowa (21-11, 7-9); 10 seed
2005-NC State (19-13, 7-9); 10 seed

Note: Arkansas (7-9 in 2000), Iowa (7-9 in 2001), and Maryland (7-9 in 2004) won their conference tournaments with sub-.500 conference regular season records. Incredibly, Clemson finished the 1997-1998 ACC season 7-9 and won just one game in the ACC Tournament. The Tigers were given a six seed and promptly lost to Western Michigan 75-72.

Both Iowa and NC State were able to fatten up on dubious nonconference schedules in which mid-majors were, in general, avoided. Certainly traveling to play a mid major was not part of the plan. This cycle allows the major to promote a glossy overall record as well as a couple of key wins over other major schools.

And why not? From 1997-2005, an astounding 276 of 428 teams (64.4 percent) from the Big Six BCS who finished their regular season at .500 or better have made the tournament. In that time frame, BCS schools have received 222 at-large bids of 307 available (72.31 percent).

If anybody knows this conundrum, it is Dick Vitale. The ESPN analyst has spent more than twenty-five years close to college basketball, and nobody has been more outspoken.

"[Mid-majors] need to go out and perform and not get caught up in worrying," Vitale said shortly before the beginning of the 2005-2006 season. "Take care of what you have in front of you. As long as the NCAA allows the automatic berth, [they should] concentrate on competing. The A10 used to spend so much time competing. Guys like [John] Chaney and [John] Calipari would play and schedule anybody."

This is what rankles coaches of mid-major programs. They know they can compete but are rarely given the opportunity to prove it.

So the mid-majors make due, working the phones into August and September to get a schedule finalized for the upcoming season. Regional matchups between mid-majors have become mainstays of schedules. ESPN entered its fourth year of Bracket Busters in 2005-2006.

It's getting the tougher games, the big games, the games against the BCS conference teams, that proves to be the challenge, and sometimes entertainingly so. When a coach finds success and wins consistently, especially if he will be returning with an experienced team the following year, it becomes next to impossible to get teams in the ACC, Big East, or Big 12 to even consider going head to head.

VCU won twenty-three games and came within one point of beating Wake Forest in the 2004 NCAA Tournament. ODU won twenty-eight games in 2004-2005 and played Final Four participant Michigan State into the last three minutes.

———

Jeff Capel and Blaine Taylor share similar stories about the frustrations of getting even a discussion going with coaches of major schools about playing, now that they are winning and gaining national attention.

Taylor laughs at retelling the joke about the coach at the other end of the phone line faking static: "What coach?...buzzzzzzzzzzz...I can't hear you...buzzzzzzzzz...must be a bad connection...buzzzzzzzzz...good luck...buzzzzzzz...no comprende........click."

Capel recounts several phone conversations. "I call my friends every year and they say the same thing right off the bat—hey how are you doing, don't ask me about scheduling."

Although both coaches laugh, it is more the laughter of "if I don't laugh, I'll cry." It's a tough spot being on the mid-major end of the phone. You are selling yourself as a good opponent for several reasons. But you can't oversell—you can be too good. What's especially tough is that the major coach on the other end knows how many games you've won and how many players you have returning.

So you end up with a phone call that resembles a dance. Each party is willing to put forth so much but not too much, each party knowing what the other wants. Too many times, it ends in failure.

Jim Larranaga had a difficult enough time scheduling games, and then he captured the nation's attention by taking his team to the Final Four. Larranaga added Duke, at Cameron, to his slate in a one-game affair. It's not ideal, but there was an opportunity.

This is where the water is not as murky as it is turbulent. Getting the opportunity to play, on television, is vital for a mid major.

Because so many times a tournament berth is predicated on strength of schedule and *who* you play, a mid major can have an outstanding season (as Utah State did in 2003-2004 when they finished 25-3 but lost in their conference tournament final) and be left out of the NCAA Tournament. In the eyes of the selection committee, though, they didn't play a tough enough nonconference schedule.

The whelp of mid-major programs is almost always the same: "How can we beat quality teams when they won't play us?" Says Vitale: "That's why the NCAA Tournament is so special. Everybody gets a chance to compete." It is precisely that opportunity that mid-majors crave.

Even a past staple, the exempt tournament, is beginning to see mid-majors slip out of favor. These are generally the early season mini tournaments that bring together eight- or sixteen-team fields to play against one another. The Great Alaska Shootout and Maui Invitational are historically the two most known of these tournaments. For example, the 2004 Guardian's Classic saw the Creighton Blue Jays, a poster child mid-major program from the Missouri Valley Conference, defeat both Missouri and Ohio State in Kansas City to claim the championship. The 2005 Guardian's Classic schedule was announced, and there was no Creighton. In fact, there was no MVC team on the slate at all. Major players Iowa, Kentucky, Texas, and West Virginia would take on Maryland Eastern Shore, South Dakota State, Lipscomb, and Wofford. At the end of the day the major coaches have a job, too. A loss to Creighton doesn't look good on a resume, especially come March. The risk involved in playing Directional State is far less than matching up and taking your chances with a mid major.

These factors combined are what exasperate coaches. It is the current "measuring stick," and the fairness is widely debated. This so-called measurement is used by the NCAA Tournament selection committee to different degrees, depending on whomever is at the other end of the conversation. Of course, this number is a team's number in the ratings percentage index—the RPI.

The RPI conundrum as it relates to a mid major is especially tenuous considering that majors have the "luxury" of playing each other during the conference season, which protects their RPI standing. Because RPI is based on opponents and their winning percentage, it is in their best interest to win early and survive the conference season. For mid-majors, the paradigm is completely different. With few opportunities to play BCS conference schools, the chance to impact their RPI in a positive way is limited; and because the bottom teams in their conferences usually carry corresponding low RPIs, even a quality nonconference schedule is undermined.

This reasoning explains why in 2003-2004 Utah State can finish 25-3 and manage an RPI ranking of forty-three, while Alabama in the SEC can finish 17-12 and boast an RPI of twenty-six. Notable as well from that season is Alabama at 4-11 in games against the RPI top fifty, a measuring stick for the NCAA selection committee. Utah State was 1-1. The opportunity is majors have it, mids don't.

The reasoning here isn't meant to say that either Alabama or Utah State was more deserving of a bid, or who was a better team. It is pointed out merely to say no one can honestly tell, because Utah State had little opportunity to prove itself. It's a familiar battle cry, even in an atmosphere where the criteria for selection into the tournament seems to be changing and evolving.

Let's take a look at the typical resumes of a major and mid major, viewed side by side, from the 2004-2005 season. RPIs are courtesy of Ken Pomeroy, a leading RPI analyst.

	Final RPI	SOS	Conference Standing	Record vs. Top 100 RPI	Nonconference Record	Nonconference Home Games	Nonconference Road Games	Nonconference Neutral Site Games
A	42	43	7-9 (7th)	9-8	12-1	8	1	4
B	45	88	12-6 (2nd)	6-6	7-2	4	5	0

When sitting on the NCAA selection committee, who do you choose?

Team A is the Iowa Hawkeyes. They traveled just once during the nonconference season, to Drake, a Missouri Valley Conference member which would finish in 2004-2005 at 13-16. Iowa beat Louisville and Texas early in the season in Hawaii. The Hawks got hot late as well, winning its last three regular season games—albeit two were against conference bottom dwellers Penn State and Michigan—and beat Michigan State in the Big 10 Tournament.

Team B is the Wichita State Shockers, which also competes in the Missouri Valley. This team beat the highest RPI team on the nonconference schedule, and the only BCS conference team it could schedule—Providence of the Big East, at Providence. Of its five home games, the highest ranked team to play WSU in Wichita was 172nd Missouri-Kansas City. Consider this as well: Last year the MVC had five of its ten teams in the top fifty-two RPI, and the conference as a whole was rated eighth (ahead of leagues such as Conference USA and the Atlantic 10). Finishing 12-6 is no small feat.

So, what's the difference? Simply, Iowa got to play teams on television. They compete in the Big 10. They were able to take advantage of the "glamorous" wins at the beginning of the season. Iowa had excusable losses to such teams as Illinois and Michigan State, so it had the luxury of taking a few nights off—losing at home to 13-18 Michigan and at 7-21 Purdue. The slate is a rather undistinguished season, as Iowa didn't beat any of the top three teams in the Big 10 during the conference season.

Mid-majors aren't asking for a reward, or even a handout. The only thing coaches want is a chance to prove their team's worth. It's about opportunity. Hofstra's Tom Pecora says it a bit resigned, but sums it up in a manner that certainly would begin an avalanche of affirmative head nods from mid-major coaches: "When all is said and done, it's a major conference tournament. The BCS conferences are making policy. They have the power and that's okay."

In a game that would prove, nearly four months later, to be wildly fitting, George Mason had the first opportunity to strike in the 2005-2006 season. After dispatching Cal Irvine of the Big West rather handily, the Patriots met eighteenth ranked Wake Forest—in Winston-Salem, no less. Wake Forest buried George Mason early, and despite a valiant rally from nineteen points down in the second half, the Patriots fell 83-78 in overtime.

That George Mason played a top twenty team close, on the road, seemed to keep in lock step with the CAAs modus operandi: Scare the majors but ultimately fall short. At some point, CAA teams would have to get over that hump if they ever wanted to become nationally significant.

"It is very difficult coming that close to victory, that close to beating an ACC team at their home court," Larranaga said after the game. "It's very painful right now." Painful, indeed, to the entire conference. The first opportunity had passed.

The pain was evident on Larranaga's face. He carries a passion not only for his team but also for the entire game of college basketball. The cornball routine the entire country would fall in love with four months later was real: He had been on both sides of this kind of game in his long career, and knows the emotions.

These emotions have helped the graying and departure of his hair, and initiated noticeable wrinkles on his face. The wrinkles, however, are mostly uncovered when he smiles, which the 6-foot, 5-inch coach often can be found doing. Everything he does has a purpose and it is a smooth gait under his frame. He is purposed, but relaxed, as if there is no place he'd rather be than exactly where he is.

For Jim Larranaga, the story of his overtime loss at Wake Forest was all too familiar. Close losses and near misses have defined his tenure at George Mason. He can easily point to the three-point loss to a top 10 Maryland team in the first round of the 2001 NCAA Tournament. He remembers vividly an almost trip to New York in the 2004 NIT, knocking off Tennessee (and then Austin Peay) before bowing at Oregon.

From 1998-1999 to 2004-2005, the Patriots finished first, second, third, second, fourth, third, and sixth in the CAA standings. Always close, always successful, yet never on top of the hill. Even in last season's magical year, the Patriots tied for the top spot with UNCW and were given the second seed.

Larranaga is one of those coaches who could sit next to you—for hours—talking basketball. He loves the sport as much as he loves the profession. He is quick to give even strangers a trivia quiz: How many Division I teams, of more than 300, have won at least ten conference games in each of the past seven seasons? Obviously, his Patriots are one of those teams.

The beauty of Larranaga is that he doesn't simply give you the answer. You literally walk, conference by conference, trying to name the teams. Larranaga will intersperse brief stories about the people or programs along the way. (My guess was twelve and I was able to name nine. The answer was fourteen.)

The fact that Larranaga is always in the hunt, yet has not coached a dominant program, is one factor that keeps the fifty-six-year-old coach motivated. So does the fact that he has a great situation for himself and his family.

"We have the PatDome, the campus, and the geography to succeed," Larranaga says. "We have a president with a vision and the place of athletics [in that vision]. My wife loves the area, and my son, when he comes home, lives close. It's a great situation all the way around." (Larranaga's son, Jon, played for his father at GMU and is now playing professionally in Italy.)

Of course, it does not hurt that basketball is the premier sport on the GMU campus. Larranaga has his system in place, and is happy with running a successful mid-major program. Some would be surprised, considering his coaching background. For eight seasons he assisted Terry Holland on the bench for Virginia, coaching alongside now NCAA Tournament Committee Chairman Craig Littlepaige. Larranaga coached Ralph Sampson in the days when Virginia was ranked #1 and played deep into several NCAA Tournaments. It was no surprise when, in 1986, Larranaga landed his first head coaching job with Bowling Green University.

"It wasn't the only place I interviewed, but it fit best. I was offered the job at Marist, but I knew what I wanted and that was not it," he says. Larranaga then leans back in his chair, looks up into the air, and muses, "I also interviewed at Providence, but they hired some guy named Pitino and I guess that worked out." Larranaga is that way. Always a story, always chatting hoops. "Facilities are so important to a mid major," he continues. "Bowling Green had the vision of a brand new convocation center. They handed me the plans for the place when I interviewed."

For the next eleven years Larranaga would lead Bowling Green to 170 wins, including upsets over many highly ranked teams, including Kentucky, Michigan State (twice), Ohio State, Penn State, and Purdue. The 1990 win over Michigan State (98-85) came when the Spartans were ranked fifth in the country.

But alas, the new convocation center was never built, and Larranaga could see the shared commitment to improve Bowling Green football. "There was football, hockey, women's sports, and then basketball," Larranaga recalls. So it was on to George Mason with the 10,000-seat Patriot Center already built.

Unfortunately, the Wake Forest game was played in Winston-Salem, and George Mason was on the defensive from the opening tap. Eric Williams, Wake's powerful and talented center, bulled Jai Lewis around in the paint and scored fourteen first-half points. A 44-29 deficit at the half quickly became a nineteen-point bulge before Larranaga began trapping and pressing all over the floor.

The move ignited a 38-18 run that gave Mason a brief 69-68 lead with just under three minutes to play. They were in line for the school's first ever victory over a ranked opponent. After Chris Ellis gave Wake the lead back at 71-69, Lewis hit two free throws to retie the game at 71-71. Mason's Tony Skinn had a good look but missed a three pointer with about a minute to play, and the game would go into overtime. The Patriots never led in the extra session, and Wake made all six free throws in the final twenty-two seconds. The final was 83-78.

Once again, close but no cigar. For Mason and the CAA.

Since an at-large berth remains a somewhat fleeting reality, mid-major coaches know that preparation for a demanding conference season, and playing your best in late February, is mandatory for success. It does more harm than good for, say, Tom Pecora to line up the top ten programs in the country to play his Hofstra team. In this climate, most if not all of the games will be played on the road, and if his team gets—to use a favorite Pecora term—tatered each time out, Pecora faces larger issues than who is on his schedule. Too many big losses can destroy a team's psyche before it has a chance at success during its conference season.

"We played the toughest nonconference schedule in the CAA last year," says VCU's Jeff Capel in reference to his team's 2004-2005 slate. "But you have to win games. You can't beat down your players because they have to learn how to win."

By balancing attractive games with winnable games, and straddling the thin line of games that will test his team with games that will build confidence and allow him to work out kinks, a mid-major coach is building up for February, when games matter most in mid-major conferences. This tack, however, certainly shrinks the universe of possible teams. This issue is even worse on the West Coast, where there are fewer teams from which to select; and don't forget logistics.

Coaches and administrators, therefore, are stuck. They need attractive games for RPI and to sell tickets and keep alumni happy. The attractive games are difficult to come by. Even the ones they get are likely to be on the road. The same stereotype Clemson receives nationally for fattening up on early in the season, nonconference cupcakes holds true for a mid major. You can only play so many Massachusetts Culinary Institutes before people howl.

Still, games can be found. The main rub for a mid-major coach is finding that high-quality opponent, so his team can show it can play with anyone, and test his team, and make fans and alumni happy. Putting North Carolina on the schedule is an all-win scenario for the mid major.

The trouble is, and this is very real, there is no way for the coach of a major school to win in this scenario. Home or away, it is expected that Kansas will beat Wichita State, that Stanford will beat San Francisco. No matter how good the mid major may be, even an eventual NCAA Tournament team that wins a game, it still will be viewed by alumni and the throng of media as a bad loss for the major. When there's no escape, the coach will mitigate this risk by agreeing to play on his home court, giving him the best chance at the win. For example, a loss to Old Dominion doesn't look good on the resume of North Carolina State come Selection Sunday, especially if the Wolfpack finishes in its customary middle spot in the ACC.

Consider this case in point: Bucknell of the Patriot League, the twenty-fourth ranked conference, waltzed into Pittsburgh's Petersen Events Center in January 2005 and beat the Panthers 69-66. Nobody beats Pitt, at Pitt. The Panthers were 43-1 all time at Petersen prior to this game. At the time, it was a bad loss for Pitt. It didn't look that bad, though, after Bucknell upset Kansas in the first round of the NCAA Tournament.

That may be a solitary example, but do you really think Roy Williams would want to take his Tar Heels team into Trask Coliseum to play UNCW, where the gym is small and warm and the fans are loud? The risk is too great.

In fact, UNC agreed to a two-game set with UNCW, but only because UNCW played their "home game" in Myrtle Beach, South Carolina, so guard Raymond Felton could play near his home town. According to Williams before the return game in Chapel Hill, "If that scenario hadn't been there, I don't know if we would be playing either one of these games."

Maryland's Gary Williams has admitted he will play the CAA's George Mason. He will play at home or on a neutral site, but never in Fairfax, where Mason has rolled up a significant home court winning percentage in the 10,000-seat Patriot Center. This is exactly why most of these games are played at the home site of the major school. The major coaches want every possible advantage. You can't blame them for wanting it this way. They have jobs to keep, too.

Interestingly, in 2005 the NCAA amended the RPI calculation to put a greater weight on road victories (1.4). It has been documented in multiple

places that home teams win 70 percent of the time in NCAA college basketball, so there's no real debate about where major teams—heck, all
teams—want to play. So the tweak makes sense. Incent teams to travel,
and help those teams without a choice. The theory goes that power conference teams would schedule a few more road games because a win
counts more than one, but the tweak thus far has not proven successful.

According to Pomeroy, a leading number cruncher in this country,
power conference teams played a *greater* percentage of home games in
2005-2006 than the average of the previous four seasons combined.
Pomeroy's numbers are as follows:

Power conference
(ACC, Big East, Big 10, Big 12, Pac10 and SEC)
Nonconference Games

	Home	Road	% Home
2002-2005	1655	341	82.9
2006	451	86	84.0

His numbers for all conference home and road games in 2005-2006
(as compiled and published on his website on October 19, 2005) are
as follows:

	Home	Road	% Home
Big XII	86	18	82.7
SEC	92	25	78.6
Big East	115	33	77.7
ACC	90	28	76.3
Pac 10	55	18	75.3
Big 10	76	27	73.8
MWC	58	26	69.0
CUSA	73	48	60.3
Atlantic 10	82	57	59.0
MVC	40	29	58.0
WCC	44	40	52.4

WAC	43	40	51.8
CAA	40	43	48.2
Horizon	35	40	46.7
MAC	34	42	44.7
Ivy League	40	50	44.4
Patriot	35	47	42.7
Big Sky	28	39	41.8
Big West	32	45	41.6
Sun Belt	41	62	39.8
MAAC	27	41	39.7
SoCon	32	56	36.4
NEC	30	53	36.1
America East	30	54	35.7
Independents	49	98	33.3
OVC	14	34	29.2
MidCon	20	51	28.2
Southland	21	54	28.0
Big South	16	43	27.1
Atlantic Sun	17	48	26.2
MEAC	16	68	19.0
SWAC	6	60	9.1

Pomeroy concludes that "teams with the big budgets are not willing to trade two or three spots in the RPI for the money that home dates bring in. This may come back to haunt one or two teams each season, thereby costing them revenue they would get from the NCAA Tournament, but most schools are willing to take that risk."

Amazingly, Syracuse's first true road game in 2005-2006 was its Big East opener at Notre Dame on January 11. (The Orange did play Towson in Scranton, Pennsylvania, in a homecoming game for Gerry McNamara.) Washington played its first road game January 12, at Southern Cal.

When asked about the importance of traveling to play a major school, Pecora is clear. "It's obscene," he says. "Travel is severe enough in conference (games). We don't need to travel nonconference."

Still, Taylor, who clearly knows his numbers, also knows who he wants to schedule. "We get more pop playing and beating Liberty than losing to Clemson," he says, referring to the RPI fact that because it is based on winning percentage and Liberty will go, say, 19-10 in the Big South and Clemson will go 10-19 in the ACC, it's better for his team's RPI to beat an inferior opponent than lose to a good one with a higher RPI.

As always, though, fans don't buy into the value of an intelligently scheduled game. Taylor himself says, "The problem is that people want to see teams so we can fill the place." After all, Liberty is Liberty.

BUSTING BRACKETS AND BEING BOUGHT

It's not as if there haven't been several well-intentioned attempts to rectify this reality. Jim Larranaga's career path—successful and respected assistant coach to head coach at a mid-major university—is almost the "market-approved" path these days in the coaching profession. The list of current coaches that took such a route could fill many pages in this book. A hurdle in this path, historically, was that these assistant coaches weren't sure how to get on the train, nor did they really know people outside their own circle of friends.

Athletic directors are in the same boat. As their coaches succeed (or fail, as is the case), they need to find quality replacements. Sure, they can spend thousands of dollars hiring search firms to help weed through candidates, but in the words of VCU Director of Athletics Dick Sander, "What do they know that I already shouldn't? It seems like a waste of time and money to me."

This scenario is precisely why VCU, through its postgraduate sports management program (SportsCenter), created the Villa Seven Consortium. The consortium is a group of mid-major athletic directors and administrators whose goal is to jointly discuss and resolve the issues facing their programs. Created by VCU in 2004 and named after its first home at the Mirage Hotel and Casino in Las Vegas, this forum is being used as a philosophical summit to gain national consensus and problem solving among mid-major universities.

Importantly, the progression and development of the meeting's agenda has become two-fold and clear: stage a reception in which thirty-five of the best and brightest assistant coaches from around the country are given a chance to meet, greet, and mingle with the athletic directors of mid-major universities. It's kind of a job fair, only without the stress of immediate needs. Secondly, utilize the benefits of getting so many colleagues together in the same place to hold a discussion on the issues and possible solutions of being a mid major.

The idea is probably most brilliant via its sheer simplicity. If an athletic director has already met and is aware of a young assistant who can take over his program, and conversely a young assistant feels he carries a good rapport with an athletic director, then when the time comes for a school to hire a new head coach, both parties have a short list.

Remember the words of Bill Hogan, AD at San Francisco. So much of the success of many of the athletic directors is based solely on who they hire as head coach. It is in their best interest to already have a knowledge of the market. This way they don't have to trust some outside source that, really, doesn't know any better.

Like Larranaga with Marist, if the coach doesn't feel the opportunity is what he desires, he can pass as well. Simply, it just makes everyone more knowledgeable, which means that better hires can occur a much greater percentage of the time.

To fully realize the potential of the idea, however, the consortium had to become much more than appetizers and an open bar for a couple of hours. So in May 2005, the Villa Seven Consortium, for its second meeting, selected thirty-five of the top men's basketball assistant coaches to attend what they called "an educational symposium" in Charlotte. The event featured coaches such as Bobby Cremins and Morgan Wootten discussing the business side of coaching, while also serving on a panel to help the assistant coaches glean a better understanding of their profession.

Frank Haith, who had just completed his first year as a head coach at the University of Miami, shared his thoughts on the first one hundred days on the job as he transitioned from respected associate head coach under Rick Barnes at Texas to head coach in the ACC. Coaches who had just finished their second and third seasons were on hand to talk about their maturation and transition.

Fran Fraschilla, former NABC Coach of the Year and current ESPN college basketball analyst, also lent his perspective. ESPNU was there to discuss television's impact on the future of college basketball. The meeting was a partnership between the VCU SportsCenter, Nike, and Daktronics and was hailed as an absolute success for all who attended.

"The programs help break down a barrier and cut down a little on the anxiety you may have toward this process," said Tom Moore, an assistant coach under Jim Calhoun at Connecticut. "You hear the names of these athletic directors and conference commissioners, and you think of these people as very professional and maybe even larger than life and unapproachable. It makes the process a little less daunting, and that's the case even if a particular athletic director wasn't there."

It is these aspects, not the x's and o's of being a coach, that are the focus of the meetings and the crux of what Villa Seven is built upon. The group understands it is accelerating the process of searching for coaches, and it helps potential coaches handle visibility and success.

Specifics such as building a staff, interacting with the athletic director, and dealing with the media are covered. Because sitting athletic directors are involved, the viewpoint is direct and legitimate, not theoretical.

Its success has been quick and obvious: of the thirty-five assistant coaches invited to the initial Villa Seven meetings, eighteen already have head coaching jobs.

The meeting has also reached its way to BCS administrators. Georgetown's Bernard Muir, one of the top young, cutting-edge administrators in basketball, has become involved in Villa Seven. Muir has worked at Notre Dame and with the NCAA. That kind of buy-in, as well as the full support of Phil Knight and Nike, has made the program nationally relevant in collegiate circles.

The success of that meeting helped springboard the July 2005 meeting in Las Vegas, in which athletic directors and conference administrators from the CAA, West Coast, Atlantic 10, Mountain West, Sun Belt, Horizon, and Southern conferences came together for two days to discuss the issues that face mid-majors. Norwood Teague, one of the top administrators from national champion North Carolina, was there to lend his perspective.

For two days prior to the reception, the agenda ranged from media exposure, to television, to scheduling, to positioning, to how people run departments. "We have a lot going for us," Sander said to open the meeting. "We need to find a way to use it to our advantage. We need to figure out ways to create a power base for ourselves."

Make no mistake. These are not "woe is me" administrators looking for a group hug and some ideas to help "overthrow" the big bad establishment. On the contrary, this is a group of bright minds, young and old, searching for progressive and creative answers to legitimate problems. They crave the same things administrators for major schools crave: success. And that really comes down to a simple tenet: situational equity.

The concept has been overwhelmingly successful and has drawn the interest and support of Nike. During the winter of 2005, Nike and VCU were in discussion about a national program that would extend Villa Seven into football and women's basketball, as well as protecting the original intent and success of the men's basketball meetings.

"We're not trying to benefit financially from this," said Mike Ellis, an assistant athletic director at VCU and the man who, along with his boss Dr. Richard Sander, is most responsible for the success of the idea. "We're just trying to put two groups together who need to get to know each other."

The biggest innovation, perhaps, has certainly received the most attention, if only because television became involved. ESPN began, in 2003, its Bracket Busters Tournament. The inaugural Bracket Buster Saturday featured eighteen teams and was played under great fanfare as a way for mid-majors to both get noticed on television and garner a late season victory over a quality opponent to "impress the commit-tee." Southern Illinois of the Missouri Valley, with a last-second victo-ry over Wisconsin-Milwaukee, was perhaps most symbolic of the event's desired result, as that victory, on national television, was cred-ited with going a long way to garnering the Salukis an at-large berth in the NCAA Tournament.

The Bracket Buster event was the brainchild of Burke Mangus, ESPN's director of college basketball programming. Mangus discussed the idea with a handful of mid-major conference administrators, all of whom resoundingly endorsed the idea, and the event was born. However, as with many well-intentioned ideas, it has grown beyond its borders. Its original purpose is also its greatest flaw.

In its second season, Bracket Busters grew to forty-six teams. That number jumped to sixty-four in 2005, and television was no longer an option for most teams. In addition, when you look at the matchups, only three had a legitimate bearing on the NCAA Tournament field: Vermont lost to Nevada (both teams made the field); Pacific defeated UTEP (both teams made the field); and Southern Illinois beat Kent State (SIU made it but Kent State did not).

In 2006, it encompassed one hundred teams and became more than just one day. ESPN would use three of its properties to televise thirteen games, the true Bracket Busters. The remaining thirty-seven games would be scheduled regionally. It was impossible, based on the number itself, to call the tournament Bracket Busters. The sheer size weakens the impetus of the event: with one hundred teams participating and per-haps five important games, many teams find themselves with merely a midseason out-of-conference matchup they neither want nor need. Eight CAA teams participated in the event, which brings into play the biggest disservice an event like this could impose on a mid major: A lesser mid major with no shot at an at-large beats a mid major who is on the bubble. That would be disastrous. Ironically, it would be a simi-lar disaster if a major school were to lose to a mid major.

Coaches and administrators, however, are most put off by its tim-ing. While it is understandable in terms of compelling programming for ESPN to stage the games in late February, almost any mid-major athletic director or coach will tell you that if it is going to be played, it should be done so in the preseason. Remember, the mid-majors already have a full slate of conference games to worry about. To toss a somewhat random game into the mix, when you don't even know your opponent until three weeks prior to the game, is, in the opinion of most, an undue hardship.

This is why involving schools from major conferences in Bracket Busters would bring the event back to its true roots and provide value. You're not going to learn a lot, and certainly not impact at-large berths, by seeing the fourth place MVC team square off against the third place Horizon team. Nor will you glean much from the resumes of, say, Southern Illinois/Vermont. Line up a Wisconsin-Milwaukee versus Alabama, Vermont versus Syracuse, UAB versus LSU, or a Bucknell versus Kansas, however, and you likely have some interest and you can tell a few things about a few teams.

These were all 2005 NCAA Tournament first-round matchups won by the mid-majors. Yet again, even under the Bracket Buster umbrella, you would be asking a major to play a mid major in a no-win situation. When you then consider that one of the tenets of a Bracket Buster matchup is that you return the game the following season on the other team's home court, you can see the additional reasons for hesitancy and the reason why we'll probably never see this occur.

Thus the constant talk among mid-majors of scheduling a conference challenge similar to what the ACC and the Big 10 hold at the beginning of each year. It's another venue to get decent teams on the schedule.

Even further, the idea has been thrown out by administrators to begin a "scheduling consortium," whereby mid-major administrators agree and commit to schedule each other for a two-game series, home and home. It's kind of the Bracket Busters idea, only created by the people directly involved with the health of the programs. The upside is that attractive regional matchups will emerge, such as UNCW against the College of Charleston.

However, this is a strained idea on the West Coast, where there are fewer teams of choice and longer travel times, which is an issue. Additional factors are the desires of the fan base and alumni.

"Our fans couldn't care less about the MAC," says Jim Jarrett, director of athletics at ODU. "Our fans relate to the Big East, the ACC. Too many [unsexy] teams erodes fan interest. We struggle with attendance and dollars, so we try to always play teams of interest."

There is no easy answer. If so, this issue wouldn't be as large as it is. So administrators and coaches are forced to get creative. One of the creative methods to play involves being paid to play at a major school in a one-game deal. This has become known in the coaching business as being "bought," or playing a "buy game." There's no three-game series or a home-and-home. It's one shot and done. You travel to Syracuse or Durham or Manhattan, Kansas, and return home with a hefty check, and most times, a loss.

If it seems desperate, it probably is, and certainly not creative. Unable to get what they need from Bracket Busters and unable to schedule their own mini tournaments, mid-majors find themselves in the unenviable position of creating attractiveness, Washington Generals style.

On one level, though, it works well. Wood Selig, athletics director at Western Kentucky, used a past relationship with Virginia's AD Craig Littlepaige to get a two-game set with the ACC's Cavaliers.

"We hate to get bought," said Selig, "but the ACC has a television package for Sunday nights with Fox. The reach is 84 million people. I get $40,000 to $50,000 and reach more than 80 million people. It's the perfect bought game." Unfortunately, the by-product of buy games is vital to mid-majors: exposure and cashflow.

With Littlepaige also installed as the chairman of the NCAA selection committee, Selig has found another angle. "It's crept into our thinking to schedule the schools of the NCAA selection committee," he says. "If we're on the bubble perhaps they remember seeing us and how well we hopefully played."

Mid-majors hate to be bought for obvious reasons. They have to go play on the home court of a major school and its usually large, raucous fan base. It's early in the season, so many times coaches aren't sure what to expect from their own team. In return, a mid major can gross anywhere from $25,000 to $60,000, and sometimes even more, from the major school just for showing up to play. Obviously an athletic department feels used, even though it's a way to help the school's coffers and get a quality team on the schedule. A coach feels an obligation to contribute to the financial well-being of the university, and gets a test for the team. While this seems to be a win-win situation in general, it's a practice most mid-major schools hate. It doesn't really solve the problem, because mid-majors are still on the road, with the deck stacked against them.

In the current climate, however, to get an attractive game and at least give coaches an opportunity to show off their team, no matter how difficult the task may be, it must happen. This is also where coaches revert to being coaches. They hate road games, and remember, home teams, no matter the level, win 70 percent of the time in NCAA college basketball. Coaches must also consider the travel, missed classes, and costs. (Pecora's boss at Hofstra, AD Jack Hayes, is quick to point out that when people talk about the money involved in buy games, they dismiss or forget about the costs involved with playing the game.)

Still, the opportunity to be on national television is compelling. Mid-majors are starved to be seen and exposed on a national basis, and if it means a trip into unfriendly confines on a Sunday night, like Western Kentucky's against Virginia, then so be it. It's tough for mid-majors to turn their backs at the numbers, mostly because television contracts for mid-majors are a different paradigm than the contracts of major conferences such as the Big 12, Big 10, and ACC. There is no Big Monday or Rivalry Week in the Horizon or WCC—at least not one that will make the ESPN airwaves.

What makes it doubly interesting is that in most business cases, and for major schools, the body that controls the product is paid by the television network for rights to "show off" that product. In a macro sense, CBS paid the NCAA $11 billion for the rights to show the tournament each season. The ACC gets paid by Raycom about $1 million annually for the rights to show conference matchups. ESPN doles out millions to program weeklong NCAA hoops mayhem and have Vitale talk about Diaper Dandies and PTPers.

For mid-majors, however, this is flopped. Not only does Comcast get paid by the CAA to show the games, but they can also sell advertising against it to make incremental money. It amounts to begging for exposure. Or, in the eyes of Jerry Baker, AD at the College of Charleston, "You take what you can get."

A typical mid-major television contract involves the conference ponying up money to underwrite production costs for a regional cable provider. Costs can run up to $30,000 per week for a game. The CAA pays roughly $600,000 per year for a men's and women's game of the week on Comcast Sports Net, a regional network.

In fact, the Horizon and its commissioner, Jon LeCrone, made the decision, as a league, to reinvest the $400,000 they paid Fox Sports to televise its "game of the week" regionally in 2005-2006. Instead, the conference embraced new technology and tried free internet broadcasting of *all* its men's and women's games. The Horizon League kept its contract with ESPN, which included the conference tournament championship game and at least two regular season games.

Jerry Baker's College of Charleston program and its conference, the Southern Conference, which was twenty-second in the 2005 RPI rankings, faces similar roadblocks and financial realities. The national television contract they play under includes all of the conference championship game, plus "two exposures" with ESPN, usually satisfied by utilizing one game pitting two conference teams against each other, opposite an NFL playoff game. During the regular season, the Southern conference additionally has a deal with Fox that puts eight games on its Fox Sports South regional cable package, which reaches 5 million people. The eight-game package is also tied in with eight football games (the Southern plays Division 1-AA football). For this reason, when an SEC school calls Baker and invites CoC to play at, say, Florida—and oh, by the way, the Gators will cut Baker a check for

$30,000—he must listen. It is why Selig couldn't pass up the opportunity to help his budget with the game against Virginia, plus get his team in front of approximately 15 times the number of people he could normally reach.

This is why even though administrators don't like it ("We need to stay away from those money games," says Jarrett.), some don't feel they have a choice. The majors know someone will pay. Everyone needs games and the majors know the mid-majors' position. It amounts to a power struggle and the way an administrator wants to run the athletic department.

Yet Jack Hayes, AD at Hofstra, knows it's not all wine and roses off the court, nor is it all about the Benjamins. "The question, in my mind, is how much?" he says. "How much do we want to recoup? How important is it in our area? The actual guarantee money is secondary. It's one factor of what you get, the upside."

Hayes points to his team's game in late 2004 against Syracuse, where the Orangemen needed a last minute surge to hold off a very game Hofstra team. "The game showed that our perimeter players can play with anybody. We were just dominated by sheer size. We played well against a Big East team in a game that made sense. It was followed and covered by every paper. The check was the last thing I was thinking about."

It's clear that in Hayes's mind, the buy game is a necessary evil. For his part, Hayes understands the pressures on his coach and on his program. He refuses to turn his coach and players into little more than glorified mercenaries, traveling the country playing for pay. Under certain circumstances, he will take on a buy game, but there are limits.

TRUE CREATIVITY

Paying for play is straightforward, but falling short of that, true creativity abounds. When Selig's basketball team—or, more accurately, head coach Dennis Felton's basketball team—at Western Kentucky began winning consistently, Selig knew he had problems. He knew he would have trouble with his schedule. He knew phone calls would be put through asking about the availability of Felton. Selig struck upon an idea he thought could kill both birds with a single shot.

"In the contract we signed with Dennis," Selig explained, "we [would be] contracted to play against the team wherever he went. It was defined by league. If he went to a top seven RPI conference it was four games, two at each place and no more than one year after he left. From conference eight seed on, it was a two-year, home-and-home series."

Selig also fully understood the give and take in his idea. "It takes a brave coach to sign a contract like that, but we've given them a chance to start their career."

Soon thereafter the calls indeed came and in April 2003 Felton was hired away to clean up the mess left behind by Jim Harrick at Georgia. Felton's first nonconference game was Western Kentucky. "He never balked or tried to wiggle out," said Selig. "Georgia handled it all above board."

Not incidental was the fact that there was also a six-figure cash buy-out included in the contract if Felton chose to back out of the game. Regardless, Selig could call it mission accomplished: He obtained a four-game, home-and-home series with an SEC team.

This idea has been widely embraced by athletic directors—after Jeff Capel led VCU to the NCAAs and within a whisker of beating Wake Forest, both Auburn and Miami inquired. Dick Sander added a similar clause to the new contract that helped persuade Capel to stay at VCU. Even if its ability to hold up in court is questionable, and it is questioned, this kind of problem solving is rampant at mid-major universities. To date, Capel has consistently maintained that a VCU and Oklahoma matchup will occur.

Selig, a bright young administrator in the business, is merely looking for answers. He wants his team to play the best possible competition, and to mitigate the problem of forcing his team is to criss-cross the country playing all comers in their building, he devised a home-and-almost-home hedge scenario.

Because of WKU's proximity to many SEC universities, it is a natural fit to get those teams on the Hilltoppers's schedule. So Selig called Auburn for a home-and-home; it, predictably, balked.

Selig agreed to play the two-game series, with the first game being on Auburn's home floor, and the return game not on the campus of Western Kentucky, but at a "neutral" site. Selig would count this as a home game and the hedge on a location suited Auburn. WKU also added Louisville to its schedule, ostensibly by agreeing to play in Nashville.

"We're able to get a 'premium' game for our season ticket holders, and we were able to minimize having to constantly go onto the home floor of power opponents."

Selig has even considered the premise, which is frequently discussed but unrealistic, of every Division I team making the tournament. It can be accomplished with one additional weekend being added to the current tournament format. The 312 teams can be whittled to 256 via play in games, or, in the language of the NCAA, the "opening round," on a Tuesday, just as the current single game dictates in the field of sixty-five. The weekend then plays out exactly as the first two rounds do now. First round on Thursday/Friday gets you from 256 to 128. The second round on Saturday/Sunday gets 128 to 64. Logistically, it works.

In Selig's eyes, making the tournament is what's driving the scheduling anyway, so why not take the #1 factor out of the equation to help gain equality?

Schools have pursued the creation of their own tournaments to solve the issue, even pondered legislation. Most have failed, though in the eyes of Pecora, that doesn't mean one stops trying. "We don't *have* to buy games," he says. His annual matchup against St. John's, played in Madison Square Garden, isn't even a money game. He also accepted less money to schedule Notre Dame this season than a similar SEC school. It was a better fit on many levels and is Hofstra's only buy game.

Still, not every team has the advantage of playing in Madison Square Garden or obtaining the reach of the New York-area newspapers and radio; so despite obvious flaws, solutions such as buy games exist as long as there is a market. So will Bracket Busters.

Both ODU's Blaine Taylor and VCU's Capel know the game, though, and work through the hurdles. There are many things that are tried and fail each year. Relationships come into play. Each has his own network of friends that really only goes but so far.

Says Capel: "Coach K loves his players but won't play them. People play up the Duke connection thing, but think about it—they are all trying to do the same thing." Capel is referring to coaches like Tommy Amaker at Michigan and even Krzyzewski himself at Duke. The first responsibility each has is to his own program, and while they will remain friends, scheduling will remain a business. Amaker cares deeply about Capel, but they won't talk scheduling.

So the coaches battle on and do their best in a tough atmosphere. These may or may not be the solutions, but coaches, regardless of setup and semantics, will still always want to balance the schedule with wins and tough games.

Then a rub of a different sort comes into play. A coach is measured primarily on one thing: wins. It's one thing to play a tough schedule and it's another to lose those tough games. In the minds of the coaches, preparing a team involves easy wins and tough tests, but the issue goes much deeper than preparing a team. Coaching is just like any other job. Just because the job involves sports and entertainment, coaches don't get a free pass. The same rules that apply to the banking business or the real estate market apply to the business of coaching. They need to be successful, which in this business means, simply, to win.

Capel laughs when asked about the importance of just plain winning basketball games. "It's the most important thing for job security," he says. "There is an old line: 'If your administration is complaining about your team's graduation rates, you're about to be fired.'" Capel is referring to the fact that while winning may not cause folks to turn a blind eye, if a coach is losing, then any excuse needed to get the coach fired will do. Graduation rates is an accommodating subject.

Coaches are in the difficult position of serving two masters: the self-preservation of winning and revenue to the athletic department. The same is true for the athletic director. He has a department to run and has a boss. The same profit and loss responsibilities exist for a college basketball administrator as do for a corporate manager. This complicates the buy game issue and is the root of the overall conundrum.

So it's no surprise that coaches and administrators are often at odds, more so than imagined, over scheduling and control of the process. Says Capel: "My dad told me never to lose control of your schedule." Capel's father coached at Old Dominion and is well-aware of the issues facing his son. The younger Capel understands that an administration, no matter how close the personal relationship, still needs revenue.

Even Capel's boss, Dr. Richard Sander, says that athletic directors should take back control of the scheduling, that the coaches hold too much power; and Sander would know. Not too many years ago, he thought he had a deal inked with Virginia for a six-game series against the Cavaliers. VCU and Virginia are approximately an hour's drive from each other, and many UVa alumni live in the Richmond area. This would be an attractive series for both schools and seemed like a no-lose situation. The particulars were agreed upon by both athletic directors.

Then Virginia hired (and has since fired) Pete Gillen, who wanted no part of VCU or the series, so Gillen demanded, "We're not going to do it," and the series never materialized. Even if athletic directors can make sense of the numbers and everybody would benefit, if a coach doesn't want the game, it won't be played.

Interestingly, most athletic directors have full control of football scheduling, yet little for basketball. (One of the sticking points for Rick Pitino to coach Louisville was that he had to have the absolute final word, and carte blanche, regarding scheduling. He got it.) Consider it college basketball's version of trickle down economics and the power struggle for scheduling. Just as a major college coach avoids a strong mid-major team, mid-major coaches crave job security.

A common theme when talking to mid-major athletic directors is they have to schedule "like teams" outside of conference play. But all college basketball coaches like the same schedule: Get a couple of wins on the schedule for your team, and add a few games that offer a chance of notoriety with a win, and don't kill your "name" if you lose.

The theory is that while it makes sense for Charlotte to play North Carolina, it also makes sense for Charlotte to play UNCW. Maybe so, but that's a game Wilmington's Brad Brownell said no to playing. In addition, Jeff Capel, after his team was humbled at home by Davidson in the 2005 NIT, wanted no part of the Wildcats during the regular season as a nonconference opponent.

The internal give and take is daily. It has to be for such a complicated and important issue.

Dr. Jim Jarrett, AD at Old Dominion, has worked out a system with his coach that both believe is fair. He emphatically states that he has the final decision on scheduling, but has outlined criteria on "how" he wants the schedule for ODU created.

"I don't have to completely own the schedule. I provide Blaine the ground rules and put the principles in place, but I give them some wiggle room," Jarrett says of his scheduling philosophy with his coaches. "I tell them you have to have X-level RPI games and so on. He has to drive X in gate receipts and that is part of his responsibility. We talk about specific teams that fit within those principles, but I let him basically go get them."

Jarrett, more so than most administrators, fully believes in spending the necessary time with his coaches to ensure everyone succeeds. "We need to remember that coaches have careers. We need to be cognizant of that. We can overschedule just as well as underschedule. We've got to get them some wins. It's a team effort. I believe an athletic director has to spend a lot of quality time with his coaches."

Hayes and Pecora have a similar relationship at Hofstra. "I talk every day with Tom," says Hayes. "We go through everything."

In the end, it's a symbiotic relationship, as it should be.

"So many of our jobs," says Bill Hogan, AD at the University of San Francisco, "depend on who we hire as men's basketball coach."

Regardless, a good relationship does not solve the ills of scheduling for a mid major. This scheduling of the quality teams issue becomes even more important when you consider many conferences are expanding and going to more league games than ever before. As conferences expand into "superconferences," league games are added to the schedule. Many have crept into December.

For example, the Ohio Valley Conference moved from sixteen to twenty league games in 2005-2006. Additionally, Bracket Busters continues to expand. The list of nonconference "game opportunities" thus gets shorter, as does the pool of teams and availability to play. Thus, administrators and coaches have a smaller window of opportunity for attractive games.

These facts lend credence to mid-majors scheduling each other, and perhaps changing the dynamics of scheduling. If mid-majors have fewer games to schedule because of expanding conference slates, playing each other essentially makes them "unavailable" to play majors. This provides fewer opportunities for the buy games. By making it difficult to match logistics, the mid-majors in essence make themselves scarce.

Fans of the major schools, the logic follows, will eventually tire of seeing glorified scrimmages against the St. Leos of the world, and major coaches will also reject playing a nonconference slate filled entirely with majors. They also have a team to prepare.

A combination of early season mid-major conference challenges, regional rivalries, and Bracket Buster matchups could eliminate the opportunity for a buy game.

This tack essentially takes the wiggle room for the majors out of the scenario. They may be forced, because they cannot find "RPI appropriate" teams to play, to travel to a mid major. The questions will be asked each March: Does a team that cannot win more than half their conference games and fatten up on the Stetsons of the world in the preseason deserve a bid over a mid major that wins twenty-five games?

We go back to the Iowa example. The Hawks were 12-1 out of conference but played just one road game. They entered the Big 10 Tournament at 19-10. Would they be a bubble team if that glowing 12-1 were, say, 8-5? That would be 15-14 overall.

Again, this is not to say that even at 15-14 Iowa wouldn't deserve the at-large bid. Playing five or six road games against decent opposition, however, instead of one road game against a marginal team, would tell the committee much more about Iowa's fate and how they *may* play on a neutral court.

It is a compelling strategy.

This is also why everyone connected to the Colonial Athletic Association, from Tom Yeager through coaches and administrators, all the way to the fans, knew that the 2005-2006 nonconference season was absolutely critical to the conference.

Old Dominion was receiving a pile of press and top twenty-five mentions, and the media knew this was a deep and talented conference. The problem, though, remained constant. Nobody could ever pull off the bellwether victory, nor sustain success. The conference was always close and always played better competition well, but could never get over the hump.

In fact, the CAA was able to place four of its teams in the postseason after the 2004-2005 season. In addition to ODU's NCAA berth, Hofstra, VCU, and Drexel all made appearances in the NIT. If you add newcomer Northeastern and its NIT bid, that was five CAA postseason teams. Their combined record: 0-5.

Mike Capaccio, Director of Athletics at North Carolina Wilmington, sat through the Villa Seven meetings with great interest. Two years ago, the school needed to replace the popular and successful Jerry Wainwright, who moved on to coach the Richmond Spiders and has since moved on to DePaul. At that time, the forty-seven-year-old Capaccio was working in development in the UNCW athletics office. Eventually he was chosen to serve as interim athletic director for seven months following the departure of Peg Bradley-Doppes and was elevated to the post by Chancellor Rosemary DePaolo in May 2005.

Capaccio's learning curve was steep, but he was right there to see the events that transpired during the search for a new head coach upon Wainwright's departure. Brad Brownell was Wainwright's top assistant and had exhibited all of the signs of a good head coach: organized, smart, motivated, dedicated. The promotion for Brownell was never really questioned, and it has never really been second guessed.

Before his promotion, Brownell served four years as an assistant coach and four years as associate head coach with Wainwright. It was a mere three weeks after the end of the 2001-2002 season that Brownell was announced as the new hire. It wouldn't be an easy start: UNCW was coming off a CAA regular season and tournament title, and had upset Southern California in the first round of the 2002 NCAA Tournament. The two best players from that team, all-everything guard Brett Blizzard and center Craig Callahan, were returning as seniors.

Expectations were high, and the Seahawks did not skip a beat. With a 24-7 record, UNCW claimed its second consecutive NCAA Tournament bid and clinched its fifth postseason berth in the last six seasons. The Hawks also had Maryland beaten in the NCAAs, until a Drew Nicholas miracle three pointer, while falling out of bounds from thirty feet, subdued them.

Despite the crushing defeat, nobody in the beach town of Wilmington was unhappy. Brownell had acquitted himself well in his first season as a head coach. In the CAA, UNCW fans are regarded as the most loyal, most traveled, and most respected. Trask Coliseum, their old, dingy, glorified high school home court is frequently standing room only. They support their team and understand the "big picture."

The 2003-2004 season could be described precisely by the Seahawks's final record: 9-9 in the conference (seventh place) and 15-15 overall. The result was not unexpected but also not encouraging.

UNCW had some good wins but also bad losses. With UNCW predicted to finish sixth by the coaches and media for the 2004-2005 season, Brownell's future was likely to be shaped by the season. He had won with good players from the previous coach. He had held steady in a season with a bare cupboard. Now, he was going to have to coach like never before: the underdog and with expectations.

All Brownell managed was a tie for second in the CAA at 13-5, 19-10 overall.

For Mike Capaccio, though, there were issues. Brownell was being noticed, and Capaccio eagerly listened to his colleagues that July day at the Mirage in Las Vegas, just two months after being named the full-time director of athletics, because he wanted to be ready when the phone call came asking about the availability of his thirty-six-year-old coach who had won fifty-eight games in his three years as a head man.

Those lessons would be sorely needed at the end of the season. Brownell's contract was up for renewal, but Capaccio, a former coach, stood firm. In the AD's mind, the beginning of the basketball season was not the best time for the coach to be concentrating on a contract. He should be concentrating on basketball.

CHAPTER FOUR

PREPARATION

"So much of our time is preparation, so much is routine, and so much retro-spect, that the pith of each man's genius contracts itself to a very few hours."
–Ralph Waldo Emerson

Everyone associated with the CAA knew this was the year that the close losses had to cease. The conference had built up a solid reputation as a strong, deep mid major that played bas-ketball at a high level. Its teams were to be feared.

After all, the history of the CAA solidified its reputation as an upset producer (or at least a tough out) in the NCAA Tournament. In fact, in 1991 the University of Richmond, then a member of the CAA, beat Syracuse 73-69 to become the first fifteenth seed to upset the second seed in the NCAA Tournament. Media pundits often point to this upset, saying it ushered in the "modern era" of March Madness.

That game was not even the first blow struck by the CAA, howev-er. Three years prior, thirteenth seeded Richmond defeated both fourth seeded Indiana and fifth seeded Georgia Tech to reach the Sweet Sixteen. In 1986, a David Robinson-led Navy squad also hand-ed second seed Syracuse an early ticket home.

Since its beginning as the ECAC South, the league entered 2005-2006 having won 37.5 percent of its NCAA Tournament games. The CAA rep-resentative had either pulled an upset (UNCW's thrilling victory over

Southern California in 2002) or taken a high seed to the wire in every year since 2000. Wake Forest needed eight straight free throws down the stretch to hold off VCU in 2004, and Maryland needed a Drew Nicholas prayer to be answered to subdue UNCW in 2003. In 2005, ODU had Final Four participant Michigan State in a one-possession game into the game's final few minutes.

The CAA needed to win these games, however, because the NCAA committee isn't interested in close losses and moral victories. To get that elusive at-large bid and be mentioned in the same breath as mid-majors like the Missouri Valley Conference—the last one for the CAA was Richmond in 1986—the conference would have to start winning the games that provided opportunities for exposure, because opportunities are few and far between.

UNCW fired the first bullets for the CAA in 2005-2006.

In order to get "name" teams on the schedule, the Seahawks planned to spend a week in Colorado to open the season. UNCW would get three games in the BCA Classic, hosted by Wyoming. The opening game would be against Butler, a mid major of note which had a disappointing 2004-2005 season. Host Wyoming, Northwestern, and Charlotte were also in the tournament. After those three games, the Seahawks would travel to play Colorado in Boulder on Friday, November 18.

UNCW eased by Butler 75-59 in a game that was not surprising for its result, but for how much UNCW controlled the game and the victory margin. Next up was the host Wyoming Cowboys.

Now, it is known that home teams will mysteriously get more calls than the visitors from the officials. This is not to say there is a conspiracy or anything of the like. It's just a human element to the game. An officiating crew generally has the home coach barking from the opening tip, "helping" the crew establish flow. The home crowd starts earlier, usually during warm-ups, with their typical evaluation of the abilities of the referees. It is also unfortunate that mid-majors most often find themselves on the road in front of hostile crowds. This would be no different.

In a physical battle, the Seahawks were whistled for thirty-two fouls and the Cowboys went to the free throw line forty-nine times, but cashed in on just thirty-two of those attempts. After controlling the entire game, UNCW misfired at the buzzer and the game would go to overtime tied at 49-49. Senior Beckham Wyrick put the Seahawks ahead for good, 52-49, by burying his only trifecta of the game with 4:35 left in the extra period.

Wyrick added two free throws with twenty-five seconds left to give the Seahawks a 61-58 lead, and after the teams traded a single free throw, Wyoming's Steve Leven missed a long three pointer from the left corner at the buzzer.

When you consider that UNCW shot sixteen free throws to Wyoming's forty-nine, and Wyoming outrebounded UNCW 52-37, and then throw in that UNCW's best player, guard John Goldsberry, would make one field goal and score five points, it is amazing that UNCW pulled out a victory in overtime. Importantly, the trademark UNCW defense held the Cowboys without a field goal for more than ten minutes in the second half.

This set up a final matchup against Northwestern, where it would be a Wildcats modified Princeton-style offense against one of the best team defense squads in the nation. It was an open joke that the final score for this game could be reminiscent of the 2001 CAA final in which George Mason beat UNCW 35-33.

The final would be 56-48, in favor of UNCW, in a game that lived up to its billing. It was a rugged, hard-nosed affair not for the weak of heart or mind. It was 23-17 at the half, with the teams combining to make just thirteen of forty field goal attempts.

"We got off to a great start defensively and competed at a high level," Brownell said. "It's been an unbelievable week for our kids. To respond like they did with one day's preparation for the Princeton-style offense is remarkable."

The CAA as a whole had won five of its first six nonconference

games, and while none were earth shattering, the list was still notewor-
thy: Butler, Wyoming, and Northwestern for UNCW; Cal-Irvine for
George Mason; and Drexel had a big win over Princeton. Only the
George Mason overtime loss at Wake Forest had prevented a perfect start.

There are worse places to be in November than St. Thomas. For
Blaine Taylor and his ODU Monarchs, the Paradise Jam early season
tournament proved to be exactly what he wanted: a reward for the
program and its fans for a better-than-expected 2004-2005 season,
and a mix of opponents that would test his team early in the new
year. After coaching ODU to its 28-5 season in 2004-2005, the most
victories in school history, Taylor was prepared to embrace success.

Taylor was, in his words, "a good player" at Montana in the late
1970s, but "I had no delusions of grandeur." With a playing career not
looming, Taylor got his business degree and was contemplating law
school, along with going back to school to get his masters in education.

Two events pushed him into coaching. First, Taylor recounts, he
had the opportunity to spend time with lawyers and realized that
while there was a bit of a sexy feel to the profession, the reality was
that he would be dealing with people who weren't always of upstand-
ing character or did not have the best interests in mind. This turned
him off. The second, but biggest, push came from his father in one of
those simple conversations fathers are so good at: "Boy," Taylor
remembers the conversation beginning, "whatever you decide, make
sure you enjoy what you're doing." Taylor's father was finished. After
Taylor did the math that his father had not received even a high
school diploma and thus spent a life working at a job he didn't enjoy,
the experience was far more valuable than any piece of paper. Taylor
knew that through athletics he'd be getting the upside of people, and
that this would be more rewarding for him as a person.

So in 1981, Taylor, then teaching social studies with half his paycheck coming from the PE department, became a graduate assistant at
Montana, working on his postgraduate degree under Mike

Montgomery. Taylor would start his own company at Montana, where he won 142 games, in order to truly "own" his coaches show. Taylor recalls spending $5,000 on digital television equipment and hiring on-air talent. "We had five major sponsors," he said. "It was quite lucrative. The school eventually negotiated back sharing the show with other sports."

Even at a young age, Taylor was showing his ability to run a program. (In fact, Taylor still laments his 1992 Montana team losing to Florida State—coached by Pat Kennedy—in the 1992 NCAA Tournament. "If I were a little better coach...") "You have to be comfortable," he says, "with your vision of what you want to accomplish in order to deal with expectations."

Although finishing dead last in the SEC in 2004-2005, the Georgia Bulldogs brought back almost everybody; and their coach, Dennis Felton, knew he had talent. Felton had been hired from Western Kentucky to clean up the Jim Harrick mess at Georgia, so he was also well aware of the dangers of a talented mid-major team. ODU wouldn't sneak up on Georgia, despite it being game one on each team's schedule.

Early on, though the game was tight, signs were pointing to a long day for Taylor. ODU trailed 11-8 when the CAA player of the year, Alex Loughton, picked up his second foul. Drew Williamson, Taylor's invaluable point guard (Williamson played ninety-two minutes in the 2005 CAA Tournament without committing a turnover), also had two fouls. Taylor, however, did exactly what good coaches do—or more precisely, what good coaches don't do—and calmly went to his bench for Valdus Vasylius, his sixth man.

Vasylius, the son of Vaclovas and Vida, is typical of the manner in which many foreign players end up on college campuses in college basketball. He came over to the United States from Klaipeda, Lithuania, as part of an exchange program, spending his junior and senior years at Norfolk Collegiate High School, just down the road from the Old Dominion campus. The international business major was the 2003 Tidewater Conference player of the year and an immediate target for Taylor.

"He was well thought of in this area but we also wanted to (recruit him) the right way, so we also went to Lithuania," says Taylor. "I think (part of the reason) we got him was that once you make a home away from home, you don't really want to do it all over again. After seeing him play more, I'm sure other schools wish they would have recruited him a bit more."

Although Vasylius' nickname is either V or VV for obvious reasons, Taylor likes to say the initials stand for very valuable or very versatile. "Valdus is a kid that's always ready to do what you ask of him," says Taylor. "There are so many kids that are high maintenance, but Valdus doesn't care if he starts or comes off the bench. He just shows up to play basketball. He's always ready and many nights gives us a shot in the arm."

Vasylius responded by going on a personal 11-0 run to give ODU an eight-point bulge. Even though Georgia whittled away the lead and tied the game at 34-34 by halftime, Taylor was encouraged. His star, Loughton, had not scored, but the game was tied.

Taylor was buoyed by the fact that he was playing a good team that was competing very hard. It was the first half of his team's first game, and they were a long way from home. They hadn't played particularly well or particularly poorly. In short, he was okay with the feel of the game, and that was his locker room message. "Nobody was going to win this game in the first half," he calmly told the troops. "Let's go out there and play like we know we can."

The message sank in. ODU came out of the locker room on a 22-7 run, including seventeen straight points, led by seventeen at the under 8:00 media time-out, and felt in control. Taylor had made a brilliant defensive adjustment early in the half by going to a zone. Of course, the game is college basketball, and one of its most apropos clichés held to form: Everybody makes a run. Taylor knew this, and when Georgia responded with a 19-4 run of its own to cut the ODU lead to 60-58 with 3:50 to play, Taylor didn't budge.

"Guys," he told the team in the huddle, "this is basketball. You're going to make runs, but you have to expect the other guy will, too." Taylor's water-off-a-duck's-back strategy paid off.

It was time for Loughton to step up and play the role of star. Loughton's bucket and free throw at a critical juncture, almost a duplicate of a play Loughton made in the 2005 CAA final against VCU, was followed by a rebound basket by Drew Williamson. The sequence restored a bit of breathing room for ODU at 65-58. The final was 74-65. Vasylius finished with nineteen points. Williamson and his back-up, sophomore Brandon Johnson, each scored twelve points and had three steals. Loughton was held to eight points, most of which came when the Monarchs needed him most. It was ODU's first win over an SEC school since beating South Carolina 59-56 in 1998-1999.

For his part, Taylor was relieved the have the season underway. He would have to do some tinkering in the early season, more so than usual, but a victory in the first game always leaves a better taste in his mouth. Much of the tinkering had to do with how Taylor would mix and match his players and the lineup. The Monarchs were only replacing one player, Kiah Thomas, but had the fortunate problem of a lot of talent ready to step in. Taylor would be getting back shooting guard Abdi Lidonde, who had red shirted the previous year. Taylor had also recruited Jonathan Adams, a high flying swingman who could step into the lineup on day one. Adams did just that, getting six minutes and scoring two points off the bench against Georgia.

Next up was the Fordham Rams of the Atlantic 10. The A10, as a conference, straddles the line of major/mid-major conference, and in many ways represents a melting pot of basketball success: You have one of the all-time greats in Temple, mixed with relative newcomers and hard chargers like Dayton and Xavier. You toss in a school with upset history—perhaps more than any other school—in the University of Richmond, and presto! You have a conference in search of an identity.

ODU rolled Fordham after a sluggish start, but senior guard Isaiah Hunter played horribly, hitting only five of twenty shots. Taylor would respond by keeping Hunter out of the starting lineup for the Paradise Jam finals against Wisconsin. This was the measuring stick game for ODU, and the matchup that they had wanted when this tournament was put on the schedule. Sure, beating a bottom-dwelling SEC team and a marginal A10 team was one thing, but Wisconsin was one of the better teams in the Big 10, one of the better conferences nationally. ODU had also been eliminated by Michigan State in the NCAA Tournament. This would be the real test early in the season.

Once again, as is the case in college basketball more than any other sport, the game lived up to the pregame hype. The game featured sixteen lead changes and nine ties. Both teams shot 45 percent from the field. ODU led by four, 36-32 at the half, and by as much as seven in the middle of the second half. The Monarchs' last lead came after Vasylius hit two free throws with 8:04 to play. ODU hung tough and had the chance to take the lead again when a Brandon Johnson floater rolled out with a tad more than 2:00 to play.

Wisconsin gripped a 76-75 lead with thirty-three seconds to play when Badgers Kammron Taylor, who scored twenty-seven points in the game, drilled a three pointer that was essentially a backbreaker. It was the one big shot in a game that was essentially evenly played.

For ODU, there was good news and bad news. The good news was that ODU played a tough major team to the wire; more importantly, Arnaud Dahi, who'd had off-season shoulder surgery, found his stroke and confidence. The junior from the Ivory Coast fired in twenty-five points on 10-15 shooting from the field. This was welcome relief to Taylor. The coach knew that for Dahi the injury was a mental hurdle. The bad news centered around senior guard Isaiah Hunter. He again looked disinterested on the court. The all-CAA performer, a mainstay in the ODU lineup since taking over a starting role early in his freshman season, played just sixteen minutes and contributed only one foul shot, one rebound, and one assist while missing all four shots he took from the floor. Brandon Johnson, a sophomore, had outperformed Hunter on both ends of the floor.

"There are three things that really contributed to Isaiah's start," Taylor said. "He's had a tender foot and we were worried about a stress fracture, so we wanted to take it easy. It's also his senior year, so he's taking more credits and carrying a harder workload than ever. I chose to hold him back in basketball to make sure he had his academics straight. Lastly, and most importantly, Hunter's father passed away a little less than a year ago. After a tragedy like this occurs, everything is a new experience—going home on the weekend, taking a vacation, holidays."

It would be especially difficult for Isaiah Hunter. His father Irv drove to every Old Dominion game—home and away—during Isaiah's freshman season after he became increasingly homesick. Irv reasoned his son would feel more comfortable if he was able to see a familiar face smiling upon him. That was the kind of bond the pair had. Holding Hunter back, so he would be more prepared for life, is the kind of coach and mentor Blaine Taylor is. "It was not an easy fall for him," Taylor explained, "as he and his father were extremely close."

Even though Old Dominion had made the championship game in St. Thomas, outplaying Wisconsin for more of the game than the other way around and sporting a 2-1 record with wins over Georgia and Fordham, Blaine Taylor wasn't happy. "We were not where we wanted to be coming out of the Paradise Jam," Taylor said. "You wouldn't want to have been a part of our program (at that point)."

On the morning before ODU's conference opener against George Mason, Taylor had a full grasp of his team. "If we win that Wisconsin game, we're probably sitting above George Washington on top of the non-BCS teams," he said. "We knew we had to sharpen up some things, make our rotations better. We just weren't hitting on all cylinders. Between the attention Alex (Loughton) has been getting and blending Isaiah back into the lineup, we also needed the freshmen and sophomores to contribute."

Perhaps Old Dominion wasn't where Blaine Taylor wanted it to be, but with George Mason and the rugged conference season looming, it was getting there quickly.

———

The CAA, thanks to Jeff Capel's VCU Rams, would get its biggest road victory of the young season at Houston. It would be a typical early season, nonconference affair. Houston fans were twenty-five years removed from the glory days of Hakeem the Dream and Clyde the Glide. Support was not as electric, and a mid major from Virginia wasn't going to stir interest in a chilly arena. Though 4,500 people would file into Hofheinz Arena, the scene was more like a business meeting than a college basketball game. It didn't help, either, that both teams were playing only their second game.

The game began exactly according to script. VCU held a 9-6 lead during the "feeling out" stages of the game when Houston went on a massive 23-4 run to build a sixteen-point lead at 29-13 with five minutes remaining in the first half. VCU managed to shave the lead to nine before the Cougars took a 33-22 lead at the break. Cougars pressure didn't allow VCU to get into its offensive sets, much less run them. "Their philosophy was to not let you get into a rhythm," Capel said, knowing he was not out of the game, not by a long shot. "Let's just improve our spacing," he told the team in the locker room. "Be stronger against their pressure and attack it. We missed some shots. They will go and then let's get into our transition game."

The second half began much like the first, with Houston still holding a 40-28 lead after about four minutes. Then it was the Rams who went on a run, 10-1, to slice the lead to three with 11:30 left to play. Capel knew his constant was defense. If all else failed, the Rams stingy man-to-man and combination zones would force Houston to work on every possession. Capel also knew this constant affront would wear down the Cougars and they would tire. Capel knew this would lessen the Houston pressure and his team would get open looks at the basket. Two Jesse Pellot Rosa three pointers, the first to retie the game at 57-57 and the second to give the Rams a 60-58 lead, signaled VCU would be there in the end.

Pellot Rosa is another of those kinds of kids who coaches love, and is always in the middle of the fray. He is a former walk-on that gives Capel effort and brings life into the team. Pellot Rosa is the team's defensive stopper and as tough as they come. He has worked diligently on his shooting ability and offensive skills and matured as both a player and a person. In fact, over the summer Pellot Rosa worked at Capel's basketball camp, not unlike many players at many schools.

Capel's camp is broken into two, one-week sessions, much like basketball camps at other schools. Pellot Rosa was scheduled to work both weeks since his family lives in Richmond and it would be a short drive over to the VCU campus each day.

Prior to the opening of the first week of camp, Kevin Brooks, VCU director of basketball operations, received a phone call. It was the grandmother of one of the campers, 13-year-old Dequane Moore. She explained to Brooks that her grandson battled autism and would therefore be a bit different than the other campers. Brooks didn't hesitate to tell the concerned grandmother that Dequane would absolutely be welcomed.

Though Brooks had prepared each of the camp counselors for the challenge, it remained an odd pairing. Pellot Rosa was a college junior and a basketball star. He was a leader at a basketball camp. He had every right to carry around an air of superiority, but he didn't. He is a rare kind of kid who combines his youthful zeal and exuberance with a maturity to understand life and its true meaning and importance.

It was on the first day of camp that Pellot Rosa met Dequane, and the two hit it off. Dequane played with the kind of spirit and zeal that reminded Pellot Rosa of his own desire, and the two began to form a close bond over the course of the week.

"A lot of the kids were picking on him," Pellot Rosa told the *Richmond Times Dispatch*. "I was telling them to just chill out, that he was autistic. You treat them the same as others. Don't make fun of them. Some people are less fortunate than others.

"I was coaching the team that he was on. He had so much energy. He didn't really know how to play, how to dribble, but he could jump high and rebound. So when he was on my team, all I had him do was rebound.

"Every shot that came off the boards, he would get it. Sometimes he would take three steps and then dribble it because of all his energy. I just told him to hold up and give it to the guards.

"After that, all the other kids saw me working with him and they started liking him also."

The most impressive part of the relationship was that Pellot Rosa wasn't just nice to Moore. He actually planned a course of improvement, so that Moore would experience success at one stage and build to the next. Pellot Rosa was careful to talk to the other campers about concepts such as inclusion and desire. The cool college basketball star was doling out a lesson that had nothing to do with a rebounding position or setting a proper screen. As the end of camp neared, it was obvious what Dequane Moore meant to the campers and especially Pellot Rosa. That kind of spirit is contagious.

One other thing Pellot Rosa had in common with Dequane Moore was that both were raised in underprivileged environments. Though every part of the relationship and story is uplifting, there remains the harsh, real-world reality that Pellot Rosa could use the extra spending money. He is, after all, a college kid.

Toward the end of the session, Pellot Rosa took it one step further. He approached Brooks and asked if it would be within the NCAA rules and okay if he donated his paycheck to fund an additional week of camp for Moore. The kid—all the kids—had benefited from the experience and the best thing that could happen would be a repeat performance.

So despite needing the paycheck for his own responsibilities, Pellot Rosa made it work for a young man to enjoy the sport of basketball and, despite his autism, be treated like any other boy.

"Jesse's not your normal young person," Capel said. "He's a lot more mature than most people his age. He comes from a great family and he gets it. He's a young man who grew up with a lot of love. You see that when you're around him."

Such are the kinds of kids Jeff Capel pursues when recruiting. It is important for him to bring in quality people as well as quality basketball players, and young men like Jesse Pellot Rosa are an example that this mission can be accomplished.

After Houston made a free throw to cut the margin to one, 62-61,

VCU missed a chance to widen the lead when a Nick George jumper bounded away with fourteen seconds to play. Houston rebounded and ran down court to set up a game winner. The Ram's stingy defense prevailed again, however, knocking a pass out of bounds under the basket with 2.6 seconds left. Following a time-out, junior forward Jahmar Thorpe missed a fall away three pointer at the buzzer, giving the Rams the 62-61 victory.

Tom Pecora was getting used to quick starts. In the 2004-2005 season, his Pride broke the school record for most consecutive victories to start a season with nine. Hofstra was one of the final ten unbeaten teams in the country when it dropped the close 80-75 decision to seventh ranked Syracuse. Questions hovered, however, as the nine victories included wins over Florida International, Longwood, Binghamton, Dartmouth, and Stony Brook. The ledger was not exactly dotted with RPI heavyweights. The Syracuse game, though, lent credence to the ability of the Pride. It was only after the season, in which Pecora had guided the team to a 21-9 record and an NIT berth, that the scheduling philosophy of Pecora was confirmed.

So it was no surprise that Hofstra, after a second consecutive season-opening drubbing of Florida International (64-51), walked into the Joyce Center in South Bend in front of 10,000 screaming Irish fans without intimidation, thinking they had a legitimate chance to win.

A Notre Dame basketball game carries more frenzy than the average observer would imagine. Though a football school, the Notre Dame students come out in full force, wearing identically colored T-shirts and chanting for the home team. It is not a sullen crowd supporting its second favorite sport on campus. The Pride players, however, carried their won swagger. Rabid fans wouldn't deter their effort.

If the players relied solely on scouting reports, the coaches knew what to expect from each other. Pecora and Notre Dame Head Coach Mike Brey had battled several times in the old America East

Conference, when Brey was the head coach at Delaware and Pecora was Jay Wright's top assistant at Hofstra. Under Wright, Hofstra defeated Brey and Delaware in back-to-back America East championship games in 2000 and 2001.

But as Pecora loves to say, it's about the players. Antoine Agudio had led Hofstra past FIU, tallying seventeen points. The figure increased Agudio's streak of games with double figures to seventeen in a row. Fellow guard Carlos Rivera chipped in fourteen, and freshman Greg "Playstation" Johnson netted twelve. (The nickname comes from Johnson's days as a child when he would put on dribbling exhibitions at Harlem's Rucker Park.)

All was not rosy. Gibran Washington, who was as much a senior leader for Pecora as he was a standout player, had chosen to leave the team. "A blow to our basketball team," said Pecora. Washington was hampered by a chronic back injury and would be graduating in December and taking a job in Florida.

Particularly troubling for Pecora, though, was the fact that his top player, first team all-CAA pick, Loren Stokes, struggled with a plastic mask he had been given to protect a healing broken nose. Stokes scored just four points, his fewest ever, and was clearly uncomfortable during the game.

Still, there was no reason to think Hofstra couldn't walk into a Big East building and win. After spotting the Irish the first six points of the game, Hofstra went on a 13-0 run, capped by an Adrian Uter (pronounced you-ter) stick back. Colin Falls stemmed the rush by hitting a three pointer for Notre Dame, and both teams settled into a rhythm for the remainder of the first half.

The second half started much like the first half ended, with both teams trading haymakers. Russell Carter hit a three to give Notre Dame its first lead since 6-5 at 37-36, and the crowd rose to its feet and made more noise than it had all night. Uter silenced the crowd with a layup that gave Hofstra the lead back temporarily at 38-37, but the Fighting Irish went on a 9-0 run, keyed by five points from Falls, to take a 46-38 advantage.

Hofstra would pull to within five at 48-43, but errant shooting doomed the Pride. After Agudio's hoop, Notre Dame ran away with a 16-3 run to take a 64-46 lead with 4:59 to go. Defense and rebounding allowed Hofstra to overcome 39 percent shooting in the opening half, but nothing could save them from the 23 percent effort in the second half (7-31). Agudio scored just eight points, breaking his double-digit streak. For his part, Uter had a double-double with ten points and twelve rebounds.

The game finished 69-50, but everyone knew it was much closer than that. It produced more questions than anger from Pecora. Loren Stokes was still not comfortable playing with a healing broken nose, and he still was not getting production from his bench. Next up was cross-town rival St. John's, the second consecutive Big East opponent for Hofstra.

The box score will show that the Pride overcame a 40-27 deficit, on the road at a Big East team, to win going away 64-51. The first thing that will pop out of the stat sheet is that the Johnnies scored a whopping eleven points in the second half. In fact, the Red Storm scored last with just over eight minutes to play on a rebound basket by Lamont Hamilton that gave St. John's a 51-50 lead. Hofstra closed the game on a 14-0 run. All are compelling numbers for a standing ovation for the Hofstra defense.

The absolutely stunning subpoint to this comeback is that Pecora played his starting five the entire second half. That's *zero* substitutions. For the record, Loren Stokes, Antoine Agudio, Adrian Uter, Carlos Rivera, and Aurimas Kieza went the distance in the second half. In fact, for the entire game the bench played just twenty-two total minutes, took three shots (making zero), made two free throws, and committed eight fouls.

Pecora once said that the "one thing I've learned about coaching that I love is its unpredictability. It's going to be that way and you can't let it bother you. I love the adjustments. You have to have a little fun with it." If this is the case, then Pecora had a blast coaching in Carnesecca Arena. This was a dismantling.

Other interesting numbers that showed Pecora made some phenomenal adjustments in an unpredictable game are that the Johnnies
were 14-15 from the free throw line in the first half and didn't even
attempt a free throw in the second half. Hofstra held the Red Storm
to only 17.2 percent shooting (5-29) in the second half, including 1-
16 from three-point territory. One could figure the guys on the court
got tired and committed a lazy foul *somewhere,* or gave up an easy
layup, but they did not.

The short bus ride home was sweet, especially considering that
Stokes finally had had his breakout game, scoring nineteen points and
dishing out five assists. Most important is that the slender Stokes
grabbed eight rebounds.

Hofstra followed up that victory with a fourteen-point win over
local opponent Binghamton in a classic trap game and was prepared
for the rigor of the CAA season. Other than one bad half against Notre
Dame, Pecora was okay with his team's performance, but not satisfied.
Stokes had had just one good game, and his bench was not progressing as much as he'd like. But they were winning, and that is the ultimate arbiter in college basketball.

———

Granted, the CAA needed the wins to gain national attention. ODU
had a chance against Wisconsin and it went by the boards. George
Mason could've beaten Wake Forest, but it slipped through their fingers. Likewise Hofstra with Notre Dame.

What Bruiser Flint and Drexel were able to accomplish in two losses was perhaps even better than any win, however. The Dragons were
scheduled to play in the NIT Season Tip-Off Tournament (the old
Preseason NIT before the NIT was purchased by the NCAA). This kind
of tournament causes a bit of a wrinkle in scheduling because a team
must win its first two games to get two more in New York.

For Drexel, this meant upsetting Princeton on the road on
November 14 and then likely getting Quinn Snyder's Missouri team,
another road game, three days later, which is truly a tough task. If

Drexel lost either of those games, it would wait until November 29 to play again against St. Joseph's.

So in order to guard against a potential two-week layoff, Flint and AD Eric Zillmer scheduled a Monday, November 21, game against Rider and a Saturday, November 26, game against Big 5 rival Penn.

If the Perfect Storm arose and the Dragons managed two victories, the semifinals would be played the following Wednesday, November 23, and the championship and consolation games on Friday, November 25.

That set up the potential for Drexel to play four games in six days, taking only Thanksgiving and the Sunday prior to Thanksgiving off. Clearly Flint and the Drexel contingent weren't counting on two wins.

While Drexel not only surprised but walked past Princeton easily, 54-41, a little school from Texas named Sam Houston State was upsetting Missouri. Flint's storm was brewing. When the Dragons slipped by Sam Houston 72-61, it all came together: Drexel would be headed to New York to play the #1 team in the nation, the Duke Blue Devils, on national television with Dick Vitale calling the game. A perfect storm, indeed.

The box scores and season summaries show that Drexel lost to Duke 78-68 and then to UCLA in the consolation game 57-56. In terms of stark record, Drexel played two games and lost them both, 0-2. (Okay, 1-2 if you throw the 72-60 victory over Rider into the mix.)

For everyone concerned, the tired adage of close but no cigar was okay this time. What the CAA was able to accomplish through Drexel's two losses could not be measured in terms of wins and losses. The Dragons played Duke even for about thirty-six minutes before fading late. Even Duke head coach Mike Krzyzewski came away impressed.

"It wasn't an easy game for us," said Krzyzewski. "They knocked us back defensively."

Duke had just played Seton Hall of the Big East one week earlier and dismantled the Pirates in an ugly fashion. The final score was 93-40, and if it's possible, the game wasn't even that close. The Blue

Devils followed that with an 84-55 pasting of Davidson, which went undefeated in the Southern Conference the previous season.

There was reason to believe this game would be just as ugly. In fact, Vitale himself said at the opening of the broadcast he expected the game to be close for awhile before Duke eventually took control. It never happened, and Drexel kept it close the entire way, with Vitale more amazed the deeper the game went.

The longer Drexel hung in the game, the better it became for the conference, because that gave Vitale the opportunity to talk up UNCW, ODU, and whatever else he could muster to help the rest of the country understand how good basketball in the CAA truly is. Vitale couldn't believe the media picked Drexel seventh in the preseason poll. Vitale knew UNCW had gone to Wyoming and beaten three quality teams. Vitale knew all about ODU. He knew about the close call with Wake Forest and the ability of Jim Larranaga.

Basically, Drexel and the CAA got two hours of nonstop love from ESPN on a holiday weekend; it continued during the Friday consolation game throughout as Drexel held the game with UCLA in its hands, literally. Once again, though, for now the result didn't matter. The fact that Drexel lost a game it should've won was secondary. The CAA had won a victory for mid-majors, and it wasn't even March.

Vitale wrote the following on his website after the games were completed.

I have to be honest. When I went to Madison Square Garden for the NIT Season Tip-Off semifinals, I thought it would be a blowout. No. 1 Duke against a Drexel team picked seventh in the Colonial Athletic Association ... are you serious?

Bruiser Flint's team hung tough and the final score (a 78-68 Duke win) was not indicative of how hard the top-ranked team had to fight to get to the winner's circle.

I was so impressed with the way the Dragons played. It reflected the personality of their coach, Flint, who is a fighter and a battler. Drexel played its style and did not try to slow down the contest. It showed passion and the

*kids played so hard, giving everything they could. I grade them an "A" for
the evening.*

*A game like this shows the mid-majors can play with the big boys if
given the opportunity. Great guard play can keep underdogs in games…*

Surely, later in the season when RPI matters and perhaps a CAA
team needed to point to a big win, it would matter that, honestly,
Drexel choked against UCLA. Right now Tom Yeager was smiling,
though, the same smile he showed after the wonderful 2005 CAA
final.

After the first weekend of action, which included a George Mason
drubbing of old CAA rival American 75-35, the league combined for
a nonconference record of 36-20 (.643). Interestingly, thirty-four of
the fifty-six games were played on the road or on a neutral court, and
the CAA was 19-15 in those games. Eight of the losses came against
teams from the ACC, Big East, Big 12, or Pac 10.

Hofstra went to St. John's and won decisively and VCU defeated
Houston, at Houston, 62-61. The Cougars went on to beat LSU and
then Arizona, both top twenty-five schools, in its next two games.
Old Dominion did what was likely expected, losing only the close
Wisconsin battle in St. Thomas.

When you factor in UNC Wilmington's season-opening champi-
onship in the eight-team BCA Invitational Tournament, defeating
Butler, host Wyoming of the Mountain West, and the Big Ten's
Northwestern, as well as the "media coverage without a victory" path
of Drexel in the NIT Season Tip-Off, there was reason to smile in the
CAA offices.

However, for Blaine Taylor, Tom Pecora, and Jim Larranaga, things
were about to get really difficult. ESPN's Andy Katz, one of the most
respected members of the college basketball media, would write in his
weekly column in early December about Hofstra:

The Pride went 3-0 last week and took out St. John's for the third straight year. They also beat Binghamton and Delaware, the latter game the opener in the Colonial. How good is the CAA going to be this year? This league keeps looking deeper and deeper.

While Andy Katz raised a few eyebrows nationwide, this was hardly news to the CAA coaches.

The battle was at hand, and each coach gripped the safety bar of the roller coaster.

CHAPTER FIVE

STATEMENT

"The most distinct and beautiful statement of any truth must take at last the mathematical form." –Henry David Thoreau

For a head coach, entering a college basketball season is a little like walking into an amusement park. The coach knows it's going to be a long haul. Days will begin early and end late. Meals are eaten on the run, and they're usually not very good. The coach will be surrounded by thousands of strangers. The kids, as well as the individual moments, are going to both thrill and annoy, but no coach would want it any other way.

Because of the new twelve-team CAA, scheduling the eighteen conference games no longer was the province of post-New Year's planning. Games had to be scheduled for early December, two for every conference team. They would be played early in the month in order to avoid exams and Christmas break. It was a chance to make a statement early in the season. (This held for every school but VCU and Georgia State, which rescheduled a February 18 game to December 20 in order to accommodate VCU's entry in ESPN's Bracket Busters tournament.)

This two-game "mini season" is like the initial scary rise to the heights of the rollercoaster. Nothing is decided, yet many things are set up for the inevitable ups and downs of the ride. You both dread and excitedly anticipate what is coming. You know both emotions

will occur. You poke the guy next to you, your top assistant, and say
those three words: "Here we go."

———

"We've got ourselves a little CAA December tournament," Tom
Pecora mused as he sat at the end of the visitor's bench, munching on
popcorn, ninety minutes before his Pride would face VCU on
December 7. Pecora seemed at odds with how important this game
was, considering it was, after all, December, and there would be sixteen more conference games to play.

"These early games are very important," he said, "but at the same
time you can throw them out the window in terms of the big picture—the conference." Pecora intimated that by the time the conference slate would be finished, CAA teams will have sufficiently beaten
up on each other to the point where one game in December wouldn't
dictate the year. "1-1 is okay," Pecora added, "0-2 might be a bit devastating." Of course, Pecora knew his team had waxed Delaware four
days earlier and could not be in the devastated boat.

Blaine Taylor was equally nonplussed by his feelings about the two
early December games. "College basketball is like a triple crown," said
Taylor in reference to the fact that the upper tier teams in the conference play twice in the regular season and then likely meet again in a
third game in the postseason tournament. "The idea is to beat the best
teams more often than not."

Granted, thanks to the new, unbalanced schedule, also highly crit-
icized by coaches, Taylor was a bit off. For example, Hofstra and VCU
would meet just once during the regular season. Taylor's point is well
taken, however. You will lose games. You cannot avoid it. Beat the
great teams in your conference and you stand a much better chance
at winning championships. Play them when they're scheduled.

Taylor held last year's championship trophy. The year before, it
belonged to Capel and the VCU Rams. But none of that mattered—
not unbalanced schedules, championships, or amusement parks. All
that mattered to Capel on a warm, sunny Sunday afternoon in North

Carolina was his game against UNCW, the team that held the previous two championships before his.

———

When you walk into Trask Coliseum, home of the UNCW Seahawks, your mind immediately and briefly returns to your junior high school. You see the glossy yellow brick walls with painted cinder block, the tile floor, and the metal stairs and windows that hearken back to the time when you prowled such halls as a seventh grader. It smells not really bad, but stale.

After you continue through a set of double doors, the big wooden ones with the vertical handle, you turn a corner and walk into a sea of teal and green. Even when you stop for a snack, at a makeshift "stand," your popcorn is teal and white. Your seat is much like your junior high gym as well, a bleacher seat numbered something like "Row D, Seat 71." You are also permitted leg room much like riding in the coach section of an airline. It's packed that tight. Because temperature is controlled by a decades-old system, it's usually hot.

Shortly before tip-off, thoughts of junior high evaporate as the almost always sold-out throng of more than six thousand rises together to greet its Seahawks as they appear for pregame layups. (Trask holds about 6,300.) There is a great deal of student support, and the alumni are ardent followers of the team. In addition, because there is no football played at UNCW, the fans also know basketball.

Perhaps this is a reason VCU, despite its annual success in the CAA, had not won in this building since the 1995-1996 season, the first time VCU played in the CAA. Nine times since that inaugural season VCU had traveled the four hours to Wilmington, and nine times, in various ways (including blowing a ten-point lead with less than eight minutes to play the previous year), VCU had left with a loss.

Then again, if you ask UNCW Coach Brad Brownell, while Trask may be a tough place for visitors to play, "I think over the years, any place that's had success and is difficult to play, the first factor is because you have good players." Touché.

Still, Capel had reason to believe his Rams stood as good a chance this year as any. VCU was coming off two nonconference wins—the second half comeback against Houston (who would defeat LSU and Arizona, two top twenty-five teams, in its next two games) and a blowout win over Elon that represented a step forward.

It was a matchup of two teams that were supposed to challenge for the CAA title. Though it was early December and only the first of eighteen conference games, there was an intensity in Trask Coliseum. The heat was there, and so were the fans. Though differing student groups supporting the team had spawned since UNCW began winning consistently, the original group, The Hecklers, were on hand.

Capel-coached teams play focused, and the coach is meticulous in his preparation. It would be a difficult hill to climb, but VCU fans had every reason to believe this would be the year they would defeat the home team.

The veritable pin in the balloon may have occurred on the game's first possession. After winning the opening tap, UNCW was forced to throw the ball around the perimeter under the usual VCU suffocating man-to-man defense. The ball landed in the hands of UNCW center Mitch Laue, whose contested short jumper rolled off the front of the rim. Todd Hendley, UNCW's gifted 6-foot, 9-inch transfer from Wake Forest, was there, uncontested, for the put back slam dunk.

The crowd, still standing but making far less noise than they had in the minutes prior to the tip-off, re-erupted. There is no greater statement than a home team jamming home a rebound dunk on the game's first possession. The noise became deafening. Although there were more than thirty-nine minutes to go, Todd Hendley's opening salvo set the tone.

Hendley was free because VCU center Sam Faulk, a player who gives Capel maximum effort but is undersized for a center, had rotated over and tried to block Laue's shot instead of picking up his box-out assignment. The missed assignment looking for the glory play got the crowd to its feet immediately. Capel preaches roles, and blocking shots was not Sam Faulk's role.

Things didn't get much better from there on for the Rams. UNCW would slowly build its lead throughout the first half. The Seahawks opened the second half with a 13-1 run, an even better tone setter than Hendley's dunk, and the final fifteen minutes turned into garbage time. VCU managed sixteen second-half points, three coming on a long three pointer from Jamal Shuler with six seconds to play. The forty points were the fewest in the school's history. They were mauled 40-24 on the boards.

It was a debacle for Capel. As the second half unfolded, a furrowed brow turned into a grimace, which turned into abject anger and finally disgust. Too many times VCU settled for long jump shots, or solo attempts at breaking down the UNCW defense. This wasn't the kind of team Capel had prepared and he was beside himself.

In the media room immediately after the UNCW game, Capel called his team selfish. "That's as selfish as we've played since I've been the head coach here," said a visibly frustrated Capel. "We didn't play together. We didn't share the ball. We were looking to go one on one. We wouldn't screen for each other."

The following day at practice Capel issued an apology to his team. If the team was being selfish, Capel reasoned, someone would've grabbed ten rebounds. No, Capel figured, "you were all just out for yourselves."

Tom Pecora knew VCU's debacle in Wilmington on December 4 wasn't going to help his team. The Pride were due to play VCU, back at home in the Siegel Center, VCU's dominating home court, three days later. The Rams were given a smack in the face. For their part, Hofstra was on a three-game roll, including a sound whipping of Delaware in its last trip to the floor.

Even though Hofstra cruised, 79-65, four of Pecora's five starters played thirty-two minutes or more. Rivera played twenty-eight. "I'm not happy with our bench," said Pecora. "I've got to find them some minutes. But it's kind of like water and flour. I need to get them minutes, but they're not ready. So you kind of put them in and hold your breath."

At VCU, Pecora would try to get them playing time, but only if necessary would there be more than one on the floor at the same time. A conference game, on the road, against a good team, is the very definition of holding your breath.

"Nothing changes tonight," Pecora said shortly before opening tip-off as he sat down, by himself, taking in the atmosphere. "This is a tough place to play. I wish they'd been in a better game instead of a blowout. They'll be ready to jump our bones."

Pecora also knew what he had to do to win. "We've got to make shots. We can't let them get running, get going, get a couple of dunks and get the crowd into it. We've got to make it a one-shot game for them. I want it slow. We'll play multiple defenses."

After rattling off those keys and a brief pause, Pecora put his hand in a popcorn bucket, popped a few into his mouth, and as he stared at pregame notes declared that "this is the best popcorn in the league." Pecora had everything scouted.

The hour before the tip-off of a game is the longest hour of the day for Tom Pecora. Once he's prepared the strategy and prepared his team, he is ready to go. He just wants to get on the court and play. He loves the games and loves coaching his kids as much as anyone in the business.

While there is nothing terse about Tom Pecora, there is also nothing that could sum up the demeanor of the Hofstra coach, nor his approach to basketball, any better. He calls them as he sees them and never appears to be under any pressure. Pecora is the kind of coach both fans and administrators love. He is quick witted and a quote machine, yet he hides a remarkable understanding of basketball behind a stereotypical New York chatterbox style. His genius is a Valvano-style genius.

Pecora honed his craft coaching junior college basketball. "I was fortunate that I was able to make mistakes on the JC level, where I didn't have five thousand people yelling at me if I made a mistake," he said. In addition, he was a longtime assistant at Hofstra before getting more of a promotion than a new hire.

Pecora is fast. His practices are fast. He talks fast. You feel like there's always something going on around Tom Pecora, and that whatever it is, it will turn out good. It is this celerity tempered with control that is most appealing because he means what he says.

Even in probably the biggest game of his brief head coaching career, a 2004 CAA Tournament semifinal matchup with ODU, when consecutive close calls didn't go his way, Pecora was nonplussed. There was no berating of the official. There was no slinging off of the coat or tie. His expression was rather like ordering off a menu at a restaurant after the waitress tells you they're out of what you want— a little wrinkle, a furrowing of the brow, and you move on to the next thing. The wheels are always turning.

It certainly was not the expression of a young coach in likely the most intense moment of his young coaching career. He simply looked down the bench as if he was searching for the next combination, or next item on the menu, that would stave off the big run of the top seed.

"One thing I love about coaching is its unpredictability," Pecora says. "I love the adjustments. You have to have a little fun with it or it will burn you out. I love it."

Although he never said it, Pecora's demeanor screams the old New York Yankees outfielder Mickey Rivers' line about putting undue stress on yourself: "There's no sense in worrying about things you've got control over," said Rivers, "because if you've got control over them then there's no sense in worrying. And there's no sense in worrying about things you DON'T have control over, because if you don't have control over them, there's no sense in worrying."

Pecora admits he followed an atypical coaching path. He didn't come from a big school or mentor under college basketball's celebrity elite. He was teaching school and running an intramural program after graduating from Adelphi University in 1983.

Pecora assisted Bob McKillop, the very respected head coach at Davidson, at Long Island Lutheran High School for four years before making a move closer to home and assisting Stu Klein at Nassau Community College in Garden City, New York, from 1987 through 1989. He got his first head coaching job, once again close to home, when he was named in 1989 the head man at the State University of New York at Farmingdale. Pecora won sixty-two games in three seasons, including a regional championship and berth in the National Junior College Athletic Association tournament.

It was then that tragedy struck Pecora, when his first wife was the victim of a drunk driver. The accident would wound Pecora deeply, while helping to shape the important things in his life: family, friends, and loyalty.

The incident, while tragic, would start in motion a series of events that would clarify his life's mission. He chose to give up his head coaching position—one in which he had coached two JUCO all-Americans and had just made a postseason tournament, also forfeiting a $57,000 salary—and leave New York. Pecora headed west to serve as an assistant (along with now-Villanova head man Jay Wright) under Rollie Massamino at UNLV. His salary would drop to $20,000, he would be in a completely different geographical region, and he'd have to adjust to being an assistant again. But he needed the break, and he got more of an education than he thought.

"Rollie made me work too much," Pecora laughs. "But I got to see how a good program is run, got to hang around with great people from places other than basketball. When I was exposed to that and saw what people like Tommy Lasorda were all about, I thought, 'I can do that.'"

Pecora learned another important thing: "I'm a New Yorker." So after one year as assistant coach/recruiting coordinator under John Olive at Loyola Marymount during the 1993-1994 season, Pecora rejoined his friend Wright, who had been hired as the head coach at Hofstra. When Hofstra needed its new head coach, it didn't have to look any farther than its own bench. "This is a lot better than I thought I'd ever do," Pecora says in a rather wistful tone. "To get the opportunity to coach on this level, fifteen minutes from where I grew up, is wonderful."

Pecora has presided over Hofstra since its first season in the Colonial, a 2001-2002 campaign that saw the Pride finish dead last in the regular season with a 5-13 record. On top of the step up in league from the America East (Delaware, Drexel, and Towson would join Hofstra in the move from the AE to the CAA), Hofstra had lost several key players and its coach. (Jay Wright moved on to take the head job at Villanova.) The rebuilding effort would be doubly difficult for Pecora, but it was a challenge for which he was ready.

Still, Pecora showed flashes of the reason he was hired as head coach. In the early nonconference season, Hofstra knocked off Kent State 67-64. At the time it was a good win, but nobody realized just how good it was until Kent State made a run into the Elite 8 of the NCAA Tournament that year. Despite finishing tenth in the ten-team CAA during the regular season, Hofstra beat the seventh seeded Towson Tigers and then upset the second seed, George Mason, 82-76. Notice had been served.

The next campaign, though, wasn't much better. Pecora won six conference games and won in the play-in round again, but Hofstra won just eight total games, losing twenty-one. Pecora had every reason to be nervous. Remember, this was a program used to winning, and winning big. Losing twenty games in the first two seasons was not a way to endear yourself to fans or the administration. A new, tougher conference was in many ways irrelevant.

Then something happened that usually doesn't occur to coaches who are 20-41. Pecora was given a three-year contract extension. "They never flinched when we were 8-21," said Pecora. "The [administration's] loyalty to me was tremendous. They understand athletics and knew that although there would be an adjustment period, we would be good again."

It turned out to be a smart move. Behind bruising all-CAA center Kenny Adeleke, Hofstra posted a 10-8 record in the CAA and avoided the play-in round in the CAA Tournament for the first time ever. Hofstra had again increased its win total in the conference and nearly hit .500 for the season, finishing 14-15.

Over the summer of 2004, the team lost Adeleke, its first team all-CAA center.

Even though Pecora knew he had a talented guard nobody had seen in Antoine Agudio (Agudio had missed most of his freshman season with an injured hand and was red shirted), it would not be a surprise to see Hofstra fall back in the standings. You don't lose a first-team all-conference player, especially in rebuilding mode, and immediately improve. Complicating matters, starting center Wendell Gibson would not return from a knee injury until mid-January.

"Our transition to guard play was not so tough," Pecora said. "We knew how good Agudio was, and at this level you have to find guys willing to play hard, set screens, because you're going to play small."

Hofstra did improve, however. They jumped quickly out of the gates in 2004-2005, winning a school record nine straight to start the season, including a ten-point win over New York rival St. John's. After that win, Hofstra's third in the past five meetings, Pecora's ode to unpredictability was consistent: "One day a peacock, the next a feather duster."

Pecora's approach and outlook is amazingly refreshing in a career path known for its hypersensitivity and burn out. "You've got to be yourself, and go with what works for you," he says.

He is like any other coach in that he is a preparation freak. But once he's prepared and the clock starts, Pecora allows his players to play and adjust to the flow of the game. The players execute at the precise opportunities they were prepared to observe, not Pecora.

"I learned a lot from Rollie Massamino," says Pecora. "The thing he taught me most was that preparation is the most important thing. If you are prepared, you can better adjust during the game when things don't go according to plan."

One aspect that makes Pecora a good coach is his willingness to allow his players to play the game. He has a philosophy, set plays, and keys. ("I play more zone defense early in the year because most teams haven't worked very much on their zone offense. I play much more man later in the year to take teams out of their patterns.") In those respects, he is no different than any other coach. His approach, however, is to allow the kids under his tutelage the freedom to play the game the way they know how, the way they've always played, yet to his specifics.

He also prepares his team in a pseudo-stealth manner. "We won't go over the other team's personnel directly," he says. "We'll work it into drills without telling them. For example, the day before a Drexel game we'll work on fighting over ball screens and drilling those fundamentals. Then in our walk-throughs [for Drexel] the kids will realize they've already done this. We sort of prepare them without them knowing. The older guys figure it out, but it's very good and useful for the younger guys."

Pecora carries with him a "no shoot around" policy on the day of games. It's something he learned from legendary Syracuse Coach Jim Boeheim, because, as Pecora puts it, "I want my guys to be excited when they show up at a gym. Besides," he continues, "getting used to the shooting background is overrated. Sometimes I think coaches use that to justify their existence in the gym."

Part of the no shoot around policy means Hofstra will conduct its walk-through (where they go over the opponents' plays and sets as a reminder) in the hotel ballroom in which they eat their pregame meal.

The room is divided, but not in half. The typical ballroom tables and chairs are huddled closely together. One table sits at the front of the room with a laptop computer. The players file in, take their seats, and view last-minute scouting film on their opponents. Pecora quizzes players on random aspects of what he believes are Hofstra's keys to victory.

The players then get up and move to the short side of the room. Tape is placed on the carpet to mock a foul lane, and a mini ball or Nerf ball is tossed back and forth, simulating the opposition. Many times, assistant Tom Parotta conducts with statements like: "Let's overplay when the ball goes wide, over by the cookies."

Tom Pecora is not flashy, just genuine. The thing about him is that he doesn't think he's smarter than everyone else. Smug is an alien concept. After being asked about his adjustments, something he loves to do, in the St. John's game that held the Red Storm scoreless for the final eight minutes of the game, Pecora laughed, saying, "I loved that they kept missing shots!"

"We do a job, establishing a foundation" he continued. "This is how we do things, but the players have to play. I like seeing how it plays out. I love the games."

Pecora's anxiety is completely invisible, though, as he sits idly, almost like he's killing time, as his players begin warming up. Inside, Pecora is the excited one. It's only a matter of minutes, however, before Pecora changes his demeanor. Not unlike almost every other team in college basketball, Hofstra heads back to the locker room at the 30:00 mark to talk matchups and strategy, and gets a last-minute game plan review. But Pecora has his team stand and join hands, everyone from players to coaches, SIDs to trainers, and bow heads. There is no prayer. Pecora only asks everyone in the room to close their eyes and take a minute to think about win. Not winning. Win.

Pecora knew they'd have their work cut out for them from the opening tap. "When it's your turn to go into the game, be ready," he implored his bench players in the locker room. "There's no room for two or three trips down the court to get loose. Be ready immediately."

The crowd began filtering in when the players returned to the court. VCU has gone 75-15 since the Stuart E. Siegel Center was built, and its crowds are at the top of the conference in terms of attendance and noise. The athletic department puts on a good show, as timeouts are busy with cheerleaders and music and giveaways, and the VCU pep band is top notch.

The atmosphere was becoming far more festive than a normal

December basketball game, and Pecora sensed this. When the players returned to the locker room at the ten-minute mark to get their final pep talk, Pecora was ready. He needed his team to know they, too, were ready.

He walked around the room looking into the eyes of his players. Though Pecora is nowhere near the size of most of his players, for some reason he was eye-to-eye with every one of them. His walk was one of purpose, one that you would normally associate with a football coach. He continued around the room and pondered the right things to say. When Pecora moved his attention directly onto the players, it was not a fire and brimstone speech. Rather, it was pointed and motivational.

"We're ready. We're ready. We're ready," Pecora repeated. "You guys deserve to win this game for so many reasons but you have to go out there and do it. Freshmen, we need you tonight to grow up a little. Don't let the crowd rattle you. Don't let the officials rattle you. We've never won in this building. Let's make history."

It was the last thing Pecora said, and it was the last thing written on the dry erase board, and it was written in red: "Let's make history."

The game began somewhat ominously for VCU. Two Loren Stokes baskets and an Aurimas Kieza follow lay-in staked Hofstra to an 11-3 lead less than four minutes into the game when Capel called time-out. At this point VCU had missed golden opportunities to score and made one of five field goals and was being pummeled 7-2 on the glass. Capel had reason to believe it was UNCW all over again.

VCU rallied, and when Alexander Harper made a quick steal and a thunderous slam dunk, VCU had its first lead of the night at 27-26. The crowd roared its approval, and the momentum was clearly in favor of the home team. ("A huge play in the game," Capel would say in his postgame press conference.)

The Hofstra weariness was evident, and after two more steals off the press and back-to-back layups, VCU led 31-26 and Pecora called a thirty-second time-out at 2:58, if only to get his guys some rest. VCU had turned up the speed meter, and Hofstra fell into Pecora's worst nightmare: a fast game with VCU running and dunking and the crowd going crazy.

Jesse Pellot Rosa swished a twenty-five footer at the buzzer to give VCU its biggest lead, 37-29, capping off a 19-3 run to end the first half.

"I thought our pressure perhaps wore them down a little bit," Capel said. "One of the things, in looking at their stats, we knew [their starters] played a lot of minutes. We felt like if we could get into their bench, it would be an advantage for us."

It got worse. After B.A. Walker hit his sixth bonus shot of the night, the VCU lead was 59-42.

Pecora sat on his bench, almost helpless against the torrent of VCU threes. Pecora subbed for the first time in the second half at the 10:16 mark, with Hofstra down by fourteen points. It took about two minutes for him to become completely fed up, and needing to get his freshmen some much-needed playing time, emptied his bench at the 8:08 mark.

"I wanted to do it at halftime," Pecora said, "but my assistants talked me out of it. Besides, the seniors (Kieza and Uter) worked their asses off and I didn't want to do that to them."

The lead got as high as twenty-seven and ended at 87-64.

Pecora huddled with his assistant coaches prior to entering the locker room in the tunnel beneath the Siegel Center. He turned and began talking with Van Macon and Tom Parotta. How would they deal with this debacle? It would be a delicate speech and he wanted to check with his assistants to see if his preferred approach was on target. Perhaps they needed a good chewing out. The quorum chose to teach a lesson. Hofstra had won convincingly throughout the early season, but in the face of adversity, they chose to fold the tents. It was settled. Screaming wouldn't teach them anything. The players knew Pecora was mad at the effort.

Pecora checked with sports information director Jeremy Kniffin regarding his press responsibilities. It was there that the coach had a run-in with a VCU pep band player; however, it was not your typical run-in.

"You guys were great," Pecora told the student out of nowhere, spontaneously stopping the conversation with his coaches and surprising the student. "You're what it's all about. Keep it up."

It was the kind of meeting most people don't ever hear. Usually a confrontation between a student and an opposing coach goes the wrong way, but Pecora understood and respected the moment: The VCU pep band had gone after the visitors loudly but fairly.

Sweating profusely, with cloth Ram horns tilted sideways on his head, the exhausted student replied, "Thanks coach, you're the best!" and shuffled down the hallway, leaving Pecora to his team. The respect was returned.

Pecora muttered about three more words and headed into the Hofstra locker room. "Well that hurts, I mean really hurts," he said as he entered the locker room after the VCU shellacking. "If that doesn't hurt you, man..."

As his voice trailed off into a nodding of the head, Pecora began telling his team a story. The plot was essentially about a salesman who was given a promotion, a big new territory, and a big salary. The salesman's boss said that if he didn't perform, he'd be given his old job and old salary back. The lesson is you have to bring your best every single day.

"Look guys," Pecora finished, "everything we do is a microcosm of life." Whether it's work or basketball, he explained, you have to bring your best effort every single day. Afterward he pointed out the keys to the game and noted that none were accomplished.

In a way, the VCU beating, although bad, may have given Pecora the opportunity for his team to receive the come-uppance he felt it needed. He definitely got his bench needed floor time.

George Mason was playing very good basketball. The Patriots had rallied from a home-opening let-down loss to Creighton to drill Manhattan, Georgia State (to open the conference season), and American. Larranaga's team waxed Georgia State in Atlanta by thirty and thumped American, 75-35.

Old Dominion, at Old Dominion, would be its first conference test. After all, these were the conference champs, playing their home conference opener against last year's sixth place team. They had been unanimously voted the preseason #1 team. The game would live up to expectations, including a hot start from the Patriots in the game's opening minutes.

George Mason stretched the lead out to 39-32 in the opening minutes of the second half, and both coaches, if they had not figured it out already, knew this one was going to the wire. What was particularly concerning Taylor was his team's defense. Normally, shooting a high percentage against the Monarchs is a feat. ODU was second in the CAA in field goal percentage defense last year, limiting opponents to 40.7 percent accuracy. However, George Mason hit 52 percent in the first half on this evening, and connected on four of its first six shots in the second stanza in building the seven-point bulge.

ODU, as both coaches expected, righted the ship, and chipped away at the lead. When Arnaud Dahi hit two free throws with a little more than eight minutes to play, ODU overtook George Mason, 47-46. It was ODU's first lead in more than seventeen minutes of action, and the crowd of nearly 6,500, short of capacity and who had been mostly sitting on their hands for thirty-two minutes, rose and cheered as loud as they had since the previous season.

At this point, both defenses dug in. George Mason's next five possessions were turnover, a Tony Skinn three pointer, turnover, turnover, turnover. However, ODU managed only a 1-5 performance from the field and 2-4 from the line and a turnover in the same span. When Mason center Jai Lewis converted a layup with 4:20 to play, the game was tied at 51-51 and white knuckles could be seen all over the Ted Constant Center. When they weren't seen, they were felt. To be tied with four minutes to play was frightening.

Lewis hit a short layup after grabbing an offensive rebound of an errant Skinn trey. There was still 2:58 left on the clock as Lewis's putback rolled through the net, and little did anyone know that would be the last ball to go through the hoop until the final second. George

Mason led 53-51, and the tension in the building got to the players.

With twenty-nine seconds left to play and Mason still clinging to the 53-51 lead, ODU chose to immediately foul George Mason and put them on the line.

Blaine Taylor's reasoning was that he wanted to have the ball in his team's hands with a chance to tie or win, and if time needed to be run off of the clock, he wanted his team to have that option. The Ted Constant Center was his building, and he would dictate the end game, even if the Monarchs trailed.

So Alex Loughton did the honors and put Mason on the line for a one-and-one opportunity. Doing the honors for Mason was senior guard Lamar Butler, who is a 74 percent free throw shooter. Butler finished third in the CAA last year in three-point shooting (more than 43 percent), but his attempt rolled off the rim and Loughton corralled the rebound.

With nineteen seconds to play, Taylor called a time-out to set up the final play. In the huddle, it was diagrammed to go to Hunter for a short jumper and overtime. Hunter was to shoot the ball with about five seconds left to give the Monarchs a chance at an offensive rebound and a stick back.

Larranaga, however, knew ODU would try to get the ball in the hands of their playmaker, and designed a defense to overplay Hunter. Brian Henderson, a sophomore who had misfired on five of six three-point attempts in the game and was probably ODU's fifth option on the floor, found the ball in his hands and, feeling he had no other option, launched a pretty jumper that spiraled out. Isaiah Hunter, who was supposed to shoot, grabbed the rebound and the ball was knocked out of his hands and out of bounds with 4.4 seconds remaining.

Out of time-outs, Taylor called the exact same play for Hunter and it generated almost the exact same result. Hunter was blanketed by the Mason defense, and with no other option, the ball was pitched to Drew Williamson near the midcourt line. Williamson took two dribbles and launched a twenty-five footer that swished as the horn sounded. It was literally a spike being driven into the hearts of the

George Mason players as pandemonium erupted in the face of the improbable ODU 54-53 victory.

A soldout crowd, routinely among the loudest in the conference in the league's crown jewel arena, exploded. The home team had trailed much of the evening, fought back, and rewarded the tension-filled fans.

Though the Ted Constant Center was barely two years old, it was lucky the roof was intact. Players jumped and hugged and chased Williamson around. Fans mobbed each other. The stories immediately began being told regarding the distance of Williamson's shot: 25 feet? 30 feet? from the parking lot?

Then, the air was nearly sucked out of the building. In all the pandemonium, the officials gathered at midcourt. They would put 0.7 seconds back on the clock and Butler would fire a long desperation shot that fell way short, but those details didn't matter. Williamson's bomb was a bolt of lightning great teams get on their way to magical seasons. The building erupted once more.

"I just wanted to get it up and give us a chance to rebound it," said Williamson. "I was actually the second option. We were setting a double screen for Isaiah Hunter under the basket. I went into the backcourt to make it a 4-on-4 deal."

It figures that the game would end that way. Last shot, and the guy who was trying to stay out of the way gets the ball and makes a play.

"You're going to need a little Monarch magic every once in a while," Taylor said. "We gave ourselves a chance and we cashed in." For his part in the glee, Taylor picked up the PA microphone and began singing the ODU alma mater along with the crowd. It was truly a festive scene that Taylor soaked in, but it wouldn't be long before he turned his attention to the reasons why this game was such a struggle.

"It's certainly no fun to lose," George Mason's Larranaga said. "Yet there are nights when I'm happy we won but disappointed we didn't play better. Tonight I'm proud of the way we played."

Even though Taylor understood exactly what Larranaga was feeling, he was happy he was on the winning side. But as everyone celebrated and finally allowed themselves to exhale, Taylor knew his team would have to play better to stay atop the CAA heap. If Taylor was wondering whether the struggle against George Mason was a wakeup call for his team, it didn't take long to get his answer.

Old Dominion's next test was against Bruiser Flint's Drexel team in Philadelphia at the venerable John A. Daskalakis Athletic Center. In this case, *venerable* means small, old, and cramped. The DAC, as it's called, doubles as a recreational facility for the school's students, and for basketball games holds a scant 1,200 people. It is usually full of screaming Drexel fans, most notably the student cheering group called the DAC Pack.

The DAC Pack was ready for Old Dominion on the conference's initial Comcast regional television game of the week. So were Bruiser Flint's Dragons. Old Dominion led 4-3 early on when Taylor's answer came. For the next thirteen minutes and ten seconds, ODU did not score a single point. The Monarchs took good shots and bad shots, but none would fall.

With 6:41 left in the first half, Drexel point guard Bashir Mason was fouled as he swished a three pointer and made the ensuing free throw. That brought Drexel's run to eighteen straight points and a 21-4 lead. Mason had just scored on one play what ODU had been able to manage as a team in more than thirteen minutes of action. The final would be 61-42, but it wasn't that close.

If the "mini tournament," in Tom Pecora's words, proved anything, it's that the preseason mantra that the CAA is a deep league was true. Dick Vitale gushed on ESPN about Drexel, and wondered aloud, for millions to hear, that if Drexel was voted number seven in the conference, he wanted to see the other six.

After the initial two-game set, the results proved the depth, albeit in a very odd manner. Exactly half of the twelve games played ended with a victory margin of twenty or better. Only three games were decided by fewer than eleven points. The conference heavyweight,

Old Dominion, had won by one and lost by nineteen. VCU had lost by twenty and beat another top-tier Hofstra team by twenty-three. Hofstra beat Delaware by fourteen. Newcomer Georgia State had won by twenty-seven (over Delaware) and lost by thirty (George Mason).

For its part, the conference had acquitted itself very well, indeed. The CAA was ranked seventh among the nation's thirty-one Division I conferences according to the first RPI ratings released by Collegiate Basketball News, which is considered to be the closest to the RPI compiled by the NCAA. The CAA trailed only the Big 10, Big East, ACC, Missouri Valley, SEC, and Big 12 in the rankings. The Atlantic 10, Pac 10, West Coast, and WAC all trailed Tom Yeager's conference.

Importantly, only the Missouri Valley Conference was ahead of the CAA in terms of mid-major conferences, and only four other conferences—the ACC, Big East, Big 10, and SEC—could boast the CAA standard of having at least seven teams ranked among the top hundred in the RPI (UNCW at fifteen, Northeastern at thirty-six, VCU at forty-one, George Mason at fifty-five, Drexel at sixty-six, Old Dominion at sixty-eight, and Hofstra at ninety-four).

The conference's 38-25 nonconference mark to this point, December 12, included victories such as ODU beating Georgia, Hofstra winning at St. John's, VCU winning at Houston, UNCW defeating Butler, Wyoming, and Northwestern to capture the BCA Invitational, and Drexel reaching the semifinals of the NIT Season Tip-Off Tournament before losing close games to nationally ranked Duke and UCLA. A full thirty-eight of the sixty-three nonconference contests were played either on the road or on neutral courts and the league went 20-18 in those games.

———

As the teams headed for an exam break and the smattering of holiday nonconference tune-ups, the only constant was that three teams picked in the middle of the pack were on top of the standings at 2-0. Conference torch bearers ODU, VCU, and Hofstra all sat at 1-1. All carried one impressive win and one depressive loss.

Old Dominion sat at 6-2 without playing what Taylor could say was a complete game. The Monarchs had the same talent that afforded the accolades. Alex Loughton would enter the DePaul game having gone ten days without scoring a point on the floor. It was now time for that talent to show itself.

Larranaga could see the pieces falling into place, but knew his squad's inconsistency must be solved. In addition to the close Wake Forest loss and the thirty-point drubbing of Georgia State, the Patriots were manhandled at home by Creighton. Three winnable home games were next, a perfect opportunity to put those pieces in place.

Hofstra was also winning regularly but still lacked any quality contribution from its bench. Tom Pecora could not keep up the pace of playing his starters thirty-two to thirty-eight minutes per game. They would wear down. He needed his freshmen to grow up in a hurry, and he needed star guard Loren Stokes to get comfortable after recuperating from his broken nose.

The question on the minds of Larranaga, Capel, Pecora, and Taylor was the same: With so much muck, so much uncertainty, what in the world would the New Year look like?

2005-2006 STANDINGS
(Through Games of December 12, 2005)

	Conference			Overall					
	W	L	Pct.	W	L	Pct.	H	A	N
Northeastern	2	0	1.000	6	1	.857	2-0	2-1	2-0
UNC Wilmington	2	0	1.000	7	2	.778	2-0	3-2	2-0
Drexel	2	0	1.000	5	5	.500	4-0	1-1	0-4
Old Dominion	1	1	.500	6	2	.750	3-0	1-1	2-1
Hofstra	1	1	.500	4	2	.667	3-0	1-2	0-0
VCU	1	1	.500	4	2	.667	3-0	1-2	0-0
George Mason	1	1	.500	5	3	.625	1-1	2-2	2-0
Towson	1	1	.500	3	4	.429	3-1	0-3	0-0
Georgia State	1	1	.500	2	4	.333	2-3	0-0	0-1
William & Mary	0	2	.000	4	3	.571	2-2	2-1	0-0
James Madison	0	2	.000	2	4	.333	2-3	0-1	0-0
Delaware	0	2	.000	2	6	.250	0-0	0-6	2-0

Hofstra's Antoine Agudio drives to the hoop.

Top:
Do-everything guard B.A. Walker hits a reverse layup at VCU's Siegel Center.

Right:
Hofstra's All- CAA performer Loren Stokes shoots a trademark floater.

Left:
Hofstra head coach
Tom Pecora is flanked
by his staff. From left:
Tom Parotta, David
Duke, and Van Macon.

Below:
Old Dominion's Blaine
Taylor waves to the
crowd after his first
CAA championship.

Left:
VCU star Nick George talks to Jamal Shuler.

Below:
Hofstra's Adiran Uter powers in a dunk in a game against St. John's.

In the CAA's most heated rivalry, VCU's Jesse Pellot Rosa dishes to a teammate while ODU's Alex Loughton tries to take a charge.

Left:
George Mason coaches and players celebrate the Patriots' first-round upset victory over Michigan State. Who knew?

Below:
George Mason shooting guard Lamar Butler answers questions about the team's Cinderella run to the Final Four.

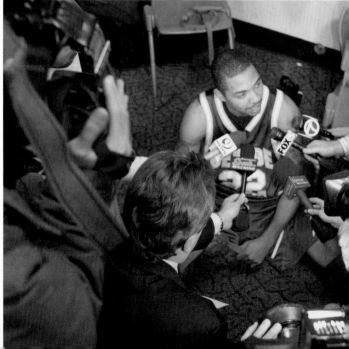

Above:
Folarin Campbell attacks the basket over Connecticut's Ed Nelson. Campbell's eight-foot fadeaway swish in overtime proved to be the signature shot in George Mason's signature win.

Left:
Jim Larranaga calmly patrols the sideline against Connecticut. The victory, his 364th overall, would send shockwaves through the sports world.

Jim Larranaga and the George Mason team are presented the trophy for winning the Washington, DC regional and earning a trip to the Final Four. Next stop: Indianapolis.

CHAPTER SIX

INTERCESSION

"Time hides no treasures; we want not its then, but its now."
–Henry David Thoreau

Having persevered through a summer in which his father had passed away, Old Dominion coach Blaine Taylor was ready for the basketball season. The routine would do him good, as he is admittedly ritualistic.

As the fall of 2005 wore on, however, pain in his joints slowly increased. What began as a rash on his leg and side had crept up into his hips and was causing discomfort. He'd had his hips X-rayed and underwent every blood and urine test imaginable, but the results showed nothing.

Taylor suspected an age-related problem such as osteoarthritis. Considering the amount of time he spent traveling, Taylor surmised, surely his body was acting out. Taylor gutted out a ten-hour flight to France on a recruiting trip, which followed a summer in which he took multiple trips to the West Coast to be with his family during their difficult time.

He would spend time in the whirlpool loosening the joints if only for comfort's sake, but Taylor would privately limp through ODU practices. His lymph glands were huge. Even the most routine action would take up to five minutes as he urged his body to beat the pain. He knew there had to be more to it than the regular aging process, complicated by the toll travel takes on a man's body.

Even as Old Dominion prepared for its opening games in St. Thomas at the Paradise Jam, when a regimen of antibiotics had eased the pain somewhat, Taylor was hurting. The side effects from the medications he was taking were horrendous as well. The nausea and sluggishness only complicated the issue because their aid was negligible. "It was awful," he said. Taylor's lymph glands were swollen and the rash became so bad that it was nearly impossible for him to even pull up his pants. It would take five doctors, seven different medications, and a harrowing Christmas Day to determine what was causing him so much misery.

Christmas at the Taylor household is Rockwell-esque. Family is important to the coach. He was not about to miss out on the biggest family holiday, especially significant in his household. "We opened up presents with our daughters," said Taylor, who was also celebrating his wife Annie's birthday, "and afterwards I told [Annie] it was unbearable. I called my doctor and he advised me to get to the emergency room." On Annie's request, Taylor didn't immediately tell his four daughters he was on his way to undergo yet another battery of tests. But he was off, and the investigation into his pain resumed.

Two miserable days later, Taylor got the call. His doctor discovered the problem was MRSA, fast becoming a prevalent and debilitating ailment in sports. Frequently referred to by its initials, pronounced "meersa" (methicillin-resistant staphylococcus aureus), the ailment is a staph infection that has become resistant to most antibiotics. According to the Centers for Disease Control and Prevention, more than 130,000 people annually are admitted to the hospital with the malady.

Because it is resistant to many of the common antibiotics and it masks itself as a rash or even the flu (with the soreness in joints), it sometimes takes doctors a while to diagnose MRSA. Its effects can be devastating. In fact, Brandon Noble, a defensive tackle for the Washington Redskins who had MRSA, was told by his doctor that if he had waited even another twenty-four hours, he could have lost his leg or even his life.

In a matter of only a few hours after his doctor called with the diagnosis, two days after being in the emergency room, and three days before a crucial basketball game against Virginia Tech, Taylor was admitted to Norfolk Hospital and underwent surgery.

"Through time, I expect strength," is something Taylor demands of his players. The coach now needed to demand that of himself.

Strength is a core value to coaches, especially in mid-major basketball circles. There's a good chance they've played their cupcakes, played well, played poorly, and played a BCS team.

The three weeks prior to the end of the calendar year is, for lack of a better word, odd in college basketball circles. It's never a surprise for a team to play at all levels, no matter the strength of the opponent, during this time. There's so much going on, and little has to do with actual basketball games.

The players finish up final exams for the semester. It is the time of year when it's easy for them to get homesick. They've been away from home for an extended time, and the "holiday cheer" doesn't translate well to the practice floor. When all other students head for home, the players often head back to vacant dorms and campus housing. The monotony of practice and time in the weight room takes its toll.

Coaches often stage a tirade so that they can throw all of the players out of practice, if only to break the monotony and attempt to refocus the players (and on more than one occasion to get some late Christmas shopping done).

However Blaine Taylor had chosen to handle his team worked. Old Dominion thrashed DePaul in the Ted Constant Center on December 17. The Blue Demons rolled into Norfolk on a high, defeating sixteenth ranked Wake Forest, at Wake Forest, soundly. Jerry Wainwright had his young squad believing they could play and win anywhere.

The Monarchs would outscore DePaul 58-21 in the second half, ending the game on a 53-9 run over the final sixteen minutes. The final score, 87-43, was the worst loss in DePaul's storied basketball history.

For its part, Old Dominion came into the game searching for answers after the Drexel debacle. They had seven days to right the ship, a one-week span in which Taylor would admit he toyed with the idea of sitting down his entire starting five. "We had a healthy exercise in introspective thought on a lot of things," Taylor deadpanned.

With a barely detectable wry smile, Taylor explained the game away as a product of "they caught us on the wrong day and we caught them on the right day." There was no hint of the pain that coursed through Taylor's body.

In college basketball, especially games played over the holidays, the first few minutes are a true feeling-out period. Both teams are adjusting to styles and matchups, and both coaches are getting an idea of how the game is going to play out, and which players are over or under their normal abilities.

For that reason, no matter the teams playing, the score is usually 6-3, 8-6, or 10-10 before a run gets one team going and both teams settle into a flow. Occasionally, a lesser talented team gets off to a quick start. Other times, however, there is a run from the opening tap.

What occurred at the outset of Old Dominion's game against the University of Richmond on December 20 defied belief. It was only two days since ODU had run DePaul out of Norfolk, and there was no reason to believe the Monarchs wouldn't continue to bring the train up to full speed.

Richmond, under first-year head coach Chris Mooney, was in a major rebuilding mode. The Spiders were implementing a Princeton-style offense and a new defense, and adjusting to a new coach. The team had also lost five players, all guards, since the departure of Jerry Wainwright (who ironically ended up at DePaul). The new system, which focused on passing, dribbling, and cutting to open spots, would be played by a team with nobody smaller than 6 feet, 5 inches tall and none a natural point guard.

With a new style, one ODU had not seen and had only two days for which to prepare, and the fact that there was only a smattering of about two thousand fans in the seats on a cold Tuesday evening, you would expect Richmond to get off to a solid start before ODU settled down and eventually ran away with the game. It's how these games typically go.

In a building that holds around 10,000 fans, the Robins Center was more an echo chamber than a dungeon. The students were on break and the feel was more of a scrimmage than a regional rivalry between teams with contrasting styles of play.

So it began. ODU turned the ball over on its first three possessions as Taylor talked to, really, himself on the sideline. The Robins Center was a light buzz—it would be a long game and many of the fans were late in arriving.

As his players ran through the plays, Taylor was coaching along, calling out where guys should be. It didn't seem to matter that he was barely audible to his assistant coaches, much less the players at the other end of the court.

Kevin Steenberge, Richmond's 6-foot, 10-inch center, hit a jump hook and then a dunk and it was 4-0.

Then 6-foot, 7-inch Oumar Sylla went over 6-foot Drew Williamson and it was 6-0.

An Isaiah Hunter turnover led to a Jermaine Bucknor layup: 8-0.

Another turnover. A Richmond layup and foul. At the under 16:00 media time it was 10-0 with a free throw upcoming. Richmond had made all five field goal attempts and ODU had missed both of its tries while committing four turnovers.

The crowd became a crowd, as it sensed what was occurring.

During the time-out, Taylor was direct but not hysterical. He noted openings in the Spiders' defense and implored Hunter to find them. He wanted the Monarchs to reverse the ball against the matchup zone: "Counter it, counter it. Sam, ask for the ball." (Taylor inserted 7-foot, 3-inch Sam Harris into the game.)

Out of the time-out, Sam Harris called for the ball and received the ball, and Steenberge promptly blocked the shot. Bucknor hit another three and the lead was 14-0. After another ODU missed shot, Jahron

Giddings, a freshman for Richmond, nailed a three and the lead was amazingly 17-0 with 12:31 on the clock. For its part, the crowd openly wondered how far the football score could climb.

Finally, Alex Loughton broke the spell a minute later with a follow-up jumper to make the score 17-2. At the next timeout, Taylor calmly told a quick joke and smiled at his team, knowing that barking could turn this game ugly.

The barrage continued. Richmond's Drew Crank beat the shot clock buzzer with a jumper in Loughton's face; Sylla then hit a layup and it was 21-2. A team that was preseason top twenty-five and being hailed around the country as one of the best mid-major teams was being pummeled, and looking bad in the process.

Taylor didn't panic. "We should have Drew run the baseline," he remarked to assistant Robert Wilkes. Two minutes later, trailing 27-9, Drew Williamson came off a screen on the baseline and swished a three.

That signaled ODU to get going, and another Williamson three with :34 remaining was the last basket of the first half. The shot cut the lead to a manageable 30-17. ODU was shooting 25 percent and Richmond 60 percent and the Monarchs trailed by thirteen points, but Taylor felt good.

"We're a basket or two from a single-digit game," he told the team in the locker room. "We're three or four good plays from being right in this thing." With that, adjustments were discussed and the players returned to the court feeling like they had a chance.

Fueled by a Williamson steal in which he crawled across the floor on all fours for a loose ball, ODU scored the first nine points of the second half and it was a 30-26 game. The teams traded baskets for the most part, and when Alex Loughton was fouled with 2:59 to play and made both free throws, ODU had forged a tie at 46-46.

With :25.3 to play and the score still 46-46, ODU grabbed a rebound and called time to set up a final shot.

The first thing Taylor did when the team sat down was make a statement and ask a question. "We have one time-out left. How many time-outs do we have?"

The entire huddle, in unison, chirped out "one."

After he got the answer he wanted, with an edge to his voice that hadn't previously been there, Taylor urged his team to "suck it up, suck it up!"

With his strategic time-out reminder and his motivational bark complete, Taylor moved in to diagram a final shot.

Richmond played inspired defense and shut down ODU's main option and counterpunch. When the play broke down, Drew Williamson drove to the basket but Steenberge, playing with four fouls, blocked the shot. It caromed to Hunter, who barely missed a baseline jumper at the horn.

Overtime.

Hunter hit a jumper to open the extra session, and then stole the ball from Peter Thomas near midcourt. The race to the basket was a tie, but Hunter forced a little contact and laid the ball in the hoop. ODU led 50-46 and the crowd was stunned.

Just as everyone was coming to grips with what was unfolding—Richmond fans wondering how they lost a twenty-point lead in a game that was going to be in the fifties, and ODU fans rejoicing in the dodged bullet—the whistle blew.

Everyone stopped as the only action on the floor seemed to be that Richmond was inbounding the ball. There were four seconds of near-dead silence as everyone reacted and reality set in.

Hunter was called for a technical foul. Taunting was the explanation. As the players headed back up court, Hunter began jawing with Thomas, who had sprinted the length of the floor in a desperate attempt to slap the ball away and rectify his mistake. After a warning, Hunter didn't back off. It would prove to be the ultimate momentum killer. Bucknor made both free throws, and that was followed by a Gaston Moliva power move and layup, and suddenly, the game was tied again at 50-50.

"I'd have loved to have been ahead four and playing defense instead of giving up a four-point play," Taylor said in his postgame press conference. "It was a pity to give it back."

The game would seesaw to the end from there. A Steenberge dunk gave Richmond a 58-56 lead, and at :27.9 Taylor called time to again play for one shot. Hunter missed badly and Richmond grabbed the rebound. The final was 61-58.

Brandon Johnson, who played with a defensive intensity that got ODU back into the game in the early stages of the second half, was not in the handshake line. He smacked over a chair on his solo journey to the visitor's locker room. His actions galvanized a clearly frustrated team.

Particularly notable was that the game was played in front of Craig Littlepaige, the athletic director at the University of Virginia. In his spare time, though, Littlepaige is also the chairman of the NCAA Tournament selection committee.

Taylor was also frustrated and still in his own personal hell, though not visibly. In the postgame press conference, there were only two themes: the 17-0 start and the overtime technical. He addressed the technical foul, at no point disputing it. "Under the circumstances, I would hope a senior would have the moxie to know that should be avoided," Taylor said. "I don't like it. It saddens me."

Taylor then gave his frank assessment. "I wish someone would take that AND1 and send it to the North Pole. But sometimes it creeps into college basketball. We have to deal with it when we're trying to help turn these boys into men." His clear reference was to the trash-talking street game that, in Taylor's mind and others', is not a part of college basketball but popularized by the shoe and clothing manufacturer.

"I know I was talking to him," Hunter said. "But he was the one touching me. I really don't feel I did anything wrong. I wouldn't call it trash talking, but yeah, I was talking."

Regardless, ODU had laid an egg, and it would only get worse. Up next was the Alabama-Birmingham Blazers, and UAB blitzed the Monarchs from the opening tap and took a 14-0 lead before four minutes had passed. The Blazers were up 48-22 at the half and finished the game with an 85-57 victory.

The team that was the beacon for the CAA, the preseason ranked team, the team that could not only get an at-large bid but also had a legitimate shot at the Sweet 16, had lost three of four, stood at 7-4, and had been blown out in three of those losses. The best team in the CAA was looking like nothing more than a middle-of-the-pack squad playing for seeding in the March postseason tournament.

Still, the opportunity existed to knock off an ACC foe in Virginia Tech and provide one final signal. One salvo to the quality of play in the CAA.

The Hokies had come within a Sean Dockery half-court prayer at the buzzer of beating Duke in Cameron Indoor Stadium, and they were 9-3 on the season. Two of the three Virginia Tech losses occurred with 0:00 showing on the clock. The horn sounded as Dockery's heave was on its way to the basket, and perhaps more shocking was Virginia Tech freshman A.D. Vassallo tipping a shot into his own basket as time expired, causing the Hokies to lose to Bowling Green, 73-72. Sure enough, Virginia Tech would enter the Ted Constant Center two miracles gone badly from 11-1.

The Virginia Tech game presented an opportunity for Old Dominion, as the Monarchs were afforded the rare opportunity of playing an ACC team on its home floor. That game was far from Taylor's mind in early December, however, as he battled the worst of his personal physical pain. Still, two days after lying on a surgeon's table, he would be on the sideline.

———

Life wasn't so tumultuous for Tom Pecora and Hofstra. His intercession slate, coming off of the road debacle at VCU, consisted of four evenly spaced, beatable opponents. The lineup would allow Pecora to get his team moving in the right direction and playing with confidence. Pecora had no way of knowing that his middle December schedule would come back to haunt him.

Of most concern was Loren Stokes. The returning first-team all-CAA player had struggled through Hofstra's first six games, fighting an aching back as well as recuperating from a broken nose. Stokes was not the fearless slasher that made him the conference's leading scorer and perhaps the most dangerous player last season.

Pecora was also desperate to get his bench some quality minutes on the court. For sure, the group played eight solid minutes in the VCU game, but it was mop-up duty. The freshmen needed to get their ears wet and the starters needed a break.

Zygis Sestokas stepped up during those four walkover games for Hofstra. He scored ten points in only fourteen minutes of action against Stony Brook, and played twenty-seven minutes in a 74-59 win over Dartmouth. The back-to-back performances also earned Sestokas the CAA Rookie of the Week.

A native of Vilnius, Lithuania, Sestokas played his senior season of high school at Statesville Christian in Statesville, North Carolina, where he averaged fifteen points and seven rebounds and shot 55 percent from three-point territory. He set a high school record with seventy-six points in a game. "If one Lithuanian could play here and be comfortable," Sestokas said in reference to the senior Kieza, "I figured it could be the same with me."

There were three Lithuanian players on the Hofstra 2005-2006 roster (Sestokas, Kieza, and reserve forward Arminas Urbutis) and a fourth on the way in recruit and a good friend of Sestokas, Mantas Leonavicius. "We get one more," joked Pecora, "and we're going to start singing the national anthem."

"When players come for an official visit and someone here speaks their language, right away there is a comfort level and that's huge," said Pecora's top assistant, Tom Parotta. "And I think their families back home feel more comfortable as well."

Sestokas was averaging eleven minutes per game and fast becoming Pecora's top reserve.

After the two patsy victories, Hofstra seemingly faced a bit more of a challenge from St. Francis. Though just 3-5, the Brooklyn neighbors had Hofstra on its home floor, Peter Aquilone Court. The Terriers had also beaten Fordham and played St. John's tough before tiring late and losing.

Pecora knew this game had the potential to provide a disastrous upset; however, Hofstra didn't let that happen and controlled play from the outset. A 42-31 lead quickly swelled to 55-33 and the rout was on. Junior guard Carlos Rivera finished with eleven points and ten assists but, most importantly, center Adrian Uter scored twenty-one to lead the Pride.

Uter had normally been Hofstra's rebounding machine since arriving from Broward Community College. In fact, the former Queens high school standout led the entire junior college ranks in rebounding at Broward his final year there. Though the Pride featured its three potent guards in the previous season, opponents knew that by attacking inside they could see some success. What's more, the lone inside presence, Wendell Gibson, would miss a significant portion of the early season with an injury.

Uter would need to step in and fill a role he was unaccustomed to playing, especially considering he was fourteen years old before he ever even played basketball. "I was excited about the chance to play," said Uter. "I just wanted to do anything I could to help the team.

"It was a big adjustment getting used to playing at this level," he said. "In junior college, I could get a lot of rebounds without really working hard. I had to learn that you need to work hard to get position before the ball even comes off the rim if you want to get the rebound." The energy he brought to the floor was never more apparent than in a late season victory over Towson in which Uter had nine blocked shots in only fifteen minutes' playing time.

This season, however, Pecora would need more than defensive presence from Uter. With Gibson graduating, Uter would need to score more than his six points per game average from the previous year. The big St. Francis game brought Uter's scoring average to ten per game, but more importantly showed he can score if needed.

"I'm really happy with the way everything worked out for me," said Uter. "I love this team and I'm willing to do anything I can to help us win. Anything the coaches want me to do, I'll do." Hofstra was now 7-2, buffeted by what some would call a very soft schedule. None of their games were decided by fewer than thirteen points. Still, as Hofstra prepared for the short drive to Philadelphia and the game with 7-1 LaSalle, Pecora felt better about the progress of his team. Not good, but better.

"They don't have a killer instinct. We're not very good right now, just okay. We have some great guys on this team, really nice guys," Pecora said. "That's great, but they need to learn to put a team away."

———

Taylor's message to his team was clear: Get tough, and play like you know how to play. Stop worrying about everything else. Losers of three of its past four games, Old Dominion had gone from at-large worthy and feared to just another CAA team in the span of two weeks. Two of the losses were horrific and nobody feared the lions, which is precisely why, when Seth Greenberg brought his Virginia Tech team into the Constant Center, it was critical for ODU to win. Critical now not because of NCAA Tournament hopes. Critical because his team needed a win in the worst way.

For Taylor, get tough was also his personal mantra. After surgery, he had been put on what is called "gorilla antibiotics." They took their own toll, and Taylor still carried pain. He would endure along with his team.

Predictably, the game was a sellout, and the intensity was present before the game even tipped off. As is customary, the visiting team takes the court first for final warmups prior to the announcement of the starting lineups and the beginning of the game. Virginia Tech warmed up in their layup line when ODU ran out. As Isaiah Hunter jogged past Tech's Deron Washington, he woofed something at Washington, who played it off, laughing and scrunching up his face in the "what was that?" mode.

If there was anything clear about this game, it was that defense would rule the day. Both teams played a grinding defense, not so much suffocating as it was physically demanding. It was this kind of defense that had forced ODU into 42 percent shooting for the season to this point, a brutally ugly 222nd in the rankings.

Typically, the game was ragged from the get-go. ODU held a 10-9 lead on an Arnaud Dahi jumper with 9:08 to play in the opening half. Though both teams had made four field goals, Virginia Tech had only attempted ten, while ODU had shot twice that number. The 20 per-cent marksmanship was bad for even ODU standards.

What was more troubling for Taylor was that Hunter seemed whol-ly disinterested on the court. He was burned repeatedly on the defen-sive end and had missed all four of his field goals and both free throw attempts.

Then it happened, again. Hunter was called for a travel, and in his continuation strolled into the interior of the Tech defense where he brushed by, of all people, Deron Washington. Both exchanged words, and Hunter went the extra step, swiping at Washington and drawing a technical. A 15-15 game became a 19-15 Virginia Tech lead and a collective groan emerged from the stands.

Taylor got Brandon Johnson into the game quickly, and changed defenses on Tech, a move he knew would help. It was his belief that while necessarily designed to confuse the opponent, switching defenses would at the very least break any rhythm.

It would be yet another brilliant move. ODU would cause three turnovers in the final 2:30 of the half in that zone, and when Johnson banked in a three at the buzzer, ODU led 25-19. But both teams were hurting. It had been a physical, chippy first half. An elbow here, a shove there; it had all added up to boiling tempers and rugged play.

The game wasn't any easier for Taylor. Still fighting the rigors of surgery, he also battled the poison oozing from his wounds. He would change pants (and bandages) at the half and follow his team back out to the floor.

Taylor would summon the strength and courage he asked of his play-ers. He would also compartmentalize his pain and focus on his goals. The third trait Taylor espoused and followed personally was to not let your opponent see your pain. He would outwardly coach his team like a preseason scrimmage or a CAA final. Nothing, outwardly, changed.

Inside, tumult and bone-gripping pain.

Things would not change in the second half. Both teams would brutalize each other as the crew of Larry Rose, Duke Edsall, and Brian Dorsey, perhaps the best in the country, tried to maintain control. It worked for most of the game. Old Dominion had taken control of the game, chipping away at the tiring Hokies. Alex Loughton converted an easy layup, one of only a handful of easy baskets for either team all night, to give ODU its biggest lead at 44-31.

Still leading 50-42 with 1:46 to play, ODU took off down court on a fast break. The ball ended up in Arnaud Dahi's hands and he rose for a dunk that would undoubtedly send the Constant Center into orbit.

However, Hokies center Coleman Collins, who had struggled all evening and was frustrated, went up with Dahi and fouled him, hard. Collins had made a play on the ball with one hand, but clearly pushed Dahi in midair with the other.

Dahi, who had earlier both injured his knee and suffered a cramp in his calf, had had enough. He scampered to his feet, fists flying, and was going after Collins, who had his back turned and was walking toward the foul line, unaware of what was occurring behind him.

"I let my emotions get the best of me and I should be above that," Dahi said in the postgame press conference. Luckily co-captains Drew Williamson and Alex Loughton were right there on the spot to bear hug Dahi and let the scene cool down.

Virginia Tech Head Coach Seth Greenberg was not about to let that happen, though. When Dahi arose in a rage, he sprinted from his spot on the other side of the gym to get into the middle of the fracas. He was incensed that Dahi did not receive a technical foul for raising his fists after a play. Greenberg and Duke Edsall were in a near pushing match as the referee was able to get the coach to back down.

For his part, Greenberg was assessed a technical foul. Dahi made all four free throws, mocking the Tech fans that sat behind the west basket with a "ssshhh" motion with his index finger over his pursed lips.

Surely that wild scene would end the game, but Tech wouldn't go down without one last surge. The game 54-44 became 54-52 after Tech's press caused consecutive turnovers, and Jamar Gordon's three with 21.1 seconds had the fans squirming.

"In my four years here, I've never seen a team make it so difficult to pass the ball inbounds," said Loughton.

After two Hunter free throws restored the lead to four, 56-52, Dowdell swished yet another three to cut the lead to one. Out of time-outs and needing to set up its effective pressure, Greenberg had instructed his players to tap the ball as it went through the basket to give the Hokies a chance to set up. Enter, again, chaos.

As the ball swished, Gordon gave it more than a tap. He grabbed the ball and "spun it" (his words). Unfortunately for Tech, the ball spun right down the tunnel leading to the ODU facilities and locker rooms. Edsall had no choice but to blow his whistle and call Gordon for a delay of game technical.

While this was going on, Greenberg had again sprinted out of the coaches' box and was giving the timer a sound tongue lashing. After the ball had gone through the hoop, the timer had allowed the clock to continue to run for almost two full seconds. Greenberg had noticed and gone ballistic. Larry Rose was on the scene, grabbing the television monitor to reset the proper game time (six seconds instead of 4.1).

After three more minutes of delay, while the officials got the clock and the sequence of events together, Hunter stepped to the line and made two more free throws to make the score 58-55. On the ensuing play, ODU threw a long pass to Hunter who, inexplicably, tried to make a contested layup and missed instead of dribbling out the clock.

Tech grabbed the rebound and threw the ball to Gordon, whose thirty footer at the buzzer fell short. ODU fans could exhale, but not after some tense moments.

"We were inept offensively," said Greenberg. "It was an embarrassment." Asked repeatedly to comment on the technical fouls and endgame incidents, Greenberg would only flatly say, "Ask the officials."

If Virginia Tech were going to opt to buy itself out of the remaining two years of its contract with Old Dominion, the decision, no matter when it was announced, was made right there.

Tom Pecora, however, was just beginning a series with LaSalle. He was good friends with the Explorers ex-coach, Billy Hahn, who had been fired when four of his players had been accused of rape. Charges would be dropped in two of the cases and the players would be found innocent in the other two, but the damage was done. Someone had to lose their job and Hahn was the easy target. (Interestingly, one of the players, Gary Neal, transferred to play in the CAA at Towson.)

LaSalle was also experiencing its best start since the days of Lionel Simmons. They came into the Hofstra game at 8-1, having lost only to top five Villanova and having beaten James Madison and Drexel.

It looked as though LaSalle would add Hofstra to its list of conquered CAA foes when the Explorers rode all-America candidate Steve Smith to 69-61 with a little less than four minutes to play.

However, Aurimas Kieza, who had drawn Smith as a defensive assignment and thus scored only two points in the first thirty-seven minutes, decided enough was enough. After Antoine Agudio hit a free throw, Kieza went on a personal 7-0 run, tying the score at 69-69 with a layup and 1:45 to play.

After Smith hit a foul shot to give La Salle a one-point lead again, Agudio ran through a screen, curled, took a Greg Johnson pass, and drilled a ten-foot jumper to give Hofstra back the lead at 71-70 with just over a minute to play. It would be the final points of the game and Hofstra again proved victorious with a huge, late game run. This time, it was 10-1 over the final four minutes.

With the win, the Pride improved to 8-2 on the year, while picking up its fourth win in a row and the seventh in its last eight games.

But all was not well. With just over a minute to play, Loren Stokes went down in a nasty spill, clutching his knee. The injury was clearly more serious than the standard bumps and bruises. Stokes was hustled to the locker room as Greg Johnson finished the game for Hofstra, providing the key pass leading to Agudio's game-winning jumper.

The MRI on Stokes's knee would show no ligament damage: a torn ACL is always the first thing that goes through the minds of players and coaches in this situation. Still, Stokes, who had fought back from a broken nose and sore back, would miss a game or two, or possibly more. It would depend on the severity of the injury and how well Stokes could respond.

George Mason capitalized on its opportunity. The Patriots followed the heartbreaker at ODU by drilling Radford, Hampton, and Holy Cross. The Holy Cross game finished 71-38 and the Crusaders coach, Ralph Willard, could not remember being beaten that badly in his long career.

The Patriots lost another tight game at the buzzer, 63-61, at Mississippi State, after leading by seven at the half.

For Jim Larranaga the result wasn't as important as the journey: His team was getting better and better. They were steamrolling weaker opponents and playing tougher teams close.

"As a coach," said Larranaga, "you can't get hung up on the end result. You have to look at the process. Are we rebounding, are we defending? Are we making our free throws? You're always disappointed when you lose, but you have to evaluate: Did we do the things we need to do to win? Overall I'm pretty pleased with where we are. We've adopted a philosophy: What we have to do is be great at what we do."

If you were to ask Tom Yeager, he'd likely say that the CAA Tournament is the most important event for the conference each year. A close second would likely be the regular season. Without football until 2007, basketball is by far and away the conference's main asset, and thus its most protected and valued property. And this reality is why an at-large bid, and the money and exposure that goes hand in hand with it, is vital to the conference.

It's also why the last three weeks of December 2005 would not soon be forgotten. If the conference were to end up without an at-large bid come March, these three weeks were the likely culprit.

First, ODU's failures at Richmond and UAB would likely be too much for the DePaul and Virginia Tech victories to offset. UNCW had its chance to make a mark, but when Wisconsin's Kammron Taylor drained a prayer that beat the Seahawks, the defeat became nothing more than a status quo close loss. And after two ho-hum wins over Coastal Carolina and UNC Asheville, UNCW dropped another of those games the CAA cannot lose, inexplicably falling in Trask to the College of Charleston 81-77. That was followed by an even more inexplicable 82-69 loss to East Carolina.

Even the middle-of-the-pack teams were losing games the conference needed desperately. During this time, Northeastern was drilled by Providence and then beaten at Wright State.

At the bottom, William & Mary lost to Maryland-Baltimore County, Towson lost to VMI, and James Madison lost to Youngstown State.

In all, the conference went 16-16 between December 10 and December 27. Only a handful of those losses could be considered "excusable" by the NCAA committee.

The conference RPI, while riding high as clear as seventh in most every rating, had fallen to twelfth nearly overnight and settled at fifteenth just after Christmas. The CAA, though not dead, was no longer a darling.

In stark contrast, the Missouri Valley Conference was riding high. Creighton bounced George Mason pretty handily by twenty in the only head-to-head matchup with the CAA.

By eschewing the buy game (and corresponding loss) and winning the games it should, the MVC found itself hanging in at fourth in the RPI rankings in late December. It was 67-22 in its nonconference games, and six of its teams boasted an RPI of better than eighty. All were better than 200.

And the usual mid-major slink toward the bottom of the RPI standings once conference play got fully underway likely wasn't going to occur as well. "As a result of the conference's exceptional depth, MVC clubs will not, during league play, race to the bottom," said Fox Sports writer Yoni Cohen. "Nor will the league's standard-bearers this season, Northern Iowa, Indiana State, Creighton, and Missouri State, be found guilty of mediocrity by association. Rather, each conference game will, by the RPI—and the selection committee—be considered a quality challenge. Wins will count more and losses less."

The resume the MVC put together was slightly different than that of the CAA. Indiana State earlier had beaten Indiana, Northern Iowa upset Iowa, and Creighton beat Nebraska. All could be traced to similar wins by the CAA, as could Bradley beating DePaul (ODU did so, very convincingly), Southern Illinois defeating Wyoming (as did UNCW), and Missouri State nearly winning at Arkansas (see George Mason versus Wake Forest, Northeastern versus California, or any CAA game against Wisconsin).

But the bad losses are the difference. The MVC avoided them for the most part, and the CAA had them. In addition, though Georgia State was able to get Kentucky and Alabama on the schedule, those buy games and the ensuing losses actually hurt the conference. The Wright States and Riders usually don't appear on MVC schedules, much less as losses.

That's the differentiator between the CAA and the MVC and why the Valley was receiving all the press. They took advantage of chances and didn't suffer the humiliating loss that sticks with the media. The Valley would be riding high in the top six of the RPI; the CAA, consequently, fell into its customary double-digit place.

Part of the issue is philosophy. You need the marquee wins but also need to avoid costly losses. The MVC has moved toward its top teams scheduling the heavyweights, with the bottom teams scheduling wins. Call it the trickle down economics of buy games.

"Just win games, really," Yeager said. "I don't care who you beat, just win games."

Ron Bertovich would still not equivocate, as you would expect from a high ranking conference official: "I am a firm believer that the NCAA Men's Basketball Committee is as thorough in its selection process as one could ever hope and expect," he said in late December. "Whether I think that 'this can be the year for an at-large berth' is irrelevant at this point."

Still, its importance was duly noted. Yeager would say in a December 2005 interview in the *Washington Post*:

Whether people like it or not, the measure of strength in the public eye is how many teams do you send to the NCAA tournament. Our mind-set all the time is we've got to think of ways to get two teams in. That's where the whole focus is; that's the number one goal.

And he was right.

The matchups to start the official conference season became boldly ironic and important: Taylor's Monarchs would face an overachieving UNCW team at home; Capel's Rams would travel to face George Mason, the team playing the best basketball in the conference (having opened its conference slate with a road win at Georgia State); and Hofstra, minus Loren Stokes, would host James Madison, a team it should beat soundly but also a team with talented players.

But too many factors were not in their control and the members couldn't worry about at-large berths, Andy Katz mentions, or wins by your opponents' opponents. There was not an expert to be found who would say the CAA had a shot at an at-large berth. Its teams had to play the conference season, just like all the others. Only in the CAA in 2005-2006, it would be different than the regular season in the Big 10, Big 12, or ACC. In the CAA, it would matter.

Every game would matter. Minor ankle sprains meant more than a lost game or two. For Old Dominion, Hofstra, and George Mason—as well as every other CAA school—every game would be a war. Only one team would be left standing in March with an invitation to the Big Dance, and that is what made basketball in the CAA, and every other mid-major conference, so compelling.

Tom Pecora knew. After the big LaSalle win, he had already begun lobbying.

"At the end of the year, if you are not lucky enough to be in the NCAA and trying to get into the NIT, these are the kind of games they look at," Pecora said. "This was a big win."

Anything could happen, and in the CAA, it likely would.

2005-2006 STANDINGS

(Through Games of January 2, 2006)

	Conference			Overall					
	W	L	Pct.	W	L	Pct.	H	A	N
UNC Wilmington	2	0	1.000	9	4	.692	4-1	3-3	2-0
Drexel	2	0	1.000	8	5	.615	5-0	3-1	0-4
VCU	2	1	.667	8	3	.727	6-0	2-3	0-0
George Mason	2	1	.667	8	4	.667	3-1	3-3	2-0
Northeastern	2	1	.667	6	5	.545	2-2	2-3	2-0
Hofstra	1	1	.500	8	2	.800	4-0	3-2	1-0
Old Dominion	1	1	.500	8	4	.667	5-0	1-3	2-1
Towson	1	1	.500	5	6	.455	3-2	2-3	0-1
Georgia State	1	2	.333	3	7	.300	2-3	1-3	0-1
William & Mary	0	2	.000	5	6	.455	3-2	2-4	0-0
Delaware	0	2	.000	4	7	.364	2-1	0-6	2-0
James Madison	0	2	.000	3	7	.300	2-4	0-3	1-0

CHAPTER SEVEN

ROLLERCOASTER

"Men seldom persevere in a vocation unless they believe or can convince themselves that it is fundamentally more important than any other calling."
–Friedrich Nietzsche

For Tom Pecora, it's about the family. It's even more than his wife Mary Beth and children (daughters Amanda and Brianna and son Sean). With Pecora, everything about him is family. Visit him for one day and you may get to see where he went to college, and where his buddy does this or his uncle did that. You might have lunch with him and his friend from grade school. They are still good friends. If you're lucky, he'll offer you his own shoes and drive you around town.

When he's organizing the Long Island Coaches Versus Cancer charity golf tournament, of which he is the co-chairman and raises more than $30,000 annually, instead of seeking the usual raffle prizes and goodie bag stuffers that have become commonplace in events like these, he seeks out books and cans of tomato sauce. These are donations from his friends, and while it is truly an "everybody wins" situation, it is refreshing to find the not-so-normal fare as a gift. After all, how many hats or pens can one person receive?

Later, you may be asked to head down to the Long Island shore, finding out where he lived when he was just out of college and attending a barbeque with friends and colleagues in the New York basketball scene.

You will always be treated with respect and made to feel like you are one of the family. It is why Tom Pecora knows the names of the facilities people at the Hofstra University Arena and can carry on conversations with them. It's why he knows that one of them will be leaving work early to attend a daughter's play.

This is Tom Pecora's way, and the way his program is run. Everybody associated with his program is his extended family, and every bit of it is sincere.

"We teach the kids about time management, a sense of preparation," Pecora says. "Things you wouldn't expect, like dressing—you don't wear black shoes and a brown belt. Our kids pride themselves on being the best dressed at the banquet. We have a guy come in and talk about gambling and agents at the beginning of the year; and have Dave Sims come in and talk about handling the media. We try to teach them the right things that will help them later in life."

And that's why on the eve on his team's game against James Madison to kick off the grind that is the CAA regular season, there is a passion in Pecora's voice when he talks about his sophomore guard, Antoine Agudio.

"Antoine is coming along; he works every day on his weaknesses," says Pecora. "His mid range game and taking ball to the basket are progressing and its making his game more difficult to stop."

It is an interesting dichotomy for the mercurial Pecora. Whether discussing strategy, coaching tactics, his background, or the weather, Pecora is animated. He can multitask with the best of them. He can start a conversation, politely excuse himself and leave the room, and then walk back into the room and not miss a preposition. He is on it.

When he starts to talk about one of his players, the motion and commotion stop, however. He doesn't measure his words, but he is very sure that you know what he is discussing is important. On this day, it is his blossoming sophomore guard.

The Hofstra media guide lists Agudio at 6 feet, 3 inches, but you could stand next to him and not immediately think "basketball play-er." Agudio carries himself in an unassuming manner, both on and off the court. He's not a vocal player but, although you may not see him, he's always right there—just like an assassin.

Agudio averaged more than fifteen points per game in his fresh-man season and was the unanimous CAA Rookie of the Year. He was also named third-team all-CAA and averaged nearly thirty-five min-utes per game as a freshman. He came to Hofstra after a stellar high school career at Walt Whitman High in Huntington Station, New York. Agudio was named all state his senior season, averaging close to twenty-five points per game, and more than one recruiting service called Hofstra's landing of Agudio "a steal."

Agudio, whose father Alex was a key player on Niagara's 1987 NIT team and still holds the school record for steals in a season (and can be seen at almost every Hofstra game), came to Hofstra with his back-court mates Loren Stokes and Carlos Rivera, but he red shirted his first season with a hand injury. That has not slowed Agudio's develop-ment as someone the big freshman class at Hofstra this season looks up to.

"He's still so unselfish," says Pecora about Agudio. "Antoine's lead-ership role is not a vocal one. Carlos is much more vocal. Remember Antoine is still a sophomore. The sky's the limit for him. He loves to play the game. He can only get better."

It was the play of freshman Mike Davis-Sabb, who was a surprise starter, that stole the show against James Madison. Adrian Uter had injured his ankle in the LaSalle game, and turned it over again while warming up prior to the JMU tip-off.

"We went to Mike and he had no time to think about it," Pecora said. "He knew five minutes before and that's probably a good thing. Early [in the game] he got a couple of easy baskets and got into the rhythm of the game."

Davis-Sabb made two layups before the first media time-out to break his previous career-high of three points, helping the Pride jump out to a quick 10-0 lead. Davis-Sabb continued to work hard through foul trouble and finished the game with sixteen points, making six of seven field goals. Importantly, Davis-Sabb led the team with six rebounds. The 87-66 win was yet another tonic for Pecora: His bench had played extended minutes, and he was able to coast late and rest. Incredibly, Loren Stokes had been injured again. This time, it was his knee; and it looked, at first, to be serious.

It turned out that Stokes had merely sprained his knee. The Hofstra basketball community exhaled as the knee could've buckled and torn the ACL. Early reports showed a sprained MCL and that Stokes would miss a handful of games. Eventually, it was determined to be the sprain, and Stokes played thirty-eight gutsy minutes, scoring ten points and handing out a career-high seven assists.

After slogging past Georgia State, the Pride moved to 10-2 overall and, most importantly, 3-1 in the CAA. They had done their job, winning home games over teams they should beat. In fact, Hofstra had beaten Delaware, James Madison, and Georgia State. The bottom feeders, by the end of this day's play, were a combined 1-12 in conference play. The Pride had miserably failed its only test, at VCU.

Four of his five starters were averaging in double figures, and Rivera, his point guard, checked in at 9.9 points per game. It was clear that any of the five starters could carry the load, but that they would need their bench. Davis-Sabb, Greg Johnson, and Arminas Urbutis would have to step up.

"We've got to get a little bit deeper as we go into the meat of our schedule," Pecora said. "We've got a big couple weeks coming up." With Uter hobbled and Stokes icing his knee every day, they would be big indeed.

———

While Jeff Capel does not consider himself superstitious, he is certainly a creature of habit. For instance, if you were to black out everything around him in the moments before a game, you could never tell if VCU was at home or on the road, or if Capel felt good or bad about his team's chances.

Every single game, without fail, just before and during his team's introductions, Capel can be found in the same spot. You will find him standing on the baseline, halfway between the basket and the corner. His arms are either folded or in his jacket pockets. He is facing the court, his team. He will pace one step to the left, then one step to the right.

It's as if he is doing his own private pregame dance. The look on his face is one of a blank intensity—there's no emotion whatsoever, yet you can tell there are several thoughts spinning through his head because of the focus in his eyes. Capel would do well at a Texas Hold 'Em table.

"I'm mentally replaying how I see the game going," Capel laughs. "It's a way I get focused. And it lets the players have their spotlight. It's their time."

As the Rams methodically filed through their layup lines prior to a big road test at George Mason, Capel made his way over to Jim Larranaga to shake hands and say hello. Because another of Capel's habits is to not leave the locker room until the 2:00 minute mark prior to the game, Larranaga was waiting at half court.

On this night, Capel battled a cold, which wasn't helped by the smattering of fans that slowly filled the Patriot Center. Games at George Mason's home floor draw around three thousand fans, middle of the pack for the CAA; but the Patriot Center holds ten thousand, so there is a vacant and cold feel to the building. The fact that the students were still on winter break didn't help.

It wouldn't matter. From the very first possession of the game, when Mason's Lamar Butler hit an improbable fade away jumper as the shot clock expired, the Patriots controlled the game. Capel implored the Rams to "play some defense!!!" at the under 16:00 media time-out with his team trailing 10-4. Capel was growing increasingly frustrated at his team's lack of emotion and, thus, production.

Capel usually spends a lot of time on the sideline talking to his players on the bench. He points out things which are occurring on the playing floor and coaches all twelve players on the roster.

As the first half wore on, Capel became increasingly less interested in his bench. He had seen this effort before, when his Rams were spanked at Wilmington. He could see how this game was going and it wasn't going to be pretty. The airspace around Capel became his primary target. He wasn't muttering, but Capel began forceful rants to nobody in particular, each one growing in intensity as the Rams sputtered. It didn't take long before an easy target became Capel's mark.

VCU center Eric Davis was called for a travel by referee Jamie Luckie on a move Capel believed to be legal. "A jump stop, Jamie," Capel bellowed, pleading his case. As if the Fates held their hands on the Patriot Center, on the very next trip down the floor, George Mason's Will Thomas made a very similar, if not identical, move and was not called for a travel. Rather, Thomas scored a bucket and was fouled by Davis. Incensed, Capel demanded to know the difference.

"Be reasonable with me," Luckie barked at Capel. The coach backed down, sensing the line that he approached. Five minutes later, with Mason in the midst of an 8-0 run, another call went against the Rams and Capel threw his arms up, screaming to nobody in particular, "Oh my gosh!"

Yes, Capel said "gosh."

The Mason lead was 36-25 at the break. VCU was being pounded on the boards (18-9) and had no answer for Will Thomas. Mason was shooting an astounding 56 percent from the field, amazing in that teams rarely shoot more than 40 percent against the Rams.

When Thomas soared over Nick George for a stick back that gave Mason a fourteen-point lead early in the second half, Capel had seen enough. Boiling, he called a thirty-second time-out and removed his first-team all-CAA player from the game. Capel's star was done for the evening, finishing with four points.

Later, with VCU mounting a comeback, George Mason guard Tony Skinn drove into the lane, out of control. He appeared to simply fall down, and the ball rolled to VCU's Jesse Pellot Rosa. When Jamie Luckie's whistle blew, the crowd was prepared for the turnover call and VCU to get the ball.

Luckie called a tripping foul on VCU's Jamal Shuler, and that was enough for Capel. He whirled around, punching the air twice, ending up not just on the court but almost at the elbow of the foul line. Luckie whistled Capel for the inevitable technical foul, and a second one was added on Capel's assistant Gerald White.

Skinn made all four free throws, and the lead was fourteen. The final was 73-60.

The most telling statistic: Of George Mason's twenty-six field goals, seventeen were layups or dunks. It's a wonder Mason did not shoot higher than 59 percent on the evening.

Most importantly, however, was the fact that George Mason had made a strong, early statement. Good basketball teams win games like this convincingly. Good basketball teams serve notice.

By outplaying Old Dominion before losing on the road on a heart-breaking buzzer-beater and absolutely mauling VCU three days after traveling home from Boston (where Larranaga's team had beaten Northeastern), that's exactly what George Mason had done.

———

If there was a team in the CAA that needed to prove something, it was Old Dominion. The Monarchs had not yet lived up to preseason media hype, but not in the eyes of Taylor.

"I keep having to address two games and a couple of minutes of another game when 80 percent of our body of work has been pretty doggone good," he said. "In a dream world, you say 'Hey, let's do something that's really off the charts.' Well, was 'off the charts' available to a team that played four of its first eleven games at home? For a team that plays seven of its first eleven on the road, you can't expect it to run the table."

Although Taylor's perspective was admirable, he privately had to be concerned about the manner in which ODU had achieved its wins. The Monarchs were shooting 41 percent from the floor, had only six more assists than turnovers, and had not scored more than fifty-eight points in five of its previous six games.

Star forward Alex Loughton, a senior, after the emotional win over Virginia Tech, chuckled. "It could be a lot worse," he said, "and we'd most certainly like it to be a lot better."

They had been a bit banged up, with Loughton, Arnaud Dahi, Brandon Johnson, and Valdus Vasylius all nursing minor injuries. Even if they weren't publicly admitting it, the Monarchs wanted to prove something to themselves. First up would be a home test against conference leader UNCW.

The game began as did many of ODU's contests. The Monarchs fell behind early; this time it was 15-8 UNCW. ODU continued its cold shooting, finishing the half trailing 25-22 and shooting just 27 percent. The Monarchs had missed all twelve three-point attempts.

UNCW was on the verge of a breakout win, and ODU a crushing defeat, when a Beckham Wyrick layup with 17:07 remaining gave the Seahawks a crowd-quieting 33-24 lead. Then Valdas Vasylius began one of those runs that coaches—and players—dream about. A Vasylius three-pointer which began a 21-3 spurt had ended the game, essentially. UNCW would claw to as close as four, but the Monarchs were too strong on their home floor. ODU doubled its first-half shooting percentage, and made seven three pointers in the second half on the same number of attempts as they misfired in the first half (twelve). Hunter scored fourteen of his sixteen points during the second half, and Brian Henderson scored a career high seventeen points.

"They key was [that] Isaiah [Hunter] was a pass-first player in this game," Taylor beamed afterward. "When he adopts the philosophy that he's going to play this game the right way instead of trying to do nothing but score, there's a noticeable difference."

Momentum would build for the Monarchs, as a road test and a trap game against Towson loomed. In what could have signaled a turnaround, ODU sprinted out of the blocks.

The Monarchs hit thirteen of their first seventeen shots and raced to a 31-11 lead in the first eight minutes. And that was that. The 85-71 sleeper was never in doubt, and it was not as close as the final score indicated.

There was no rest for Taylor and his team. The Monarchs, thanks to the new CAA scheduling policy of Thursday/Saturday games, would bus home late Thursday night from Towson, arriving in the wee hours of Friday morning. There were Friday classes, practice, and a noon tip-off Saturday with Northeastern.

Citing an opportunity to reduce the number of travel days and thus missed classes during the season, the CAA office had chosen to move to a Thursday/Saturday format for its conference games. Traditionally, the games had been spread out an even Wednesday/Saturday.

The rigor of the change didn't go unnoticed by coaches, who to a man didn't like it. Hated it, in fact. Their players had less time to recover; scouting opponents became a jumbled mess. The argument of fewer missed classes was a negligible statistic because most teams traveled on Wednesdays anyway.

First there would be the beatings, and then the travel. The first trip through the Thursday/Saturday scheduling was not greeted warmly by the coaches. Pecora said that he was "telling anyone that will listen that it's a bad idea." Capel agreed, saying flatly, "I don't like it. I don't like it at all." Brad Brownell was more candid. "I'm only outspoken on one issue. I'm very disappointed with the Thursday/Saturday schedule. When you travel like we have to travel, I don't know if we're doing the things that are the best for the programs. We talk about doing the things [we need to do] for a second bid...most of the television games are on Saturday afternoon after a Thursday game. I worry about the product. I don't think this can continue. I know it was done for academics but it doesn't help us there either. I don't think over two months it is helpful."

VCU's Capel backed down to a more practical approach. "It is what it is and we just have to get used to it," Capel said. "Players are players...they play two to three games a day in AAU." Capel did, however, concede, "But I'd like more time for my guys to recover."

It would be a quick turnaround for the Monarchs, made more difficult by the fact that Northeastern was largely an unknown quantity to the CAA. In its first season in the CAA, the Huskies began 3-1 with

victories over Towson, James Madison, and Georgia State. It had lost
only at home against George Mason.

Particularly of concern to Taylor was that Ron Everhart's team featured two of the best players not only in the conference, but also in
the country. Jose Juan Barea, Northeastern's barrel-chested point
guard from Puerto Rico, was leading the nation in assists with nine
per game, more than two assists greater than second place.
Additionally, Barea was in the top ten in scoring, averaging nearly
twenty-five points per contest. In short, the ball was in Barea's hands
much of the time, and it was in good hands. CBS Sportsline had rated
Barea the nineteenth best guard and fortieth best player overall in its
preseason rankings.

Everhart also featured Shawn James, a wiry 6-foot, 9-inch shot
blocker. James led the nation in that category, with more than six
rejections per game. His very presence inside changed the way teams
attacked the Huskies.

For his part, Everhart said his two biggest adjustments to life in the
CAA was first the Thursday/Saturday travel situation. "It's been a huge
adjustment," he said. "[When it was Wednesday/Saturday, like in the
America East] we could get guys to class on Thursday before turning
around and having to travel again on Friday. Plus, the AE was a bus
league. [The addition of] flying creates a whole different world. For us,
it would be better to have that extra day to travel."

Prior to his job in Boston, Everhart spent seven seasons as the head
coach at McNeese State in Lake Charles, Louisiana. You might say he is
well connected. While at McNeese he coached "Pistol" Pete Maravich's
oldest son, Jaeson Maravich, who was a walk-on for the Cowboys.
During his playing days at Virginia Tech, Everhart roomed with long-
time NBA standout Dell Curry during the glory days of Virginia Tech basketball, when Cassell Coliseum was always full to the rafters and always
loud. He is also a cousin of Mary Lou Retton, the first American woman
ever to win the gold medal in the all-around in women's gymnastics.

Everhart, who had won seventy games at Northeastern (losing
sixty-three) and improved the Huskies' record each of his four years as

head coach, winning AE coach of the year in 2004-2005, had also had his eyes opened to the depth of the CAA. It was different than the America East.

"There are four teams in the CAA that can play with anybody, anywhere, on any night," he said. "Every team that is productive can reach into their bench and not have a drop off. Teams can get guys off their bench and get better. You can play well on any given night and not have an opportunity to win."

This could easily be the case as the Huskies traveled to Norfolk.

Ever the philosopher, Taylor remained collegial about the constricted time frame. "The reward for becoming a better a program is you get to play Saturday afternoon games," he told his team, trying passively to impart the message that they were both good and not tired.

He may have been wondering if the message had sunk in, and if his team had indeed turned a corner against Towson on one of the first possessions of the game. Shawn James blocked three Monarch shots, and within two minutes had also hit a three pointer of his own. By the time the teams reached the under 16:00 media time-out, Northeastern led the game 13-4. It was a typical ODU slow start, fueled by Barea carving up the Monarchs' man-to-man defense.

The Huskies' lead ballooned to 20-6 on a Barea three and Taylor took a time-out. Northeastern was making ODU look slow, not just in terms of foot speed but also in terms of the ability to make moves with the basketball. James had five blocked shots and the game was barely eight minutes old.

ODU would need answers, and they found them in a zone defense and in James getting into foul trouble. A Brian Henderson three at 15:30 cut the lead to 49-45. Arnaud Dahi hit another three a minute later to make it 51-50, but Northeastern's Bennet Davis immediately responded, and both coaches realized this one was going to the wire.

Shawn James, who earlier in the half was mistakenly whistled for his third foul when in actuality it was Bennett Davis, picked up his fourth foul trying to block a Vasylius shot. The basket and free throw from Vasylius at the 13:42 mark made it 56-53.

With James on the bench, ODU, especially Isaiah Hunter, began attacking the basket at will. Hunter's layup gave ODU its first lead of the game at 64-63 with just over ten minutes to play. Another layup gave the Monarchs a 71-66 cushion, and the teams ended the game 85-79.

"I thought we gave great effort. I thought we had them," said Everhart, no doubt remembering his "play well and lose" quote. "They changed defenses and made it a difficult second half for us. They made great plays to get back into the game." Just like any other coach who knows his kids played hard and well, but came up short, he took it on the chin. "I have to do a better job with our depth, our front line depth especially."

ODU's Hunter scored nineteen of his twenty-one points in the second half. Henderson added sixteen, most of which when his team desperately needed him. This was somewhat surprising to ODU fans, who had grown accustomed to Henderson's defensive abilities and intangibles.

"I don't want to act like I'm an Amazing Kreskin," said Taylor, "but I'm not surprised by Henderson. We red shirted him and invested in him. As a freshman he was a player for us and he made us a better team. He's stepped in and become a steady player. He's been man enough to knock some [important] shots when he gets the chance."

Henderson was but one of the Monarchs stepping up when their time came. In its eleven wins, ODU had five different players each step up and be its leading scorer.

It took all of one week in January for the much-hyped depth of the CAA to take effect and prove itself true. Nobody was undefeated. Only the Atlantic Sun, Ohio Valley (who had played seven conference games), and Pac 10 conferences could boast that balance. After five games, seven teams were separated by one game, either 4-1 or 3-2. Towson drew the line at .500 (2-2), and the bottom four teams (Georgia State, William & Mary, Delaware, and James Madison) had combined for one win.

At the top, where the teams were barely discernable, the battle would rage for an all-important top four seed. Since the conference added Georgia State and Northeastern, that meant that teams five through twelve would play what had become less of a play-in round and more like a first round in the CAA Tournament. The extra game meant that in order to win the CAA Tournament, three wins in three days wouldn't be good enough. A team would need four wins in four days, which is daunting, to say the least.

Only one clear trend was emerging. On Saturday, VCU had beaten Drexel in Richmond and ODU had taken down Northeastern in Norfolk. This followed ODU squeaking by GMU (in Norfolk), GMU beating VCU (in Fairfax), Drexel beating ODU (in Philadelphia), and VCU beating Hofstra (in Richmond). The trend was simple: Hold serve at home.

From the national perspective, things were looking up. While the conference had been written off only ten days prior, Old Dominion had seen its RPI shoot back into the mid-twenties. Five other CAA schools were in the top hundred.

It was also helpful that of the CAA nonconference wins, many were well placed for more important reasons than an on-court victory. UNCW defeated Butler, which plays in the Horizon, whose commissioner is Jon LeCrone. Drexel beat Princeton, whose athletics director is Gary Walters, and played well before losing to UCLA, whose athletic director is Daniel Guererro. LeCrone, Walters, and Guererro all sat on the NCAA Tournament selection committee.

When asked in early January, Taylor called the conference race "wild and wooly." By the middle of the month, wild had left the barn. Wooly wasn't far behind.

2005-2006 STANDINGS
(Through Games of January 11, 2006)

	Conference			Overall					
	W	L	Pct.	W	L	Pct.	H	A	N
Old Dominion	4	1	.800	11	4	.733	7-0	2-3	2-1
George Mason	4	1	.800	10	4	.714	5-1	3-3	2-0
UNC Wilmington	4	1	.800	11	5	.688	5-1	4-4	2-0
Hofstra	3	1	.750	10	2	.833	6-0	3-2	1-0
Drexel	3	1	.750	9	6	.600	5-0	4-2	0-4
VCU	3	2	.600	9	4	.692	7-0	2-4	0-0
Northeastern	3	2	.600	7	6	.538	3-2	2-4	2-0
Towson	2	2	.500	6	7	.462	3-3	3-3	0-1
Georgia State	1	4	.200	3	9	.250	2-3	1-5	0-1
William & Mary	0	4	.000	5	8	.385	3-3	2-5	0-0
Delaware	0	4	.000	4	9	.308	2-2	0-7	2-0
James Madison	0	4	.000	3	9	.250	2-5	0-4	1-0

CHAPTER EIGHT:

CIRCUMSTANCE

"The only use of an obstacle is to be overcome. All that an obstacle does with brave men is, not to frighten them, but to challenge them."
–Woodrow Wilson

When Dr. Wayne Edwards went searching for a head basketball coach, he knew the one thing he needed was someone who knew how to win. More importantly, Edwards wanted someone who would win in a way that would reflect well on Towson University. This would not be a "win at all costs" hire. Edwards was rebuilding an athletics program and obviously scandal was not part of that plan. He also knew that his coach had to be patient and have a history of turning around basketball teams and programs.

For their part, Towson needed a turnaround. The Tigers were an annual heavyweight in the Big South Conference in the early 1990s. It was in 1991 that the program made its last NCAA Tournament appearance under head coach Terry Truax. Towson would move up to the America East in 1995 and quickly became residents of the AE second division.

Fan interest was on the wane, but when the opportunity arose to move up once again for Dr. Edwards as part of the group that was joining the CAA, it was a natural move. Basketball would take its lumps, but the football program had ties to Johnny Unitas and desperately wanted to jettison its football program to the next level. This move would allow the Tigers to play in the Atlantic 10, one of the most respected Division 1-AA conferences in the country.

Edwards was right. After middling success in their first CAA campaign (7-11, sixth place), the Tigers would win twelve games total and five in conference in the next two years. Head Coach Michael Hunt was fired and interest was near flatline. Edwards knew he needed a winner and a personality.

It was only natural that Dr. Edwards' search for a new coach to lead his moribund Towson University basketball team found its way to Pat Kennedy. "I knew who Pat was, but I didn't know Pat," said Edwards. "I knew that he had been around and that he had been successful at the next level."

Knowing Pat Kennedy is knowing a basketball coach—he is the poster child for the position. Kennedy stands less than 6 feet tall and carries a perpetual harried appearance. His hair is mussed, tie crooked, and though he always wears a suit, it looks probably one-fourth its retail price. He gets excited often, and his face turns a glowy red. He talks fast and is very sure of himself.

But that surety is not false bravado. Pat Kennedy is known for reclamation projects. He was able to win at Florida State (202 wins in eleven years) in a time when winning basketball games at Florida State was considered impossible. Kennedy presided over the Seminoles' transformation from the Metro Conference to the ACC. Florida State was already predominantly a football school. While the move would obviously benefit basketball, it was expected that the Noles would take their lumps for a long time. Playing Duke, North Carolina, Maryland, Georgia Tech, and Wake Forest twice a year has a way of slowing progress.

In his debut season in the storied conference, Kennedy "managed" an 11-5 mark, finishing behind only Duke, which would go on to win the national championship. The following year Kennedy would guide the Seminoles to a school-record twenty-five wins and fall in the Elite Eight to Kentucky.

Kennedy made it to Florida State after guiding Iona to two NCAAs and two NITs in his six seasons as coach. He was promoted at the young age of twenty-eight, taking over for another young coach named Jim Valvano. After 124 wins at Iona and graduating 95 percent of his players, Kennedy moved on to Florida State.

With nothing left to prove, Kennedy left FSU, and on June 12, 1997, took the helm at DePaul. The Blue Demons carry one of the deeper traditions in college basketball. Names such as George Mikan and Mark Aguirre were players, but it is a coach, Ray Meyer, that most defines the Blue Demons.

In his forty-two years as head coach of DePaul from 1942 to 1984, Meyer compiled a record of 724-354 (.671). In his career, thirteen of his teams advanced to the NCAA Tournament and seven of his squads played in the NIT. His 1943 and 1979 teams advanced to the NCAA Final Four, while his 1945 team, featuring Mikan, won the NIT when it was considered the national championship.

The court on which DePaul plays its home games is named after Meyer.

But the Blue Demons had fallen as far as a program could muster: The year before Kennedy arrived (1996-1997), the Blue Demons were 3-23. Kennedy's initial 1997-1998 season showed slight improvement at 7-23, but the following year he rallied the Blue Demons to the biggest one-season turnaround in DePaul history. They finished with an 18-13 record and participated in the NIT. The following season DePaul made its first trip back to the NCAA Tournament in eight years.

The rigor of a budding program would take its toll, however, as Kennedy faced players leaving early for the NBA draft, and he suspended three of his top four scorers in 2001-2002 for a variety of offenses including elbowing another player. It is noteworthy that the players were eligible by DePaul and NCAA standards, but not by Kennedy's, so the suspensions stood at "violations of athletic department policy."

"I stood back and said 'whoa,'" Kennedy says of his last days at DePaul. "It's fragile."

He left, and after a two-year stint at Taylor's alma mater, Montana, Kennedy accepted the rebuilding job at Towson.

"Pat applied for this job, along with some head coaches and top level assistants," said Edwards. "We met in the Minneapolis airport and had iced teas at a TGI Fridays for four hours. I went there convinced it wouldn't work. But after four hours I was convinced it would. It was clear to me I could work with him."

Tom Pecora, who had been warned when he became the head man at Hofstra that the coaching ability in the CAA was higher, top to bottom, than most conferences, and knew the bar had once again been raised. "We knew Pat was going to get it going down there," Pecora said. "He's a helluva coach. I turned to my guys [when it was announced Kennedy was hired at Towson] and told them we'll have about a year before he gets it going in the right direction."

Towson spent its first four seasons in the CAA as the laughingstock. The Tigers had always been the get-healthy game, the get-your-bench-minutes game, the homecoming opponent. Towson had won eleven, four, eight, and five games. The total (twenty-eight) is the same number of victories as Old Dominion managed in the 2004-2005 season alone. Its conference victory total of seven, one, four, and two was one fewer than ODU's 2004-2005 season.

Then things changed in 2005-2006. Towson had equaled, on January 7, its conference total and surpassed its overall victory total from last year. In the words of Towson's coach as he prepared for a matchup with Hofstra, "It's not a fluke."

The turnaround had been helped immensely by the sudden arrival of a talented guard named Gary Neal.

The story of Gary Neal had been much publicized and written about in some of the country's largest newspapers. Neal, a star player at LaSalle who had scored more than a thousand points in his first two years, was accused of rape by a women's basketball player from the University of New Haven who was a counselor at LaSalle's summer basketball camp. Her account was that on the night of June 24, 2004, some late night drinking after a LaSalle youth basketball camp turned very wrong. She had had far too much to drink, and Neal and teammate Mike Cleaves were accused of the crime.

The facts and merits of two underage, intoxicated college basketball players can be debated without end, but the summary of the situation is not unfamilar for all college students: two young adults putting themselves in a tenuous position, their lack of maturity, and their inability to handle the consequences of their actions and to understand their situation. In the end it was a situation far greater than he said/she said when he said/she said wouldn't do. However, in the end a jury found Neal innocent of the charges.

"We put our faith in the jury system and they didn't let us down," said Wendy Goldstein, who represented Neal. "I hope he can get his life in order," she said. "His life has been on hold for a couple years."

The allegations would cost both the men's and women's head coaches at LaSalle their jobs, and Neal left the school, unsure of his future.

Neal told the Towson University student newspaper that "there was a period of withdrawal, where you don't want to go in public." He didn't play basketball for six months after the arrest, turned off his cell phone, and disappeared from view. It was an event in his life that had nothing to do with basketball and it deeply affected him. Gary Neal was not a punk or a troublemaker. In many respects, this made Gary Neal like any other kid, and being a basketball star had nothing to do with it, which was an odd paradox: The thing that most defined him throughout his life had nothing to do with his greatest challenge.

This was, perhaps, his greatest challenge and what made him withdraw all the more. Because he was a star athlete, the stereotypes would fit: spoiled, used to getting his own way. He would be cut no slack in a terrible situation and deservedly so. It was the remarkable pull of the sports media that would hurt him, the innuendo and blather of the airwaves. Gary Neal knew he was not a bad person. Neal also wouldn't let it end his future.

Few people realized that Neal took out a loan and enrolled himself at Towson as a student in January 2005. It was eight weeks later that anyone realized Neal was on campus, and it was only after a student newspaper article about some guy named "G" that dazzled fellow students at Towson's Burdick Gym in rec league pick-up games that brought him back into the limelight.

"He had a student ID card but nobody knew," said Edwards. After the article was published, Edwards still felt it inappropriate to discuss the matter with Kennedy, who had begun his own investigation. There was a trial and a verdict that needed to play out, and nobody knew anything about Gary Neal.

As the fall of 2005 wore on, Neal would have uncomfortable conversations with his teachers, telling them he couldn't be in class to take care of a legal matter. Neal continued to manage his classroom workload, netting a near-3.0 grade point average through the stress and emotion of a trial that would decide possibly the next ten years of his life, if not the rest of his life.

It wasn't until November 2005 that Neal was acquitted on the charges. Four days after the jury rendered its not guilty verdict, Edwards was greeted in his office one morning by Pat Kennedy, who knew this was the appropriate time to discuss Gary Neal. Edwards still believed he could not or should not give a snap decision on the matter. "Just let him play," Edwards knew, was not the right answer.

After meeting with Towson president Bob Caret, Edwards decided to set up an administrative committee to review Gary Neal and the circumstances surrounding the young man. Pat Kennedy would not be involved, as this was a university matter. Edwards chose the university chief of police, the university attorney, the vice president of student affairs, and the vice president of student judicial affairs to join him in the investigation and decision on Gary Neal.

"I met with Gary personally," says Edwards, "to see what kind of person he is. I wanted him to tell me what happened and what he learned. (I came from) that meeting believing the young man was not a rapist. This was a mistake that the young man would learn from."

So the investigation proceeded. Edwards obtained Neal's records from LaSalle and conducted a thorough investigation into Neal's background, his friends, family, and how Neal conducted his life.

"There was nothing else in his background," says Edwards. "And you also have to rely on the judicial process."

Even though Edwards would okay Neal's acceptance onto the Towson basketball team, there would be a probationary period. Neal would not be provided a scholarship his first year, and it would be Kennedy's decision after that. He also had to stay out of trouble.

President Caret approved the plan, and the next day Edwards laid it all out to Neal and Kennedy in the same meeting.

One day later, Gary Neal practiced for the first time with his new teammates. In his first game back on the court, Neal made his first five field goal attempts, three of them three pointers. Edwards also spearheaded a $35 million renovation of the school's football facilities, and led a planned $7 million renovation of the Towson Athletic Center, its basketball home. When your annual budget hovers around the $12 million mark, this is a significant undertaking. Towson had also signed a radio deal with powerful WBAL, who had covered the University of Maryland for twenty-five years.

Though Edwards would call the 2005-2006 season his last, retiring to a multitude of options, the Towson ship was pointed in the right direction.

So when the ball was tossed up to start the Hofstra/Towson game, perhaps only the coaches and Wayne Edwards really believed this was a different Towson team, one that could challenge and win in the CAA.

This was especially true as Hofstra's bruising center, Adrian Uter, would miss his second straight game with a high ankle sprain.

"One day it's going to bite us," Tom Pecora said as he watched his team warm up. "I hope it's not tonight."

Uter had been slow to return to the court not because he wasn't tough enough, but more so because of the way he plays basketball. Uter is very athletic and active on the court, rebounding so well, as much due to his superior positioning and hustle as to his sheer size. Because of that activity, the high ankle sprain is particularly painful, and slower to heal, than if he were a standstill shooter or a pure post man.

Mike Davis Sabb would start in Uter's place, and with the Towson students still on winter break, the atmosphere was cold. You could hear the yelps of the coaches, barking out instructions, over the smattering of fans.

The students would not return to school until January 30, an amazing vacuum for a mid-major school trying to build a program. Half of the Towson home games would suffer without the students, and it was the enthusiasm that Edwards would miss the most. He knows that revenue generated from concessions and parking, while important in the grand scheme, is meager.

"You're not going to make money (off of sports) at this level," Edwards concedes. "The benefit is what sports can do for your university."

Towson scored the first five points and led most of the first half, but a Loren Stokes three with 2:45 to play tied the game at 35-35. Hofstra would take its first lead of the game on a Stokes layup at 42-41, and a Zygis Sestokas three at the buzzer gave Hofstra a 45-43 lead. Despite thoroughly outplaying the Pride, Towson found itself down by two and facing a waking up of the echoes they didn't want.

The second half was a back-and-forth, and when Kennedy called curl play off an out-of-bounds possession, the resulting bucket made it 77-72 Towson.

"Same play he ran twenty-five years ago at Iona," said Wayne Edwards.

An Antoine Agudio three retied the game at 86-86 with 1:09. In the final minute, the ball would be almost exclusively in Gary Neal's hands. His final two free throws went down with 5.3 seconds and gave Towson a 94-91 lead. When Agudio's three, a good look, fell harmlessly away, Pat Kennedy could finally exhale.

The victory was much more than a 94-91 win over a conference foe, more than the Tigers shooting 57 percent and turning the ball over a measly nine times against a quality team that plays, usually, at least three guards. It was more than Gary Neal's thirty-four points, or Lawrence Hamm's 10-15 shooting, or freshman point guard Tim Crossin's ten assists with zero turnovers. (In fact, Crossin teamed with fellow freshman Velmar Coleman, both to combine for eighteen points, fifteen rebounds, fifteen assists, and two turnovers.)

"I think this is the first time in my career here we've been over .500 in the conference," Hamm, a senior, said in a muted jubilance.

There was a new look and new feel inside the Towson Arena.

As Hofstra was losing to Towson, Old Dominion casually strolled over Georgia State, 77-62. VCU dispatched of James Madison in equally easy fashion, going to Harrisonburg and winning 76-48. Eleven Rams netted double-figure minutes played.

More importantly, both victories set up the game most people who follow the conference were anticipating: the rematch. Old Dominion and VCU would see each other for the first time since their epic CAA final the previous season.

The rivalry is the most storied and arguably most heated in the conference, going through three conferences and seventy games since they first played in 1968. VCU held a 36-34 advantage. Both schools, which are separated by about a hundred miles down Interstate 64, are largely urban universities with commuter students. The rivalry goes far deeper than even games, leagues, and school demographics.

Jeff Capel's father had coached at Old Dominion from the 1994-1995 season until the 2001-2002. His tenure bridged the gap between Oliver Purnell, now at Clemson, and Blaine Taylor.

The elder Capel went 122-98 in his seven seasons, but it was the way in which he departed that left an impression. Many at the school had felt Capel mentally had checked out, searching for the next big job. After all, his teams had won consistently and had played in two NCAA Tournaments. Capel Sr. presided over the Monarchs' stirring three-overtime upset of Villanova in the 1995 NCAA Tournament.

Capel's on-floor success landed him a job interview with Rutgers at the conclusion of the 1996-1997 season. This was not surprising, as Capel had also taken his North Carolina A&T team to the Big Dance in 1994. He was clearly a smart coach who knew how to win.

It is also an unsaid pitfall to mid-major coaches that their names will come up for major conference jobs in media speculation, even if no discussions between the coach and the school have taken place. It didn't help that even Capel's peers were stating the obvious, without specifics.

"I think Jeff's marketability right now—in a market that's a buyer's market—is at an all-time high," then-UNCW coach Jerry Wainwright said in a March 1997 interview. "Like all of us, he wants to be playing in the Final Four. At this level, it's hard to do that. I think this is the year of a multitude of opportunities for good coaches like Jeff Capel."

Capel's contract at ODU was to run for another three years, and his total compensation at the time was said to be in the neighborhood of $150,000. A step up meant a tripling of that salary and benefits.

It didn't help matters that Capel Sr. was never big on glad-handing ODU alums. The social scene was not in his bag of tricks. Making the alumni—especially the rich donors and program sponsors—feel not just part of the program but special is a significant measure for athletics departments. The elder Capel was kicking the last leg of the stool out from under himself. Folks aren't happy when they don't feel appreciated or feel a sense of loyalty.

The truth of the matter lay somewhere in the middle of the speculation, but Capel eventually resigned his position as head coach at Old Dominion, taking with him a young assistant named Jeff Capel III, who would sign on at VCU as an assistant to Mack McCarthy.

No matter how great a man Jeff Capel III had become, his last name was C-a-p-e-l and ODU fans have long memories.

There clearly were some hard feelings then, and Jeff Capel the VCU coach was asked about it six years later in the press conference after Old Dominion's victory over VCU in the 2005 CAA final. Though it had nothing to do with the game and was an event from a different decade, even century, the question was not unexpected. The entire press room braced for the explosion. It took all of the restraint Jeff Capel could muster, but he was able to answer the question without stepping over the line of disbelief and into rage and fury. Yes, this rivalry is heated.

As the ODU students began pouring into the Ted Constant Center an hour prior to tip-off, Blaine Taylor was sipping coffee, sitting back, and taking in the big game atmosphere.

"The kids are getting used to playing in this environment," he said. "We should be comfortable, but this is such a big rivalry. I'm sure both teams will be a little nervous at the beginning."

Robert Wilkes, Taylor's assistant, agreed. "It's tough to top the last two games," Wilkes said, referring to last season's CAA final overtime thriller and the Monarchs' 82-76 win in this building the previous year. Wilkes then also allowed himself to soak it in. "It's fun to see these guys go at it. It's such a good rivalry."

Two minutes prior to the tip, after receiving final instructions, both teams converged in the tunnel that led to the floor. Usually the visiting team appears first. They congregate in the tunnel, huddle and chant or clap or cheer or yell. The goal is to get their game faces on squarely and hit the floor in a victorious mindset. They will be running out first to a cascade of boos.

The home team follows with their own version that ends in the home crowd standing and cheering, and the pep band playing. But on this day there was a timing error, delaying the VCU entrance to the floor. Both teams stood face to face, out of the sight of the crowd, with only one security guard on hand. They seemed as surprised as anyone, and for just a moment they stood there wondering what to do, frozen. It was as if they were in the middle of a twenty-five-man game of hide-and-seek.

The scene that ensued could only be described as comical, yet apropos. As you would expect, the trash talking began, but it was the gentle walk into trash talking. Players from both teams mainly shouted into the air and kept their distance, though it was only about two feet. When members of both teams began bouncing up and down on their feet, they began woofing at each other. There was no more than a centimeter between the players' noses, yet there was never contact—just a torrent of words and pregame banter. The lone security guard stood by, helpless but amused.

It was clear that even in the middle of a tremendous smack-talking war, the two teams respected each other and the game of basketball enough not to cross a line. It was a wonderful reflection of what both Capel and Taylor teach the kids in their charge.

Alex Loughton, reigning player of the year in the CAA, stood in the back watching and laughing.

The game began just as Taylor had thought—a bevy of turnovers and missed shots signaled nerves. Both teams eventually settled into the rhythm of the game and the game became a donnybrook.

ODU took control when Brian Henderson rattled in a three with 8:30 to play. The score rose to 60-48 and the sellout crowd went berserk. An Alex Loughton dunk one minute later restored a double-digit lead at 62-51. It was the kind of dunk that is a punctuation mark signaling the end of the game, in most games, but this was VCU/ODU.

Two minutes after the Loughton dunk, VCU marksman Jamal Shuler swished an NBA-range three to make it 62-60, and VCU center Eric Davis, who managed two fouls and three turnovers in the first half hit a layup to knot the score with 4:21 to play; the game would also end the way everyone knew it would.

It was going to be another VCU/ODU wild finish.

In the final four minutes Isaiah Hunter would keep VCU at arm's length, only to see Shuler drain another three to keep it close. Hunter hit two free throws to give ODU their lead back, and then Hunter hit a three with just less than two minutes to play to give ODU a 69-64 lead. Two more free throws restored the lead to five at 71-66.

It was clear that ODU had withstood the VCU rush and it was just a matter of running the clock. Nobody told Shuler, though, who hit two more NBA threes to bring VCU back to 75-72.

Loughton hit one of two free throws with 2.6 seconds left to give ODU a 78-75 lead. Capel called time-out and everybody in the sold-out Constant Center knew where the ball was going. Shuler had nailed five three-point shots in the final seven minutes, three of which defied belief because they were so deep.

"The play was designed for whoever is open," Shuler would say after the game. "I flared and both (defenders) went with me. Nick took a good shot."

Nick George, who finished the game with twenty-seven points, nine rebounds, and four steals, got a good look. A better look than Taylor wanted.

However, George's three-pointer bounced harmlessly off the back rim. Even so, the shot took a high carom, and for that brief instant all of the air was sucked completely out of the Ted Constant Center. It was one of those stop-action scenes out of a movie, where the director cuts from actor to actor showing each emotion as it appears in that moment. The split second of real-time action is covered by about ten seconds of film. The building fell completely silent. And then someone turned on the fans, literally and figuratively, when the ball did not find the net.

After the final, furious minute, one in which VCU's Shuler showed unbelievable range and resiliency, you would have to look hard to find a Monarchs fan that did not think George's shot was going in and the game was going to overtime. It seemed fitting.

It was a game in which nobody walked away griping about officials, wondering why his team did or did not do this or that, or felt badly about how it was played. Most people only said, "Wow, what a college basketball game." Big players played big in a big game.

Capel said in the postgame that Isaiah Hunter gives ODU a swagger, and when pressed on what he meant, Capel was blunt: "He is cocky. And I mean it's a good cocky. Guards are flashy and flamboyant and his team responds to it. He has that 'it' inside him."

———

Meanwhile, Tom Pecora's Hofstra team was gutting out an important home victory over UNCW, the Pride's fourteenth consecutive victory at home. "The first thing I told them before the game was the most intense, toughest team is going to win this game." Pecora knew that UNCW would come flying at Hofstra.

Though Pecora would call the victory a "total team effort," Loren Stokes played his best game of the season, scoring thirty points and handing out seven assists with three steals in the 92-87 triple overtime win. The white-knuckler knocked UNCW out of first place in the CAA, further crowding the standings.

The Pride led most of regulation play, taking its largest lead, 48-33, on a layup from junior guard Carlos Rivera with 12:59 left. In the next eight minutes, UNCW would score on fourteen consecutive possessions, tying the score at 58-58 with a little more than five minutes to play.

Antoine Agudio answered with a short jumper, but UNCW senior guard John Goldsberry answered the answer, hitting a three pointer that gave the Seahawks their first lead of the night.

The teams went back and forth down the stretch, with UNCW's T.J. Carter missing a jumper with 0.4 second left on the final possession of regulation play to send the game into overtime tied at 70-70.

UNCW led for most of the first overtime, but a contested three pointer from Agudio knotted the score 76-76 with 1:25 left. Carter's second attempted buzzer beater missed at the end of the first overtime, and Stokes obliged at the end of the second overtime with the score tied at 82-82. Stokes redeemed himself by starting the third overtime session with back-to-back three pointers to give the Pride an 88-82 lead and Hofstra held on.

"The second half was crazy," UNCW Coach Brad Brownell would say nearly a month later, the result fresh in his mind. "It was back-and-forth action and kids made plays."

Stokes's thirty points was one shy of his career high. Stokes also set a school record with fifty-four minutes played. While those numbers are truly impressive, few people knew that Stokes had led his team to victory despite a badly injured right thumb (his shooting hand). He had dribbled most of the evening with his left hand. "I couldn't let it bother me," Stokes would tell reporters of the pain. "We needed this one."

For UNCW, Carter shot 11-22 on the night, including 6-11 on three pointers to reach his career high of thirty-one points. Goldsberry added sixteen points and a game-high ten assists.

The mantra was as clear as ever. Hold serve at home and try to steal a few on the road. The road is where Hofstra was headed, to Norfolk and defending champion Old Dominion.

———

The vibe at the Ted Constant Center for the ODU/Hofstra game was noticeably different than for the VCU game. The mind does not immediately call up these two teams when thinking of rivalries or grudge matches. There is no sexy angle like players facing each other in pickup games during the offseason.

These two teams simply have no history, nor do they share geography. It was certainly a series progress forged. Before Hofstra became part of the CAA in 2001, the teams had played each other just once— a 92-66 ODU thumping of the Flying Dutchmen at the Norfolk Scope in the 1993-1994 season.

Hofstra has a new nickname, ODU has a new arena, and the series has quietly become one of the best in the CAA. Both games in 2004-2005 were won by the road team, and both games came down to a buzzer-beating shot that went astray.

Hofstra won at Old Dominion 66-63 last February, which at the time of the game stood as the only home loss in the last two years the Monarchs had suffered (22-1). ODU, meanwhile, defeated the Pride at Hofstra Arena by a 67-66 score. Hofstra had not lost a home game since (a fourteen-game streak; 21-2 in its last twenty-three home games). That's 43-3 at home in the past two years, and two of the three losses were inflicted by the other team in this series. Six of the eight regular season meetings between the schools in the last four years had come down to the final seconds. ODU had missed winning or tying shots just before the buzzer three times, and Hofstra missed last year's game-ender at home, and it also missed three tying three-point attempts in the closing seconds of a 71-66 defeat in Norfolk in 2003-2004. ODU had knocked Hofstra out of the CAA Tournament in each of the last two years.

Adrian Uter would return for Hofstra. His high ankle sprain was not necessarily feeling well, even though it felt good enough to give it a go. Though he was noticeably hobbling, Uter's presence alone required a reckoning. With Uter back and ODU playing increasingly better each game, this game appeared to add to the budding rivalry.

Taylor had chosen to start Brandon Johnson and Valdus Vasylius over Arnaud Dahi and Brian Henderson. Johnson, ODU's best defender, was tabbed to check Loren Stokes, but Vasylius's start was due more to Dahi's lackadaisical manner in practice than anything Vasylius had done.

"Arnaud needs to do the things he's good at doing," Taylor would say after the game. It would be a simple explanation, but reading between the lines was easy. As the teams moved to midcourt and shook hands as starters do, Taylor stood with his arms at his sides, clipboard in one hand with the dry erase Sharpie stuck in his hand like a cigar. He stared intently at his players.

"I'm pretty ritualistic," said Taylor. "My interactions [before a game] are not words, they are more watchful. I'm not into the hoopla or like to give the Knute Rockne speech. I like to notice the little things, and sometimes they are not good."

Tom Pecora eyed his star. Loren Stokes looked like a refugee from a Frankenstein movie, complete with a wrap on his knee and his thumb still heavily taped. Still, the Hofstra road blue uniforms shone well in the bright lights of the Ted Constant Center.

It was no surprise that the uniforms, despite the bruised and cut bodies of the players who wore them, looked slick. The blue background sets off a gold and white-trimmed Hofstra flag across the front of the uniforms. The numbers are a pointy font not seen in most uniforms and trimmed in gold. While most NCAA teams get jerseys from Nike or Adidas or whomever else provides the team its shoes, not Pecora.

Hofstra gets new uniforms—home and road, as well as practice uniforms and coaches' wear—designed, produced, and sent to Hempstead from the little town of Aprille, which is located just outside of Milan, Italy. Nando Diablasi, who grew up in Queens, does the honors. Diablasi's father was a master tailor in Manhattan and relocated the family back to Italy when Nando was fourteen years old.

Pecora was introduced to Diablasi by Bob Oliva, legendary head coach at New York's Christ the King High School. Diablasi makes it back to the United States to visit with Pecora three or four times each year, including at the Final Four.

In a game that was as ragged as it was compelling, Hofstra's Carlos Rivera hit all ten of his free throws down the stretch, and the Pride pulled the upset for the second year in a row, 76-68, outscoring the home team 48-33 in the second half.

Loren Stokes was again the leading scorer for Hofstra with twenty-seven points, but it was a series of plays in the second half that Stokes made that led the Pride. On several trips down the floor, Stokes beat his man one-on-one and flipped in a soft floater. He dished to Aurimas Kieza for a layup and to Chris Gadley for a dunk. Finally, he dashed from one side of the court to the other to swipe the ball away from behind an unsuspecting Brandon Johnson that led to another Hofstra hoop.

"He was in that zone where he's impossible to guard," said Pecora after the game. "When I was younger I didn't think putting four [players] on the baseline was coaching," he continued. "Now that I'm older it's great."

The entire press room laughed.

The CAA was seeing its typical season: barnburner games, quotable coaches, and solid play. The problem, however, to this point was fairly typical. Because conferences are measured on bids to the NCAA Tournament and advancing in that tournament, "typical" for the CAA wasn't going to get it done. It had been twenty years since its last at-large bid.

Conversely, something special was occurring in the Missouri Valley Conference. Long considered another mid-major conference, the MVC had been quietly successful over the past seven years. It sent at least one team to the NCAA Tournament as an at-large participant in each of those seasons, and has seven first-round victories and two Sweet Sixteen teams in the past ten years (Missouri State as SW

Missouri State in 1999, Southern Illinois in 2002).

In 2005-2006, it was a top six conference in terms of RPI, frequently topping the PAC 10 and Big 12 conferences. It routinely placed five teams in the top thirty-five of the RPI as well.

It was clear that the MVC had arrived at the destination the CAA coveted. This season, the MVC also entertained a similar battle for the top spot in its conference—Northern Iowa, Creighton, Wichita State, Southern Illinois, and Missouri State all parried at the top of the standings, vying for position and an at-large resume.

But what was the difference? How had the MVC, which was in a similar position to the CAA, moved up so quickly in the national scene?

Since the 2000-2001 season, the conference regular season champion won the MVC postseason tournament exactly zero times. In the CAA, the regular season champ won the tournament *every* time. (In 2000-2001, Richmond won the conference regular season title, but the Spiders were deemed ineligible for the conference tournament after announcing the school's move to the Atlantic 10. George Mason finished tied for second and won the tournament.)

The "perfect storm" of a mid-major's best team being knocked off in the conference tournament, thus opening the potential for an at-large team, never occurred for the CAA. The storm revolves around related events unfolding precisely. A mid major needs one team to nail an early-season, eye-opening win. That team then needs to roll through the regular season, losing just once or twice. They consequently roll up a gaudy record of 25-4.

This team, for whatever reason, loses in its conference tournament to a hotter team. Still, the NCAA Committee is hard pressed to overlook such a great performance, so they get two bids. But for the CAA the backdoor exposure was unavailable. The #1 seed kept winning it all.

The MVC's at-large selection during the last five seasons was always the regular-season champ. In 2005, Northern Iowa received an at-large berth despite finishing tied for third in the regular season.

"The yardstick of success, the measurement of success for us every year is multiple berths, and obviously along with that, success in the tournament," MVC Commissioner Doug Elgin had told various media outlets in January 2006. This is precisely what fuels the success.

A big portion of the $11 billion contract that CBS signed with the NCAA is wrapped up in what the NCAA calls its "Basketball Fund." The fund is essentially monies sent to NCAA member schools for making the NCAA Tournament and advancing into deeper rounds.

According to the NCAA:

The basketball fund provides for moneys to be distributed to Division I conferences based on their performance in the Division I Men's Basketball Championship over a six-year rolling period (for the period 2000-2005 for the 2005-2006 distribution). Independent institutions receive a full unit share based on its tournament participation over the same rolling six-year period. The basketball fund payments are sent to conferences and independent institutions in mid-April each year.

One unit is awarded to each institution participating in each game, except the championship game. In 2004-2005, each basketball unit was approximately $152,000 for a total $113.7 million distribution.

In short, over a six-year period a conference receives $152,000 per year, or a $912,000 check. To the Big 12 or Big 10 this may be a rounding error. To the MVC, it meant an additional $912,000 for each team that made the tournament, and one more share for each victory. (When Maryland's Drew Nicholas nailed a buzzer-beating, falling out of bounds, three-point shot to beat UNCW in the 2003 NCAA Tournament, it truly was a million dollar shot.)

It becomes a circular proposition: The money earned from the NCAA helps a conference (and thus its schools) gain exposure on television. It helps the teams not have to schedule buy games in order to help their individual budgets. This way, member schools have a little more freedom in the manner in which they schedule games. Top teams can schedule top nonconference opponents with the goal of winning marquee games and impressing the selection committee, while at the same time not taking a huge RPI hit and avoiding the dreaded "bad loss." Weaker teams can schedule smartly, getting themselves victories as opposed to a shellacking in Lawrence, Kansas, or Durham, North Carolina. Winning—whether at the top or bottom of the conference—fuels interest from fans and recruits, which fuels more winning, higher RPI, more exposure, and, of course, more NCAA tournament berths. This all means another $912,000 check (or $152,000 over six years) and a better chance at winning in the tournament, and then the cycle begins anew.

For the 2005-2006 CAA season, with no fewer than five teams with a legitimate chance to get to the magical number of twenty victories, and with the bottom of the conference feeding those victories and the top of the conference getting some much-needed separation, the planets were aligning for the CAA the way they had for the MVC ten years earlier: Its best team stood a good chance of *not* winning the conference tournament.

There was so much talent at the top of the league that it was a reasonable guess that the top team could easily lose in the tournament. They kept winning, however, even though teams had better records. Plus, multiple teams had the eye-opening victory early on. Thus, there were many options for the CAA. Speculation was rampant, and it wasn't yet February.

CHAPTER NINE:

DOGFIGHT

"We fight, get beat, rise, and fight again." –Nathaniel Greene

The statement released from Old Dominion University was terse, but it was also complete:

At approximately 10 p.m., Wednesday, Jan. 25, Old Dominion University men's basketball player Brandon Johnson (Orlando, FL) was shot as he exited his residence in the University Village Apartments. Brandon was treated at Norfolk General Hospital for a fractured right clavicle and released. He will miss action until he is re-evaluated in approximately five to six weeks.

Old Dominion University Police are assisting the Norfolk Police Department in the investigation, which is ongoing. The university has expanded its policing and security coverage of the entire campus.

On the night before Old Dominion was to take on the Drexel Dragons, in the middle of a season that saw the Monarchs battle injuries and transfers, and exactly one month after the team's coach had been rushed to the emergency room with a serious medical condition, sophomore guard Brandon Johnson had been shot in the upper body.

A basketball team—the entire team, meaning coaches, trainers, and managers—becomes extremely close. Calling the team a family is one of those clichés that is a cliché because it is the truth.

The group eats, lives, trains, works, shares, and plays together for a significant portion of their waking hours. They fight for the same goals, both on and off the court. When one of them hurts, they all feel the pain.

For the kids, the game is their bond. It is the great equalizer in any conversation, transcending backgrounds and upbringing. It is what each player, coach, trainer, and manager can point to as the basis for their togetherness. After all, the players have been doing this since they were about five years old. Coaches, too.

It is an odd bond, too, since they compete for floor time. One man's sprained ankle is another man's opportunity. The competition is always there, and that actually spawns the togetherness. They all feel the pain because at some point in their basketball lives, each has felt that pain. This pain was different, though. A teammate and friend had not suffered a sprained ankle. He had been shot. So they were all able to harken back to their common denominator and root for their friend.

It would be a long night for the team as they gathered first at the hospital, and then in Isaiah Hunter's apartment afterward, the apartment he shared with Brandon Johnson. There would be discussion, reflection, emotion, and even introspection. Children—and let's not fool ourselves; even though these were twenty-year-old men, they were children in this situation—were coming to grips with the emotion that tugged at them. Because most were many miles from their families, they shared with their current family, their close family.

The night quickly became early morning.

"Let's just say my alarm clock didn't go off this morning," said team co-captain Drew Williamson, playing the role of spokesman.

Blaine Taylor refused to let the situation paralyze his team. "I told them we need to bounce the ball around and go get some rest," he said. Taylor wanted to ensure that his team had a perspective of the moment. "I've dealt with worse, and you are going to [deal with worse as well] in your lifetime," he said. "The bottom line is your friend is okay and we have to move on to a better place. In this world there is violence and you have to be aware that you are vulnerable at all times."

With that, there was a light practice and the team was released to do exactly what Taylor wanted: rest.

The Ted Constant Center filled up quickly in the early evening of Thursday, January 26. There was a nervous murmur, an almost restless feeling to the building as word spread as quickly as the rumor. Certainly Drexel Coach Bruiser Flint and his talented swingman Dominick Mejia were not the topic of discussion.

The students were ready, complete with media guide blowups of Brandon Johnson's picture, in the event that Johnson would be in attendance. Nobody really knew.

As the clock dipped below the 1:00 mark prior to the start of the game, an ovation slowly grew in the Ted Constant Center. Brandon Johnson, twenty hours after being shot in the shoulder, escorted the Old Dominion coaching staff to its home bench.

Johnson showed no emotion and a very quiet expression as he walked the straight line to the bench. He provided the home fans only a short wave of his hand. Wearing a turquoise sweater pulled over an untucked white shirt, he spoke to nobody; and nobody engaged him either as Johnson took at seat at the end of the bench, arm in a sling, with the team managers.

It makes one wonder just what you say to someone in that situation. Players on a basketball team become lifelong friends; but Johnson is just a sophomore, and that means there is only so much time beyond books and basketball to get to truly know someone. Frequently, because of differing backgrounds and geography, it is easy to fall back on stereotyping in order to communicate and get to know one another.

Unfortunately, the downside to this is that you don't really know someone. Yes, you are a family, but in this moment the lack of its true family roots makes it an awkward situation. So when a situation like this occurs, nobody is sure of the right thing to say.

Taylor, however, knew exactly what to say after Drexel's Mejia hit four consecutive three-point shots to break open a nip and tuck basketball game. The words weren't nice but they were pointed. ODU responded with a spirited 7-0 run of its own to retake the lead at 25-24.

Brandon Johnson sat motionless during both barrages, his head in his left hand, contemplating. His body was in the Ted Constant Center, but his head was nowhere near. It couldn't have been. Though the game was tight and it was a very important conference game, life had its way with Brandon Johnson's mind.

Drexel settled into a rhythm and took a 32-27 lead into the locker room. ODU had played twenty minutes of listless but focused basketball. It was not spirited. It was determined.

This would turn into an evening of wills. It was sheer will that brought Johnson into that building. Nobody would have said a word had he chosen to skip. The fans who had filled the Constant Center would do anything to will their team and their injured hero to victory. Taylor's will was similar.

Coming out for the second half, the hallway just outside the ODU locker room was quiet. The ODU players congregated, waiting their turn to take the floor for warmups. Not a word was spoken and they stood, in eerie silence, just waiting, as if they were in line at the grocery store. It was as if every bit of goodwill that was thrust their way was not ignored; rather it was uncontemplated. This was a team that was clearly going through the motions.

It was not until freshman Jonathan Adams, who had played only three first-half minutes, spoke up and chided the team that there was a hint of emotion. The last man on the team that should have been expected to rally the troops was trying just that.

"It's quiet back here," Adams said. "I don't hear anything. You guys are quiet. It's too quiet back here." But Adams was greeted with only a smattering of applause and little emotion. What display was shown was forced. Taylor followed the team out the door, steely-eyed and willful.

Old Dominion's first possession of the second half turned into a Drew Williamson prayer that was an air ball and a shot clock violation. Drexel promptly went down the court and Frank Elegar scored and was fouled by Loughton, sending the deficit to 34-27.

As Elegar ambled to the line—he had been hit pretty hard on the play—you could sense the feeling in the building had turned from a hopeful urging to a dispirited pleading. It would be very understandable for the home team to fold its tents and call it a night. Their wills were being tested.

Suddenly a building full of energy, that for the past hour had been suffering a slow leak, let out a gaping sigh. The signs were lowered to the floor. The students just looked at each other. Long-time alumni and season ticket holders sat in disbelief or on their hands. It was a bit like falling victim to a last-second halfcourt shot. Disbelief was turning into resignation of what had just occurred.

The Monarchs needed to come out of the locker room and hear the plea of their freshman. The crowd needed it. The team needed it.

On successive trips down the floor, Old Dominion had taken a punch, not delivered one. Though less than two minutes into the half, players' hands tugged at their shorts. Heads bowed. There was nary a hint that eighteen minutes of basketball were left to be played.

Arnaud Dahi heard the pleas and came to the rescue. Dahi hit two short jumpers to close the gap. He then made a steal that led to free throws and converted a dunk on an inbounds play, the latter trimming the margin to 36-35. Dahi hit another layup then drew a charging foul on Mejia.

A minute later, after Drexel Coach Bruiser Flint was whistled for a technical foul, Valdus Vasylius hit a free throw to finish off an old-fashioned three-point play. The hoop and shot closed a 13-2 Old Dominion run and the Monarchs had a four-point bulge at 40-36. The crowd was back in the corner of the home team, making as much noise as it had all night.

Brandon Johnson, meanwhile, busied himself opening a bag of Skittles.

Old Dominion would slowly pull away in the second half and eventually win, 74-67. The Monarchs were now 8-2 (15-5 overall) and tied for first in the conference with George Mason. Faint echoes of an at-large bid remained.

After the game, Taylor had never looked so tired. He simply appeared out of gas. Taylor, who is always gregarious and straightforward with the media, also proved himself a poor liar. Rumpled and downtrodden, even after a big victory, Taylor muttered "I'm half spent, to tell you the truth." Taylor was clearly completely spent.

Interestingly, Taylor had been more expressive than usual during the game, even at the previous season's CAA Tournament final, leaping from his seat to call plays and barking at officials. It was only after the game that he allowed the past eighteen hours to slouch his demeanor.

"I'm proud of our maturity," Taylor continued. "Our kids did a good job of compartmentalizing [the situation]."

Drexel's Flint, perhaps, summed up the past eighteen hours in the life of Taylor better than Taylor himself. "What do you do when you have to call a kid's parents [with news like that]," Flint said, shaking his head and staring at the floor. "It's not a sprained ankle. It's tough, man."

Resolve. It was a concept Taylor knew his team had learned and would take to heart when he challenged them after the Drexel game.

"How much better are we going to be?" was the simple question.

Who was the Monarchs' opponent on Saturday, less than forty hours after the Drexel victory and less than sixty hours after Brandon Johnson had been shot? The George Mason Patriots.

———

On the night Old Dominion gutted out its victory over Drexel, Hofstra busied itself with Gary Neal and the Towson Tigers. The 82-70 Pride win was most notable for the battle between Neal and Loren Stokes. Neal poured in thirty-six points, making seven of twelve three-point shots, but the rest of the Tigers managed only thirty-four points combined. For his part, Stokes set a career-high with thirty-one points, adding eleven rebounds (another career high) to his stat line.

VCU kept pace with an underwhelming performance at Delaware, rallying from five down at the half to win 54-52. With UNCW and George Mason lambasting James Madison and William & Mary, respectively, all of the top teams in the conference had won again, further creating separation among the haves and the have nots.

GMU	8-2
UNCW	8-2
ODU	7-3
Northeastern	7-3
VCU	7-3
Hofstra	6-3

January 28, 2006, was more than the slate of the last conference games to be played that month, signaling February and the real grind. It also proved to be the single most exciting day of conference play in a season in which every weekend had been dotted with unbelievable games and storylines.

Jim Larranaga's George Mason Patriots would play Old Dominion for a share of first place. Likewise, UNCW hosted Northeastern.

Commissioner Tom Yeager was on hand to watch the George Mason game, which would feature the team everybody talked about in November when "at-large berth" was the subject of discussion, Old Dominion, and the current topic of at-large conversation, George Mason. Yeager took his courtside seat and was flanked by NCAA Tournament Selection Committee Chairman Craig Littlepaige, who had driven up from his Charlottesville, Virginia, office, and George Mason Director of Athletics Tom O'Connor, who moonlighted on the selection committee.

While every game would be of importance in its own right, the Old Dominion at George Mason matchup was the beacon. Littlepaige would see, by his own estimation, more than a hundred games over the course of the season. When you throw in television games, phone calls, tapes, and newspaper reports, the jumble of teams can be maddening; and March Madness was still more than thirty days away.

A well-played game was one thing. Press row niceties and Littlepaige's appearance was another. But there was actual pressure on this Saturday, and it had little to do with zone defenses and free throw percentages. A statement would have to be made. A statement that would stick with Littlepaige, the most important man in the building.

The Monarchs, who came into the game having won eight of their last nine contests and reasserted themselves as a favorite in the conference race, looked like the ODU of old. The players were loose, joking around, and showing the kind of emotion one comes to expect in a game of this magnitude. They had the talent.

Conventional wisdom says the second game is more difficult than the first in an emotional situation. On the bus ride to Mason from Norfolk, according to ODU assistant Rob Wilkes, everybody sacked out. It was the rest and healing they needed as a team. They had rested.

For its part, Mason had won thirteen of sixteen. The Patriots came into the game leading the conference in both field goal percentage made and field goal percentage defense. Memories of Drew Williamson's twenty-seven-foot buzzer beater to give ODU the 54-53 victory over GMU on December 7 remained fresh. George Mason had the momentum and the home court and, importantly, the edge. They sought revenge, and they had the perfect audience.

Even with a good student turnout, though, the Patriot Center was barely 40 percent full. Part of the problem certainly was the fact that it was a sunny sixty-five degrees in Washington, D.C., on a Saturday in late January.

Valdus Vasylius, the strong ODU forward whose rumpled hair and sleepy eyes always make him look like he just got out of bed, hit a layup ten seconds after entering the game. The surprising move prompted Larranaga to grab Sammy Hernandez, his beefy freshman forward, and state rather calmly "You cover Vasylius, the left-handed kid." Larranaga immediately turned to his assistants and asked, "Who do we want covering Vasylius," after Vasylius wriggled free for a second layup before Hernandez could reach the scorer's table.

Of course, the head coach wasn't actually asking for advice or a change in game plan. It was more of an assurance. Coaches get that way after their teams give up back-to-back layups.

Mason led 12-9 when Jordan Carter, the backup point guard, drained a twenty-seven-foot three pointer and ODU's John Morris was whistled for a foul. In fact, Morris didn't come within a foot of Carter, but no matter. The four-point play turned the tide of the game from a battle royale to a blowout.

The run would reach 16-2 and the score of the game 28-11 before Taylor had seen enough. He called time with 7:48 to play. George Mason had made ten of thirteen field goals, though to be fair, many were layups and dunks provided by the Patriots overplaying defense.

Taylor, who admits to being a creature of habit, will walk to the baseline at the end of the ODU bench by himself when he's truly disgusted with something: his team's play, the officiating, etc. After ODU's eleventh turnover of the first half was followed by a Tony Skinn three pointer for George Mason, Taylor seemed to almost take root down by ODU trainer Scott Johnson. Skinn's bomb, George Mason's fifteenth field goal in twenty attempts, opened the lead to 42-19. The Patriots had made all nine free throws as well and were putting on a clinic, much to the delight of the home fans.

"The art of field goal percentage comes down to two things," Larranaga says. "One, make a shot; two, get shots you want to make."

When Mason star shooter Lamar Butler, who holds the school record for three pointers made and is also the winningest player in school history, got behind the defense for only his second field goal—notable in that Mason's best player was invisible the entire afternoon yet the Patriots still rolled—Taylor called time-out. The score was 62-38 with 5:11 to play.

Taylor knew it was one of "those" days. He would later say "the story is not what we did not do, it's what they did."

The "oh-ver-ra-ted" chant started with about three minutes to go. "Hey-hey-hey good-bye" was one minute later.

Meanwhile, Tom Yeager chewed the ear of Littlepaige, inaudible above the din. Certainly the word *impressive* was part of the conversation. George Mason had made its statement in a convincing manner; Yeager had his two minutes for final arguments. Yeager knows his numbers very well. You could wager, and probably win, that the conversation planted seeds in Littlepaige's mind about the strength of the conference and the team that was on top.

If it didn't leave a mark, Larranaga, who shared a bench with Littlepaige when both were assistants for Terry Holland at Virginia in the late 1970s and early 1980s, made sure.

As part of his postgame comments, Larranaga was clear to point out, in front of Littlepaige, that "last season [the CAA] played thirty-eight home games. The Missouri Valley played sixty-four! The difficulty we have is scheduling."

It was a soliloquy filled with a directive purpose. Larranaga finished his comments: "As a coach you have different philosophies. We've adopted that what we have to do is be great at what we do. I like my team. I like the way we're playing. It's about playing well."

Littlepaige left Fairfax that day thinking about the at-large bid for the CAA. He wasn't thinking about Old Dominion.

—————

Sports information directors don't come more conscientious than Hofstra's Jeremy Kniffin. Members of the media can expect timely and complete game notes, as well as quick recaps to all Hofstra games.

"Whenever I'm on the road and want to get a press release together really quick after the game," says Kniffin, "I always type in one paragraph for a win and one for a loss in advance, and then delete the one that doesn't apply."

The preparation, while helping his ability to work better and faster, can also hurt him. Nearing the conclusion of Hofstra's game against Drexel, Kniffin admits, "I deleted the 'win' paragraph with thirty seconds to go in overtime down by six."

Kniffin was referring to the wild finish to the Pride's 76-75 over-time victory in Philadelphia over Bruiser Flint's Dragons. For drama, TNT has nothing on this game.

A three-point Hofstra halftime lead had held up during an intense second half. The Pride led 67-61 as the teams trudged back onto the court at the under 4:00 media time-out. Drexel, however, held Hofstra scoreless over the last 3:51 of regulation and the first 3:53 of overtime to turn the six-point deficit into a 73-67 overtime lead.

Hofstra still trailed 75-69 with thirty-five seconds left, but Antoine Agudio missed a free throw (after making the first) and the Pride grabbed the offensive board. Carlos Rivera then knocked down a three pointer to cut the lead to 75-73 with eighteen seconds left, and Hofstra drew a five-second call on the ensuing inbounds pass.

Rivera was then fouled attempting a three pointer with 6.3 seconds to play, and Drexel's Flint was called for a technical foul for leaving the coaching box to argue the call. When you consider how little time Flint actually spends in the coach's box during an entire game, to draw a technical foul at this juncture is interesting; but Flint left the officiating crew no choice.

As if scripted, Rivera missed the two technical foul shots. Rivera regrouped to make the final three provided by the original foul to give Hofstra a 76-75 lead. Bashir Mason's twenty-five footer rimmed out at the buzzer.

"That's as wild a finish as I've been around," said Pecora. "That's why you have to play it out. That's what separates basketball from other sports."

Stokes scored seventeen points, but it was his defense on Drexel star Dominick Mejia that merited praise. Mejia did not score in the second half and finished with ten points, twenty-four fewer than he had scored at ODU. Stokes also played through a painful thumb injury that required heavy icing.

The final game of consequence on Showdown Saturday saw UNCW come from nine points down at the half to defeat Jose Juan

Barea and the Northeastern Huskies 46-44. Barea came into the game in the top ten in the nation in scoring and was the nation's leading assist man. Clearly, everything Northeastern did ran through Barea.

On this day it would, once again, be the UNCW defensive effort that would prove the difference. Barea was held to five points and committed an astounding nine turnovers, much to the delight of the Trask Coliseum students. In fact, the difference in the game could be attributed to one statistic: assist to turnover ratio. Barea had seven assists to go with the nine turnovers. UNCW senior point guard John Goldsberry matched Barea with seven assists but had just one turnover.

It was good enough for a first place tie with George Mason and set up an important game seven days later for the Seahawks. Their opponent then was George Mason, naturally.

As the calendar turned from January to February, it provided the opportunity to talk about the CAA on a national scale. On February 1, ESPN would be announcing the matchups for Bracket Buster Saturday.

Though Old Dominion had faltered, the Monarchs were still within striking distance of the coveted at-large bid. VCU, UNCW, and Hofstra were winning important games; and, of course, George Mason steamrolled along.

The question about the at-large berth and the difficulty of this conference race was both natural and increasingly frequent. To a man, the coaches all had different versions of the same answer: It's way too early to talk about this, but what we need to see is some separation. We need to have two or three teams get ahead of the pack.

Taylor knew this. "I've encouraged our crew not to look too much into things," he said in early February. "If you're going to accept that the race is going to be a dandy, then you have to accept that every team is going to take some lumps."

Taylor was on point: the five teams that could legitimately offer postseason hopes. It wasn't out of the realm of possibility that two could separate from that pack. Judging from Towson's victory over Hofstra, or VCU's struggle with Delaware, an upset wasn't only possible, it was probable.

While the conference race was meeting expectations, the teams were beating up each other, not neutral opponents. Fortuitously, the conference still had one proving ground. It had one place where it could make a mark and not worry about the defeat of another conference foe: ESPN's Bracket Busters.

Remember, the concept of the Bracket Busters was to provide mid-major schools the opportunity to play a similar opponent with the potential for a win to strengthen a team's "resume" and impress the NCAA Tournament Selection Committee.

The setup and payoff had been etched from its inception: a mid major gets the game it desperately wants. It may not be against Syracuse, Kentucky, or Kansas, but the opponent would be strong. RPI would be helped as teams were matched against each other in this one-game series.

It was important for the CAA as well. George Mason would be the ideal matchup. This was the matchup Yeager wanted. It was the chance to prove itself in the Valley.

The national media was coming around to the CAA. Andy Katz wrote the following on his ESPN.com blog in early February.

The Colonial Athletic Association is pretty confident this is the year that it can get that at-large bid—the first time in 20 years that the conference would get a second bid. Commissioner Tom Yeager said having a number of teams in the RPI top 50 (3) and six in the top 100 should carry weight. Yeager is talking about George Mason (32), UNC Wilmington (43) and Old Dominion (48) as possible candidates. Hofstra (63), VCU (65) and Northeastern (96) also are in the top 100.

It became doubly important for Tom Pecora. Though he had already scheduled a home game against Longwood for that Saturday—designed to be more of a tune-up than a battle—Pecora allowed himself to be persuaded to play in the event.

"Initially we weren't going to play in it," Pecora said. "We had a full schedule and the conference asked us to play in it. It's a good way to play a team with a significantly lower RPI."

Pecora already had a home game, so that carrot fell on deaf ears. It was the lure of a decent RPI team, as well as a chance to get his Pride on television that convinced him. Pecora also felt that this would be great exposure for the CAA in the north.

It had only been five years since the old America East teams had joined the CAA, and this was Northeastern's first season. Despite having teams in Boston, New York, and Philadelphia, the CAA was still viewed nationally as a southern-school conference. This would give Pecora some wonderful ammunition to bring to the fickle New York media who knew very little about the conference. It would be a chance to remove the stigma of a southern bias. With the data in hand, Pecora called Longwood and had the game postponed. He cleared February 18.

When the announcement of the teams that would comprise the Bracket Busters event was made—the thirteen games and twenty-six teams that would be on various ESPN television networks—the Hofstra Pride were nowhere on the board. Instead, George Mason would play a road game, televised nationally, while Old Dominion and VCU nabbed a home television game.

George Mason drew perhaps the most interesting team possible, Wichita State of the Missouri Valley. The Shockers carried an extremely similar resume to George Mason. Both teams were in the high twenties in RPI and both were considered a mid-major power. National pundits viewed the matchup as a potential "at-large elimination" game. The Patriots also drew a prime time television slot. The winner could stake a claim to at-large positioning. The Mason game was one of the three best in the format, along with Bucknell at Northern Iowa and Missouri State at Wisconsin-Milwaukee.

None of this pleased Pecora, and he wasn't shy in telling ESPN's Andy Katz about his displeasure. In an online column, Katz related his conversation with Pecora:

"It's like a February exhibition game," Pecora said of the importance of playing Siena on Feb. 18. "[Fellow CAA member] George Mason playing at Wichita State is a good game. So, too, is Bucknell at Northern Iowa. Those make sense. These other games don't."

The reason this occurs is the conferences make a number of teams available for the event and hold open a date. So, when they're not picked for one of the TV games, they still have to fill the schedule. That's what happened to countless teams like Hofstra and UC Irvine and Montana and many more."

For Pecora, it became just another February game, which he already had with Longwood.

Unfortunately, Pecora didn't have much time to sulk. He had to prepare his team for its most important game yet—a rematch against an Old Dominion team missing Isaiah Hunter, its catalyst and most explosive player.

Whether it was desperation, willpower, or just plain talent, ODU came out flying against the Pride. In front of a record student turnout, and the students were boisterous like college students can be, the Monarchs scored the first seven points of the game.

ODU looked like a different team than they had against George Mason, and Brandon Johnson looked different as well. He was up at every stoppage in play, urging his teammates on. He was slapping fives when they came off the court, and he cheered as loudly as any active player on the bench.

In college basketball, however, emotion can only get you so far. Hofstra was able to settle down, and started making shots. Loren Stokes flipped in another of his patented floaters and Hofstra led 27-16. The 27-9 run had whipped the crowd into a frenzy. Taylor was forced to switch to a zone defense to slow the Pride, and once again a Taylor adjustment worked. The Monarchs were able to close the gap to six, 34-28, by the half.

Trailing 62-54 with just over two minutes to play, ODU again awoke.

Alex Loughton and Arnaud Dahi quickly hit back-to-back threes. With 1:25 to play it was a 62-60 game, and the noise now was coming from the two hundred or so ODU fans that made the trek to Long Island.

On its ensuing possession, Hofstra ran down the shot clock and got a good look from Carlos Rivera that rolled out, but Adrian Uter grabbed the offensive rebound for Hofstra and zipped a pass to Antoine Agudio with twenty-four seconds. ODU was now forced to foul, and they hacked Agudio, a phenomenal dead-eye shooter but only marginal free throw shooter. Agudio promptly hit the back iron on the front end of the one-and-one and Dahi collected the rebound.

ODU called time to set up the final shot. The play that was called was exactly the same one that freed up Loughton a minute ago. The defending player of the year would take the final shot. However, Hofstra denied the pass with less than ten seconds to go, and Drew Williamson was forced to improvise.

In a play eerily similar to his buzzer-beating swish to defeat George Mason two months ago, Williamson swished a twenty-five footer to give ODU a 63-62 lead.

The only difference was the 5.4 seconds left on the clock; and in the words of Pecora, "We've practiced this situation and we can get the ball the length of the court and get a good shot in 3.5 seconds."

After a Hofstra time-out, the ball was inbounded to Stokes to the surprise of nobody. Stokes sprinted down court, dribbled behind his back, and flipped a pass to Aurimas Kieza. With no time to think but enough time to set his feet, Kieza faced the hoop and let fly. The ball hit the back of the rim hard and settled into the hoop. Hofstra had won 65-63, and as Williamson lay prone on the court, unable to believe what had just happened, Kieza was mobbed by teammates and students. Nobody worried about Kieza's healing nose. He had broken it a week ago and wore a protective mask—the one that had belonged to Stokes earlier in the year—in the first half, but discarded it because it was uncomfortable and fogged up.

Kieza was jubilant afterward, admitting he really didn't realize it had gone in until "I got tackled." Kieza also noted that it was the biggest shot he had hit in his career "so far."

Pecora, however, wasn't as lighthearted as one would imagine. "That's living life on the edge," he said. "I knew our poor free throw shooting was going to bite us. Not everybody brought their A game tonight. They manhandled us in the first half. Win or lose, I guess, you learn."

When it came time to discuss the final play, Pecora did, however, lighten up. "It was Loren making a play. I get a kick out of coaches who take credit for [these things]. I trust Loren to make a play whether it's a shot or pass."

When finally asked if he considered throwing the ball to half court and calling time to set up a play, a strategy embraced by many coaches, Pecora flatly and quickly said, "That's power basketball and that's not what we do."

Once the floor had cleared and the Hofstra Arena had emptied, it dawned on Jeremy Kniffin that there likely is not a rivalry in the country played closer than Old Dominion at Hofstra.

The Monarchs had traveled to Long Island five times to play at Hofstra Arena since the Pride joined the CAA and four of the games had come down to buzzer-beaters. Oddly, Hofstra had won three of those four games. The first three were all one-point games where the buzzer-beater missed (including Old Dominion's 67-66 win the previous season, Hofstra's last loss at home). The only ODU/Hofstra game at Hofstra Arena that did not get decided at the buzzer occurred in 2002-2003, when Hofstra won by the relatively huge margin of 69-65. It was even two foul shots with five seconds left that avoided the last-second heroics. The five all-time meetings at Hofstra Arena had been decided by a combined nine points.

More importantly to Pecora, the Pride moved to 15-4 on the season and stood a half-game out of first place.

———

While Hofstra was scraping by Old Dominion, the rest of the leaders—George Mason, UNCW, VCU, and Northeastern—were all winning as well, providing further separation for the top teams. The victories set up a Saturday that would feature two games that would determine seeding—VCU traveled to Boston to face Northeastern and UNCW would battle for first place at George Mason—and two walkover games. Old Dominion and Hofstra did their part, soundly beating William & Mary and Delaware.

For VCU, it meant a trip to the conference's newest member and northernmost outpost. The Rams would initially consider themselves lucky, as on this February day in Boston the temperatures hovered in the mid-forties and the sky was clear. One week later it would snow two feet.

Mathews Arena, home of the Northeastern Huskies, is quite different. VCU and ODU have state-of-the-art facilities. Hofstra has also built an on-campus facility. You get a distinct college feel visiting William & Mary's Alumni Hall or JMU's Convocation Center. Even Trask Coliseum, the venerable and stale home of the UNCW Seahawks, oozes basketball charm. Mathews is cold. The seats are uncomfortable. The basketball floor is plopped-on boards that cover the ice surface. You look into the rafters and the banners are not NCAA or NIT basketball memoriam. Women's ice hockey and the Beanpot hockey tournament dominate the ceiling.

Still, the building reeks of history. It is dubbed the "world's oldest hockey arena," and it served as the original home of the Boston Bruins, the Boston Celtics, and the Beanpot. The Arena has hosted Northeastern hockey since the program's inception for the 1929-1930 season. Groundbreaking for the arena: October 11, 1909.

Two fires, one in 1918 and another in 1948, were unable to destroy the building, and the arena has undergone numerous renovations, most recently new seats and new locker rooms for the men's and women's varsity hockey teams. Though the basketball team didn't call the arena its home until 1981, the Huskies first played a game there in 1936. Free public skating remains a staple.

The other staple of Northeastern basketball is the attacking style of its point guard, Jose Juan Barea. What makes Barea so dangerous is that he is always moving forward, pressuring the defense to do something. Anything. It doesn't matter what the offense and defense calls, because Barea is attacking the defense to make a decision and he reacts. Once the defense makes its move, Barea reacts. This is why Barea is much more valuable scoring twenty points and handing out ten assists than scoring thirty-four and dishing out four assists.

And so it went in the frigid Mathews Arena. Barea made breakneck dashes down the court and fed Bobby Kelly or dumped to Shawn James. The wiry James started the whole cycle by swatting away a shot or corralling a rebound. It was a precision game being played by Ron Everhart's team. VCU never stood a chance.

The modus operandi ended in Northeastern's 79-74 win. Barea had several nearly uncontested layups, but he also found a teammate wide open on the times the defense shifted over to cover him. Many times it was center Shawn James, who managed an unconventional triple double—twenty-six points, ten rebounds, and ten blocks.

"Barea was as good as we advertised," said VCU's Capel. "But Shawn James was much better than we expected. He was far better than he looks on tape."

While VCU was losing in the frigid Mathews Arena, George Mason was playing, again, for first place. It seemed every time George Mason stepped onto the court, they were playing in the conference's biggest game. This time, the Patriots were hosting UNCW, and the game represented the fourth time in the past month that Mason would take the court with its first-place standing on the line.

The Patriots had lost to the Seahawks two weeks ago 69-63, the only defeat against nine victories for George Mason since the calendar turned to 2006. The Seahawks had won five straight and eight of nine themselves, and both teams were 10-2 in conference play.

This meeting looked eerily familiar, right down to the very end. The 6,700 fans in the Patriot Center grew louder as the home team fought back from eight points down, 56-48, in a second half full of runs. The last big run was made by George Mason. Trailing by 59-56, Lamar Butler drove the baseline and hit a tough layup that ignited a 7-0 outburst. The Patriots held UNCW to just one field goal in the final 4:28. Free throws would spell the difference in the end, in the 69-62 Mason victory.

"Right now, what's important is that we continue to play well," said Larranaga. "There's a lot of good teams in the league and there's really no time to look back. You've got to look forward."

———

After protecting its first-place standing on three occasions, George Mason knew its work was not done—not even close. When asked about a potential at-large berth for his streaking Patriots, Larranaga cautioned, "It's way too early to start talking about that. We're still [only] two-thirds of the way through the conference season. This week is big for everybody. We're playing some very, very good teams on the road."

First up would be a date with Capel's VCU in Richmond. Though the Rams had fallen out of the race for the conference title, they were still one of the most talented teams in the conference.

Capel had spoken to his team: "We've talked a lot about what this week means," he said in reference to this game against George Mason and the following tilt against arch rival Old Dominion. Two wins and the Rams were back in the thick of things. As for the Patriots, Capel was brief: "We feel good about having them at home."

That's the way it began, too. Mason missed nine of its first ten shots and VCU jumped out to an 11-4 lead. The Patriots were in trouble, and the final play of the first half typified the afternoon.

With 1.5 seconds to play, Jai Lewis knocked the ball out of bounds underneath the George Mason basket. VCU would get a seemingly harmless possession to end the half. Instead of the requisite pitch to a guard and fruitless heave from three-quarters court, VCU's Jesse Pellot Rosa, a former all-state football player, sent a rocket toward the VCU basket.

Eric Davis collected the pass and calmly laid the ball through the hoop at the buzzer, giving VCU a 36-22 lead. More importantly, it gave VCU added momentum.

Larranaga had some ugly words for his troops at the break, and the

Patriots came out with renewed vigor on the defensive end. They harassed VCU into several difficult passes thirty feet from the basket on the first possession of the second half. The ball eventually landed in Nick George's hands, who then swished a three from the top of the key as the shot clock expired.

There was no reason to believe Mason stood a chance. VCU still held a seventeen-point lead with about fifteen minutes to play on a B.A. Walker layup when everything fell apart. The George Mason press forced two quick turnovers and the Patriots ran off seven points in forty seconds, forcing a Capel time-out.

Still, the Rams led by ten points and had the ball and the home crowd. Though it was understandable that they would get sloppy with a big lead, a Jeff Capel team is mentally tough. They may give back part of a huge lead, but not all of it. Nobody seemed overly concerned in the Siegel Center.

After the teams came back onto the court, it got worse for VCU. Folarin Cambell hit a three, and Lewis scored again from the block. It became a clinic: precise, devastating offense combined with hard-nosed defense. George Mason was imposing its will on VCU.

This just didn't happen to VCU at home, but it wasn't about VCU. The Patriots were in the middle of a special run in a special season. It was as if Larranaga gave the "now" command and the lights turned on. It was about George Mason. Will Thomas hit a layup with 6:32 to play, giving George Mason its first lead, 53-52. Tony Skinn followed with a bomb to cap an astounding 24-3 run.

Though VCU trailed by just four with four minutes to play, the game was over. George Mason had done the unthinkable: The Patriots had broken the spirit of their opponent, on their floor. The final tally was 73-61.

It was the kind of win, in the words of Capel, "that champions do." The fact that George Mason shot 74 percent in the second half backed up Capel's assertion.

Larranaga was just as factual in his assessment. "We're fortunate we didn't give up on ourselves. I haven't seen that 'oh, no' in their eyes in a long time." The response was the hammer on Capel's point. Champions respond to adversity in the manner in which George Mason had just done: They stepped on the gas pedal.

But alas, Larranaga knew the reality: "We've been playing good for a long time now."

———

The separation that all of the coaches had been saying was necessary for the CAA was taking place. After all, the separation was step one in the two-step process to overcome the one-bid stigma.

This is something the Missouri Valley Conference had done several years ago when its regular season champion began losing in the conference tournament. The MVC's at-large selection during the last five seasons was always the regular season champ. The conference was afforded the opportunity of having both its best team and its hottest team playing in the same NCAA Tournament. Thus, more upsets were possible.

That kind of success surely built the elevation of the MVC to media darling status. The conference would go into the Bracket Buster games with national writers talking about three, four, even five bids to the NCAA Tournament. This was important in that each team that makes the NCAA Tournament grosses its respective conference one credit, or $912,000, under the current system of NCAA basketball revenue distribution. A victory is another credit.

Still, money was a long way from the minds of the coaches and players. It would be a battle to the end as the conference season entered the home stretch. George Mason would have to travel to Hofstra and could not forget an important Bracket Busters trip to Wichita, Kansas, to face the Shockers of the MVC. UNCW would host Hofstra and travel to VCU. Hofstra, of course, faced the two games mentioned. ODU also would travel to VCU and then close with three of the bottom feeders, albeit all three on the road.

2005-2006 STANDINGS
(Through Games of February 11, 2006)

	Conference			Overall					
	W	L	Pct.	W	L	Pct.	H	A	N
George Mason	13	2	.867	19	5	.792	10-1	7-4	2-0
UNC Wilmington	12	3	.800	19	7	.731	10-1	7-6	2-0
Hofstra	11	3	.786	18	4	.818	10-0	7-4	1-0
VCU	10	5	.667	16	7	.696	11-1	5-6	0-0
Old Dominion	10	5	.667	17	8	.680	11-1	4-6	2-1
Northeastern	9	6	.600	13	10	.565	8-2	3-8	2-0
Drexel	7	8	.467	13	13	.500	9-3	4-7	0-3
Towson	6	9	.400	10	14	.417	6-5	4-8	0-1
William & Mary	3	11	.214	8	15	.348	5-5	3-10	0-0
Delaware	3	12	.200	7	17	.292	4-6	1-11	2-0
Georgia State	3	12	.200	6	17	.261	3-8	3-8	0-1
James Madison	2	13	.133	5	18	.217	3-10	1-8	1-0

CHAPTER TEN:

STRETCH

"Drive on. We'll sweep up the blood later!" –Katherine Hepburn

The stage had been set. The conference would have its annual ESPN2 game on a Saturday in February. It was at the tail end of what ESPN billed as rivalry week, and the game would feature the conference's biggest rivalry—Old Dominion at VCU.

What's more, the two teams always seem to bring out the best in each other—well-played, close, hard-fought games between two teams with a mutual respect. The Alltell Pavilion at the Siegel Center would be full, and rocking. It would pit the past two years' conference champions.

Indeed, everything was set. The only problem was that this encounter was a battle for fourth place. UNCW, Hofstra, and George Mason were all, technically, having much better seasons. Unfortunately, you schedule television games far more than four days in advance.

The thing going for the CAA was its two teams that could get a television story's argument for an at-large bid, something the CAA was back in contention for. Remember, in December Dick Vitale wondered aloud how Drexel could be the seventh best team in the conference, and that was exactly their place. For two hours the story would be about two good teams and the depth of the CAA. It was also VCU and ODU, longtime rivals that are annually in the top three or four in attendance. This matchup is always a sellout.

Steve Gordon, who would be lead official for the game, said beforehand that he arrived at 3:45 for the 6:08 tip-off and students were lined up around the building and down Harrison Street. The buzz was there: painted faces, spontaneous cheers, smack talking among fans, and lots of smiles. This action was outside the arena.

It was also Homecoming for VCU, an odd appellation for a school that does not play football. In fact, "Not Football" was the theme of the week. As if on cue, the Alltell Pavilion would break a record with 7,838, a number that would get the attention and interest of fire marshals.

Inside, the scene and the temperature was hot. The ESPN announcers sat at half court in front of the bright lights as fans milled about, trying to get themselves some background face time. Signs written in homage to the worldwide leader in sports waved randomly. The crowd was a din and a fever pitch.

Brandon Johnson wore no sling and found himself sitting right next to Taylor, wearing a shirt and tie. It was very different than the Drexel game two weeks ago.

The jump ball to start the game was very mid major: 6-foot, 7-inch Arnaud Dahi jumped for ODU against 6-foot, 8-inch Sam Faulk.

As every opponent would try first against VCU, ODU pushed the ball inside for an Alex Loughton layup. The show was clearly back on for the CAA, and Isaiah Hunter. It appeared Hunter spent as much time adjusting his shorts and talking smack on the offensive end as he did running the plays.

It burned ODU when VCU's Michael Anderson, a pure athlete, blocked the dunk attempt of Arnaud Dahi. VCU quickly transitioned and Jamal Shuler, Hunter's man, drained a three pointer that gave VCU a 22-11 lead.

The half ended with VCU holding a 38-32 lead. Most notable was VCU's Jesse Pellot Rosa, who had already hit his career high with seventeen points. VCU was holding its own on the boards and shooting 52 percent. When the ball went to Pellot Rosa on the first possession of the second half, the defense collapsed and Pellot Rosa hit Sam Faulk in stride for a VCU layup.

Sometimes the adage "truth is stranger than fiction" applies. After Nick George drained a three to build VCU's lead to 50-37, Taylor called a time-out. Larranaga had done the same thing at nearly the identical spot in the game, right down to the momentum of the home team and the time on the clock. While VCU did not wilt, another adage held true: In college basketball, everybody makes a run.

Controversy seems to follow Steve Gordon and VCU. With 6:50 to play and VCU holding on to a 60-57 lead, Alexander Harper drove the lane and ran into ODU freshman Jonathan Adams. Manny Upton, five feet from the play, signaled a block on Adams. However Gordon, from a full twenty-five feet, signaled charge, and there was no more discussion. The teams headed to the other end of the floor, and Capel, despite his best arm-flailing attempts, could do nothing about it.

"That's bad," he repeated, at least eight times in some form, to anybody that would listen. More importantly, it was Harper's fourth foul. Loughton followed with a short hook that scored on an Anderson goal tend to slice the lead to one.

Thanks to a tremendous hustle play by Pellot Rosa, VCU maintained possession after a miss, and VCU freshman Eric Maynor hit a floater as the lead was restored.

Though VCU would hit its free throws down the stretch and win 80-74, the first question Capel would face would be the "repeat of Thursday" point in the game, referring to the second half collapse against George Mason. VCU had led ODU by thirteen in the second half and allowed the Monarchs back into the game.

"There were no visions of Thursday," Capel said. "I got an email from Dr. Trani on Friday [Dr. Eugene Trani is VCUs president] that said, 'Tomorrow is another day.'"

Capel continued: "Sometimes you have to fail—big—to get better."

Jesse Pellot Rosa had led the way.

"I was in my office [Thursday night after the George Mason game],"
Capel said in a voice that was of respect. "We were watching tape and
I looked down and Jesse was shooting, still in his uniform. (His good
game tonight) is not a coincidence."

For Pecora, his game against Northeastern was the beginning of a
critical stretch for the Pride. They needed to maintain pace with the
top of the league, and they needed the victory for tiebreaker purpos-
es. The Huskies had defeated the Pride on January 21, and the sweep
gave Northeastern the advantage.

Hofstra did just that, winning its sixth in a row and bringing its
record on the season to 18-4 overall and 11-3 in the CAA.

Hofstra guard Carlos Rivera retook bragging rights with
Northeastern's sensational senior guard Jose Juan Barea. Rivera and
Barea have known each other since they were five years old and
played for one season together at Miami Christian High School in
2001-2002, when the team went 38-2 and set a Florida state record for
victories in a season.

Hofstra prepared itself for a Wednesday trip to the beach to play
UNCW in a battle for second place in the CAA.

"I put the standings up on board in the locker room," said Tom
Pecora, "and they understand the importance of it. Our goal is to win
the league. If we're tied with Mason and beat them at our place we get
the tiebreaker."

Before Hofstra could worry about its February 23 potential tiebreaker matchup with George Mason, the Pride would have to contend
with a trip to UNCW to face the Seahawks in an actual battle for second place.

It was a game Brad Brownell would call "like a tournament atmosphere...bodies were flying all over the place." One of those bodies was
Carlos Rivera. The Hofstra junior injured his ankle five minutes into
the game and never returned. Hofstra also played six minutes of the
second half without senior forward Aurimas Kieza, who needed five

stitches to close a cut over his eye after he butted heads with teammate Loren Stokes.

The defenses would rule the day. Hofstra held the Seahawks without a field goal for the first 5:45 of the game, but led only 4-1. UNCW used Rivera's absence to turn its defense up another notch, finding its stride to take a 30-16 lead, settling for a 33-25 halftime advantage behind T.J. Carter.

The Seahawks would hang on to the margin most of the second half, as every Hofstra run was met by a UNCW answer. The 77-68 final score belied the defensive effort that was given on both sides. It was UNCW's twentieth victory on the season, an important number in the eyes of the NCAA Tournament Selection Committee. The Seahawks also ran their conference record to 13-3, garnering sole possession of second place, one game behind first place George Mason (14-2). The Seahawks also improved to 5-0 all time against Hofstra in Wilmington. Senior guard John Goldsberry had fifteen points, six rebounds, and seven steals to once again fill the stat sheet for UNCW.

The loss was particularly damaging for Hofstra, a team that needed every big win it could muster. Not only did the Pride miss an opportunity to impress the NCAA selection committee with a top-fifty RPI win, it also slipped closer to a dreaded fifth seed and the Friday game in the CAA Tournament.

Larranaga couldn't complain. If there was anything he could count on this season, it was that his team was giving consistent effort and playing well. It was primarily due to the leadership of his three all-conference seniors, Tony Skinn, Lamar Butler, and Jai Lewis.

Despite winning, Butler had been, in the eyes of many of the Patriots faithful, slumping. Larranaga was not concerned.

"Lamar Butler's problem is that he's too coachable. He listens to me too much," said Larranaga before his team's game against Drexel. "His assists are up and his turnovers are down. I had a conversation with him yesterday and I expect Lamar Butler will be Lamar Butler the rest of the season. I told him 'you're the leading three-point shooter in school history (and you've won more games than anyone at George Mason). Be sure you to continue to play like Lamar Butler.'"

Larranaga's real problem was beginning to look like the loss of Tony Skinn for their huge Bracket Busters game against Wichita State. After beating Towson 65-53 in a very workmanlike manner, George Mason would face the always tough and always combative Drexel Dragons. The Patriots were well on their way to a 67-48 victory, when on a rebound play Skinn got tied up with Drexel's Bashir Mason. According to the *Washington Post:*

> *Emotions flared late in the game when a scuffle broke out on the court involving Drexel's Bashir Mason and Kenell Sanchez and George Mason's Tony Skinn. The game was delayed for approximately 10 minutes as officials met to discuss the penalties. After the officials reviewed the videotape several times, Sanchez and Skinn received technical fouls and were ejected from the game with 5 minutes 43 seconds to play. Because of the ejection, Skinn may not be allowed to play on Saturday at Wichita State. School officials expect to learn his status today.*

In reviewing the game tape, the original call, before the officials went to the monitor, was simply an over-the-back foul on Skinn. The officials properly separated the players and then met at half court to inform the coaches.

Drexel's Flint, however, saw Skinn flail his leg at Sanchez in the skirmish, a point he loudly made, berating the crew to review the play. If Skinn were to have kicked, he would've been tossed from the game and forced, under CAA rules, to miss the next George Mason game. This was also where the controversy and mistake came into play.

After the officials went to the video, they chose to assess both Sanchez and Skinn dead ball flagrant technical fouls. By rule, however, officials cannot use video replay to make this kind of call. The officiating team of Curtis Blair, Michael Stephens, and Mike Eades spent about ten minutes reviewing video of the mini-fracas, and in an attempt to get the call right, got it wrong. Oddly, if they had stuck with their original call, the correct call, there would be no controversy.

With that in mind, the conference made its ruling early the following day in this press release:

RICHMOND, Va. (February 16, 2006) - CAA Commissioner Tom Yeager determined today that George Mason University's Tony Skinn and Drexel University's Kenell Sanchez, both ejected from Wednesday night's men's basketball game for receiving dead ball flagrant technical fouls, will not be subject to the CAA's Sportsmanship Rule violation and the accompanying minimum one-game suspension due to misapplication of specific playing rules by the game officials.

Yeager concluded that because of the misapplication of specific video replay rules, the penalties and accompanying ejections should not have been assessed. Both Skinn and Sanchez will be eligible to participate in their respective school's next scheduled contest.

The officials have been notified of these findings and any follow-up with the officials will be handled as per CAA policies and procedures.

The show would play on, with George Mason leading the way.

While the top teams in the CAA were busily brutalizing each other, and the separation that needed to occur to provide the appropriate regular season finish for a potential at-large berth was occurring, the Missouri Valley Conference continued to receive high honors from the national media.

There would be a three-page color spread in *Sports Illustrated* that would come out the week of Bracket Busters. Just as readers would have time to sit down and flip through their magazines, the MVC would be tipping off several high-profile games on ESPN. The CAA would not be without its love, garnering a column and a half in the same issue in the magazine's "College Basketball Roundup" section.

But the placement and treatment was noticeable.

Larranaga openly spoke of the old Rodney Dangerfield motto of getting no respect. He meant it for the entire league, not his George Mason team. There would be a huge chance to change the tide. On Saturday, February 18, at 8:00 p.m., his Patriots would go against the MVC leader in their soldout and frenzied building. ESPN2 would televise the game.

Though nobody would admit it outwardly, everybody knew. Outside of a tournament game, this was likely the biggest game the CAA would play out of conference in fifteen years. It was likely an "at-large elimination" game for the Patriots, and for the league. It would serve as the biggest win for the conference, RPI-wise, and it would come at the perfect time of year.

A month prior, Larranaga, in his predictably understated but straightforward manner, had said that he liked the Bracket Busters setup, only because his team was winning and getting national attention. "The nice thing," he said, "is that whoever we play is going to be good."

Wichita State qualified as good. The Shockers had just slipped past Creighton—the same Creighton team that had waxed George Mason, in Fairfax, by a 72-52 score on November 22—in overtime on a three-pointer by Matt Braeuer with .5 remaining to take first place in the rugged MVC. Five teams, very similar to the CAA, were battling for first place.

The Shockers also carried with it history, something older Wichita State fans cheered lustily to recapture. The 1980-1981 team won twenty-six games and advanced to the final eight. During the four-year span from 1980-1984, Wichita State produced a 92-29 record. Perhaps its best-known alum is Xavier McDaniel.

So it was no surprise that Wichita State's "Roundhouse" was jammed full of 10,500 yellow-clad, screaming Shockers fans.

Shortly after 8:00 p.m. local time, and two hours after Old Dominion had secured the CAA's second Bracket Buster win in two games, Will Thomas lined up to jump center for George Mason in

Wichita. Tom Yeager was on hand, and though he carried the cool demeanor of a man enjoying his surroundings, his insides were flipping like when you ring the doorbell on a first date.

His luggage had not arrived from San Antonio, where he had been attending NCAA meetings. He was forced to buy a tie from his hotel gift shop, and it had not yet become the magic tie that helped carry George Mason to the Final Four. It was a rather dubious beginning to an important evening.

If dating is truly the apt metaphor, then Yeager spent the entire evening with sweaty palms, wondering if a grand evening would go horribly wrong in an instant.

There was little reason to think differently. The Roundhouse is loud. The fans are close to the court. They were nearly all wearing gold. It was television in the midwestern outpost of Wichita, Kansas. Because of this, there are no NBA teams, NFL teams, or MLB teams to distract fans. Wichita is a college basketball town and this was a college basketball night.

George Mason surged early, taking a five-point lead, but Wichita State fought back. It was a 22-20 Shockers lead when Tony Skinn hit a three and the Patriots closed the half on a 13-7 run to take a 34-29 lead into the locker room.

The second half was much of the same, though Mason led the whole way. The Patriots would build an advantage, only to see Wichita State rally to cut the deficit. It seemed every time the home team would make a couple of defensive stops and get the game close, Tony Skinn or Folarin Campbell would hit a three to stem the tide and quiet the boisterous crowd.

George Mason rebuilt its lead to thirteen points, 57-44, with 8:49 to play and appeared poised to put the game away; however, Wichita State wouldn't wilt. The lead stood at six with 3:53 to play when Jai Lewis, the George Mason center who is listed at 6 feet, 7 inches, 275 pounds, but is closer to 300 pounds, drained what appeared to be a heartbreaking three pointer. Lewis came into the game having made just five bonus shots in twenty attempts. On this night, Lewis was two for two.

The Shockers pressed on though and rallied yet again, pulling to within three on a three pointer from Karon Bradley at the 2:00 mark. After two fruitless possessions for Mason, Sean Ogirri swished another three from the right corner and the game was tied at 67-67 with 28.7 seconds on the clock.

They say that it takes seniors to win ballgames; big games. Coaches will tell you that they "get it." So it wasn't a surprise that George Mason ran down the clock to fifteen seconds and pitched the ball into the paint to Lewis. The senior center drew a double team and kicked the ball on the right wing to senior Tony Skinn.

With twelve seconds to play, on the road, and in a tie game, most players would opt to pass on a long shot attempt to dribble back to the top of the key to ensure his team got the absolute final shot. It seemed even the Wichita State crowd, very knowledgeable fans, knew this and expected it. Many glanced up at the clock to see if their team had time for a steal of an entry pass. Home fans are like that.

Not Tony Skinn. The senior from Takoma Park, Maryland, realized he was wide open and fired. The ball was in the air before the moment sank in to the fans. He shot the ball! The gasp came late but it was there. The building fell silent for the most split of split seconds.

It was the kind of shot you get from a senior: Skinn had set his feet and never hesitated. For Tony Skinn, it wasn't about what was expected. He saw an opportunity and capitalized. He lifted comfortably and confidently. Swish. George Mason 70, Wichita State 67.

Dagger.

The Shockers had used their time-outs to rest and stave off George Mason runs, so they had to inbound and shoot without a diagrammed play.

All Wichita could manage in that frenetic final ten seconds was a desperation, fall away three from P.J. Couisnard as the clock ran out. Wichita State Coach Mark Turgeon told the media afterwards that he would have preferred the ball in Ogirri's hands. Ogirri indeed had the ball near the top of the key, but chose to pass to Couisnard with time running short.

Couisnard and Ogirri are both sophomores.

The elated Patriots players sprinted across the Koch Center floor, where the home team had just lost for only the second time this season. They hugged each other, mobbed each other, and celebrated among the shuffling fans and opposing players. There weren't tears of heartbreak: The Wichita State players knew this wasn't the end of their season; rather a huge missed opportunity. Likewise for Tony Skinn and the Patriots. They bounced and smiled and danced to the locker room.

They knew, immediately, the significance of their achievement. "All we want is a chance," is the refrain. They had gotten theirs and proved something.

Larranaga didn't even need the stat sheet to tell him the difference of this game. It was his team's defense. It was something he had preached since the end of last season. The players on his team didn't need to see that the opponent had shot 41 percent to their 52 percent. They knew, too, what had won them this game. The seniors especially knew.

Now, so did the Shockers. "Our defense just wasn't good enough," said Turgeon. Ogirri concurred: "They just scrambled all around a lot," he said. "You would dribble the ball and they would come at you. You would feel rushed—a lot of chaos."

Far to the north, in East Lansing, Michigan, the Michigan State Spartans were beating up the Michigan Wolverines. Nobody would know the importance and irony of that game for another three weeks.

It would be a much-savored victory for the Patriots. An odd, yet significant moment occurred next. As Larranaga walked into the locker room after the game, his jubilant George Mason players, all of them, were chanting "C-A-A, C-A-A, C-A-A."

Tom Yeager smiled approvingly as he left the Koch Center, wiping the sweat from his palms before every handshake.

———

Hours prior to tip-off, Pecora had prepared his team as best as he could. This wasn't the game he had wanted—it wasn't on television, and his team was beaten up. The toll of all the minutes his starters were forced to play showed up not in their effort—the Pride played as spirited and with as much energy as ever—but manifested itself in a steady torrent of nagging injuries.

Loren Stokes had fought through an injured foot, knee, ankle, thumb, nose, and eye. Carlos Rivera had twisted a knee and an ankle. If it wasn't those players, Adrian Uter battled on a bum ankle or Aurimas Kieza was getting smacked in the nose or the eye (by Stokes, no less).

So Pecora openly wondered if he shouldn't rest his horses for the CAA Tournament. The Siena game offered him no upside. Hofstra was at the far end of the NCAA Tournament at-large bubble, yet the Pride had played well enough that an NIT home game would not be destroyed by losing this Bracket Busters game against Siena. Plus, Pecora wanted a healthy and full squad for the CAA Tournament.

Kieza, Uter, and Stokes talked him out of the idea. The three—two seniors and the team's best player—wanted to protect Hofstra's seventeen-game home winning streak, third in the country. Plus, kids always want to play. Period. Pecora should have known better. He wasn't going to win that discussion even though he was the coach.

With Adrian Uter playing the best game of his career, Hofstra shook off a sluggish start and a four-point halftime deficit to drill Siena 76-62. Uter scored twenty-seven points and blocked four shots. After missing his first shot attempt, Uter hit on his next twelve.

Perhaps the game's most exciting moment came in the first half when Siena Coach Fran McCaffery was tossed from the game after picking up two technical fouls arguing a call with the officials. After McCaffery retreated to the locker room, however, his wife Margaret, pregnant and toting two children, appeared and also began to berate the officials. In an instant she, too, was thrown out of the game.

Pecora, though, had to privately worry if his starters—four of them played thirty-four or more minutes—were going to wear down. Only Rivera, still hobbled with the ankle injury and foul trouble and playing just fifteen minutes, was able to rest. He had a 400-mile bus ride to

Williamsburg and a game against William & Mary in forty-eight hours to worry about.

Old Dominion had its own issues. The Monarchs had won three of its last four games, but the wins were by eighteen, nineteen, and twenty-one points against lower tier teams—James Madison, William & Mary, and Georgia State. Its loss was the setback at VCU.

Taylor also had to face the distraction of junior Janko Mrksic. The reserve center from Canada decided to leave the team at the end of the year to use his last year of eligibility at a lesser division school. It was strictly a playing time issue. The burly center had played in only eleven games, totaling twenty-nine minutes. Mrksic, a fan favorite, had scored four points and grabbed four rebounds all season.

Marist came into the Ted Constant Center a dangerous team. They played smart and featured the national assist leader in Jared Jordan. Marist also had bulky James Smith clogging up the middle. They were just the kind of team that could give ODU fits.

ODU would trounce Marist 84-71 in front of a soldout crowd, pulling away quickly in the second half and cruising home. It was senior day for Alex Loughton and Isaiah Hunter, and emotions ran high.

The last home game and national television audience, though, were not the big story. When the horn sounded to usher the players back onto the court with 5:27 left in the first half and the score knotted at 30-30, Valdus Vasylius and Abdi Lidonde were joined by none other than Brandon Johnson.

"On Friday at practice, my trainer said let's edge him into a few drills and see how he takes to contact because he was healing faster than we thought," said Taylor afterward. "Doggone if he didn't go through the whole practice. The trainer was in a coma trying to figure out how he did it. But for him to be back out there playing buoyed the spirits of our student body and our school and our team and everybody in the league."

Capel has his VCU team say a short prayer before each game. Since being shot, Brandon Johnson was always a part of that prayer.

Johnson would play harassing defense for the eight minutes he was on the floor. He didn't score (nor attempt a shot) but that wasn't the point. Three weeks and three days after being shot while coming out of his dorm room, Brandon Johnson was back on the playing floor.

———

The very next day, when the analysis of the 2006 ESPN Bracket Busters would be completed, the tide began to turn.

George Mason found itself ranked in the *USA Today* and AP polls. They were the first Colonial Athletic Association team to be ranked nationally since Navy, with a guy named David Robinson, was ranked eighteenth in the AP poll on January 20, 1987.

The CAA had gone 6-2 over the weekend in the Bracket Busters event, importantly with its best six teams posting the wins. The CAA won all three games that were televised—George Mason, VCU, and ODU. It had two teams with twenty wins, and Hofstra stood with nineteen and ODU eighteen. The conference, for the first time since the 1988-1989 season, would have four teams with twenty wins or more.

The MVC had gone just 5-5, and national writers and broadcasters were taking note. The *USA Today* ran a story touting the success of the CAA and the struggle of the MVC.

Mike DeCourcy of *The Sporting News,* one of the nation's leading and most respected columnists, wrote on February 21:

The best league in college basketball is not the Big East or the Big Ten. Those are the strongest leagues, but the league worth every dime it is charging for its conference tournament is the Colonial Athletic Association, which has six teams with double-digit victories and a team as strong as Drexel, which made a good accounting of itself against Duke and UCLA in the NIT Season Tip-Off, at two games under .500.

The king of this league is George Mason, which might have turned the CAA into a two-bid league by visiting Wichita State in the Bracket Busters event and left with a 70-67 victory. GMU has won 14 of its past 15 games. It is going to the show.

Suddenly, the planets were aligning for Tom Yeager. Winning big games on the road in February has a way of helping that occur.

———

Three minutes into the William & Mary game, Pecora screamed at Carlos Rivera: "Hey, what's your problem!" Rivera had just picked up his second foul on a ticky-tack reach in, and it was his sloppy turnover that created the foul.

As much as he tried to make it a tough game, Pecora could see how this was going to go. His team shot 74 percent in the first half, and it wasn't due to a rash of layups and dunks. Adrian Uter had made all six of his field goals, giving him eighteen consecutive field goals made, a school record.

Pecora's team was overpowering the Tribe. His only concern in the second half was having his team build on its low-teens lead instead of allowing it to shrink below ten. He could then rest his starters.

The Pride turned up the heat and blew out William & Mary, 82-57. It was Hofstra's twentieth win of the season.

Everything was going in the right direction for the conference. Its top teams were winning. It was getting the national press it craved. Some even had three CAA teams in the Big Dance.

On Thursday, February 23, George Mason would travel to Hofstra to play the Pride in a game that had more implications than players. UNCW would drive down I-40 and up I-95 to its closest geographical rival, VCU. The Rams rarely lose in the Siegel Center and had rallied from eighteen down to the Seahawks with less than six minutes to play to defeat UNCW in the previous season. It was senior day then, and it was senior night again.

———

Tom Yeager had already acknowledged the importance of the events unfolding in front of him. "We're coming up on the twentieth anniversary of the last time we got an at-large berth," he had told reporters. "We'd like to put that in the closet."

Yeager was also well aware of the odd statistic that the CAA's #1 seed had won the conference tournament in every season since 2000. With George Mason having already seemingly won its way into the NCAA Tournament via its big victory over Wichita State, the Patriots were clearly the league's best team.

UNCW and Hofstra were fast on their heels, however. The Seahawks had flown under the radar all season long. A horrid couple of games after the Christmas break had relegated the team to undiscussed status, but UNCW had strung together eleven wins since the first of the year. Their only losses were at ODU, at Hofstra, and at George Mason.

All Hofstra had done was go 16-3 since its brutal defeat at VCU, losing at Towson, at Northeastern, and at UNCW.

Clearly these were two teams playing their best when it mattered.

With this in mind, even if Yeager would not admit to cheering for any one team; it would be understandable if he had a 51 percent rooting interest in Hofstra holding serve at home, and UNCW stealing a road victory at VCU. After all, both victories would enhance the conference's ability to get more than one team into the NCAAs.

As it stood in late February, even though George Mason had seemingly locked up its NCAA bid, if the Patriots won the conference tournament there was a better than average chance the CAA would fall victim to the same fate: its best team and #1 seed winning the conference tournament.

In a game that would be the first in the nation in the 2005-2006 season to feature two teams with twenty or more victories, Hofstra took control of George Mason early in front of a packed house at the Hofstra University Arena. The Pride's students had come out in full force and made noise with every Hofstra basket. Hofstra was hosting a ranked team for the first time in school history, putting its eighteen-game home court winning streak to the ultimate test. The fact that it was also a conference game escaped nobody.

Hofstra used a 14-2 run to take a 33-24 lead with 5:24 left in the opening half. The Pride led by eight at the break, 41-33, and matched its largest lead of the game at 53-42 on a layup from sophomore guard Antoine Agudio with 13:35 to play.

George Mason, though, answered the challenge and cut the lead to three at 61-58 when Mason sophomore guard Folarin Campbell hit a three pointer with 7:37 to go. A Campbell layup with 4:13 to go again brought the Patriots within three at 65-62, but Agudio made a tough double-clutch jumper in the lane and then threw an alley-oop to Kieza on the next possession to give the Pride a 69-62 lead with 2:33 to go. The final was 77-66.

Loren Stokes's twenty-six points led Hofstra. He was making it known why he should be voted conference player of the year. Stokes averaged 22.4 points on 51.6 percent shooting against the top five teams in the CAA. He had at least one twenty-five-plus scoring night against each of the other top five teams in the league—big players playing big in big games.

George Mason was led by senior center Jai Lewis, who had twenty-three points on eight of twelve shooting from the floor. Senior guard Lamar Butler added fourteen points, while senior guard Tony Skinn had eight points to reach the 1,000-point plateau in his career.

The win was the Pride's ninth in its past ten games, the kind of strong finish that catches the eyes of the selection committee. So does a win over a ranked opponent. The Pride also essentially clinched the third seed in the CAA, which gave them a by in the CAA Tournament. Hofstra also extended its home court winning streak to nineteen games, tying it with Duke for the second longest in the nation behind Gonzaga (thirty-six). The win was the Pride's first ever against a nationally ranked team in its thirty-three-year history at the Division I level.

However ironic it proved, the CAA's ranked team (George Mason) had lost and it was good for the conference. Its second-best team (Hofstra) had benefited.

There was a lot to celebrate on that evening, but it would be short-lived. Because of the Thursday/Saturday scheduling, Hofstra had Bruiser Flint's Drexel Dragons coming to town less than forty-eight hours later.

While Hofstra was putting the clamps on George Mason, UNCW was struggling in Richmond. The Seahawks trailed 42-29 in the second half and were being outplayed. At some point during the VCU game, word that George Mason had lost at Hofstra filtered its way to Brad Brownell. While he didn't use it as a direct motivator for his team, he knew that if his kids knew they were playing for first place, it could be the spark they needed to overcome a tough road environment.

It worked. UNCW rallied for the 61-54 road victory and the Seahawks had tied George Mason with a 14-3 conference record. Tiebreakers showed the conference's official leader was the little school located at Wrightsville Beach.

For Capel, the loss was especially difficult. VCU had given away a third second-half, double-digit lead and lost. Capel awoke the next morning and faced, for the first time in his tenure as coach, serious questions about his team. "Crash and Burn" was the headline in the following day's *Richmond Times-Dispatch*.

After his team followed its big win over ODU with a listless loss at Towson, Capel had asked VCU SID Phil Stanton for a minute to calm down before he faced the media. Capel knew that even though his team had won a few games in breathtaking fashion, they had escaped. There was no escape in Towson. Capel's emotions were due more to knowing how he had been feeling about the team.

Capel was beyond angry at his team. He had clearly moved into bewilderment as he searched for an answer to his squad's inconsistency. "Our guys don't know how to handle success. You would think we would enjoy that feeling [the win over Old Dominion]," he said. "It's amazing to me we didn't come out here with more energy. It's on me to figure it out."

Regarding the inconsistency, Capel was more to the point: "That's not the way I want my program run. I'm disappointed in myself [for allowing the inconsistency]. I pride myself in running a program that gets better [through the season] and hits its stride in February," Capel said after practice. "[The emotions] are a culmination of a lot of things. Maybe I internalize things too much. I wish I could be a coach that doesn't care what people think. I feel the letdown part when we don't play well. I want us to have a good product on and off the floor."

Capel would call it easily his most frustrating year since he became the head man, and none more so, likely, than his talented big man Renardo Dixon. Over the previous summer, Dixon had attracted NBA scouts to his workouts. The Marshall transfer was as athletically gifted as any player in the country. His 6-foot, 8-inch wiry frame allowed Dixon to get up and down the court with grace and ease, and he could both rebound and shoot from outside.

Unfortunately, Dixon was prone to concentration lapses and also would fall back on strict athletic ability instead of hard work. These were two areas that Capel demanded his players have. Even though it was Dixon who tipped in the winning basket against Houston in November, his minutes waned as the season progressed. Frustration grew on the part of both the player and the coach. So after healing from a minor knee injury, without word, Dixon simply vanished from the VCU bench.

———

As important and weighty as the regular season's final Thursday proved—Old Dominion had also won handily at James Madison and Northeastern had done the same hosting Towson—the final Saturday proved incredibly anticlimactic.

The top six teams in the conference—UNCW, George Mason, Hofstra, Old Dominion, Northeastern, and VCU—all played and defeated the bottom six teams in the conference.

Hofstra held on to defeat the Drexel team 70-68, but it was an ankle injury to Loren Stokes that grabbed the headlines. Stokes would say that he heard a pop, and early tests revealed the ubiquitous "some ligament damage." However, the extent wouldn't be known for days, and Stokes would rest in the week leading up to the CAA Tournament. Hofstra was fortunate to receive the best of all possible draws in terms of rest. As the third seed, the Pride would not play until Saturday night at 8:30. Stokes, and the rest of the starting five, would have a full week to heal, rest, and prepare.

The games closed a regular season that worked exactly in the manner in which Tom Yeager and Ron Bertovich would've drawn up. The top six teams in the conference didn't lose a single game against the bottom four teams. The top teams were also able to separate from the middle teams.

Four teams had won twenty-one or more games, and two others—VCU and Northeastern—could do so as well with a successful postseason. George Mason had established itself as an at-large team, yet it technically finished second. Three teams—George Mason, UNCW, and Hofstra—had legitimate at-large hopes.

Perhaps most importantly, any of the top six teams could make a legitimate argument that they could win in Richmond.

And although the usual nervous preparation existed for the CAA Tournament, there were added stressors for Larranaga, Pecora, and Taylor. It wasn't about winning it all this time. Who you beat and when you lost were significant data points.

The country would be watching.

2005-2006 STANDINGS

(Through Regular Season)

	Conference			Overall					
	W	L	Pct.	W	L	Pct.	H	A	N
UNC Wilmington	15	3	.833	22	7	.759	12-1	8-6	2-0
George Mason	15	3	.833	22	6	.786	13-1	7-5	2-0
Hofstra	14	4	.778	22	5	.815	13-0	8-5	1-0
Old Dominion	13	5	.722	21	8	.724	13-1	6-6	2-1
Northeastern	12	6	.667	17	10	.630	10-2	5-8	2-0
VCU	11	7	.611	18	9	.667	12-2	6-7	0-0
Towson	8	10	.444	12	15	.444	7-6	5-8	0-1
Drexel	8	10	.444	15	15	.500	11-3	4-9	0-3
Delaware	4	14	.222	8	20	.286	4-8	2-12	2-0
Georgia State	3	15	.167	6	21	.222	3-9	3-11	0-1
William & Mary	3	15	.167	8	19	.296	5-8	3-11	0-0
James Madison	2	16	.111	5	22	.185	3-11	1-11	1-0

CHAPTER ELEVEN:

INTERLUDE

"There comes a pause, for human strength/Will not endure to dance without cessation." –Lewis Carroll

I t became very clear after Hofstra's defeat of George Mason that the planets were indeed aligning for Tom Yeager and the Colonial Athletic Association. Not only had the top teams beaten the bottom teams, but every time two of the top teams played each other, the team the conference needed to win—for the good of the conference—would step up and win.

It had happened with UNCW and VCU in November. It happened when Old Dominion beat both DePaul and Virginia Tech in December. It happened throughout the conference season with George Mason going 15-1 in January and February, culminating in its big win over Wichita State (the lone loss: at UNCW); and it happened when Hofstra knocked off the ranked George Mason Patriots.

The CAA was acting very un-CAA. It had largely avoided the bad loss and featured a handful of somewhat marquee victories. What it lacked in sex appeal it made up for in tenacity. Its best teams were winning, and winning big and often, late in what many were calling, without hesitation or a wink, the greatest season in the history of the conference.

As the calendar turned to March and signaled the official beginning of March Madness, the conference was receiving unprecedented acclaim by the national media. Joe Lunardi of ESPN, the best-known "Bracketologist," had George Mason in the tournament and an eight seed. UNCW was also in with a nine seed. Hofstra was among the "Last Four Out."

Gregg Doyel of CBS Sportsline had George Mason a ten seed and both UNCW and Hofstra in at twelve.

Fox Sports, SI.com, and RPI guru Jerry Palm all had Mason a seven seed. Palm and Fox had UNCW at twelve and SI.com had the Seahawks at eleven. Palm had Hofstra at twelve.

No matter who would eventually be proven right or wrong come Selection Sunday, there was one consistent theme: There was a very good chance of at least a "2" appearing next to the number of CAA bids to the NCAA Tournament. It had been a banner season.

"Drexel set the tone early," said CAA Commissioner Tom Yeager. "Who knows what the final exam will say but now I think I'd be disappointed with two [bids]. It's what we've strived to do for years. You really feel good for the coaches and players."

As the teams gassed up the buses for Richmond, the common theme was that the conference was not only strong, but also stronger than even they had anticipated. To be sure, the fact that the CAA had a team ranked in the top twenty-five was not a shock.

What was somewhat surprising was that Hofstra and UNCW were also listed in the polls in their summary "Also Receiving Votes" category. Interestingly, the team everyone had pinned their hopes on in November, Old Dominion, was not there despite winning twenty games. That fact alone spoke to the depth of the league.

"Our top four teams deserve very serious consideration no matter what happens this weekend," said Larranaga. Always one to know his numbers, Larranaga at this point in the season was able to run through the February records and important victories for his team, UNCW, Hofstra, and Old Dominion.

Larranaga went on to talk about the recent slippage of MVC teams, noting that the CAA certainly deserved to be mentioned in the same breath. It was indeed odd, for those that had been around the conference for many years, to hear multiple coaches talk about their own NCAA at-large chances.

"To the extent our names are being bandied about, this is very good," said Yeager. "They are not 'unthinking' about us."

The coaches were no more forthcoming than Yeager. Indeed, perhaps, they were collectively superstitious and didn't want to discuss it.

UNCW's Brad Brownell said that he had "no idea. Do I feel like we deserve to be? Yes. [But] what happens with the committee you never know. In our league we get good television exposure but we still aren't like the [major conference] that you see two or three times in the last week of the season. A team like Indiana who is on the bubble...I worry about the lasting impression of a team like that overriding the success of a 'mid major.' This is a year where we need to get multiple bids to the tournament." (Brownell was referring to Indiana's win over Michigan State that weekend.)

Larranaga became testy when asked to assess his team's chances should George Mason lose in the quarterfinals: "I don't think in the negatives and I don't try to create hypothetical situations," he snapped.

Ever the realist, Pecora was right on it. "If we lose in the first round [of the CAA Tournament] we're going to the NIT," Pecora said. "If we get to the finals, beat Mason in the semis, I believe we're going to get into the NCAA Tournament. Our RPI would jump. [But] by winning you solve all your problems in regards to basketball."

As it turned out, Pecora was both right and wrong. He got his desired path, but he also didn't win, setting up the drama that would unfold.

Nobody could've forecast how those four days in March would reshape the conference. George Mason, with its overtime escape of Georgia State, had punched its ticket. It wasn't apparent at the time, but the drama surrounding Tony Skinn's punch to Loren Stokes would only serve as the appetizer.

The new neighborhood had brought new challenges, but no matter what had occurred, Tom Pecora had a job as a leader of young men. He believed his team was going to be selected to the NCAA Tournament, after Hofstra's loss in the CAA finals, after the punch, after the long season, and after now not really knowing what his team's basketball future would hold. Even after shaping the lives of the college kids under his charge who at that very moment were in an incredible basketball moment—granted a very difficult moment, but a basketball moment—the last thing Pecora told his team in the locker room after the UNCW loss contained his message: "Everybody is in class tomorrow morning," he said. "We're going to check and you'd better be there."

———

Of the mid-major conferences, the CAA was hand in hand with the MVC in carrying the success flag. Only the Mountain West—with Air Force and San Diego State—and Conference USA with Alabama Birmingham and top five Memphis could boast the threat of multiple bids to the NCAA tournament.

The MAC spent the season cannibalizing itself, CAA-style. The WAC had Utah State on the outside peering in. The Sun Belt—the former conference of Old Dominion and VCU—featured a very good Western Kentucky team that would be highly favored to win the conference tournament. Out west, Gonzaga ruled the West Coast and nobody else, like St. Mary's and Pepperdine had done in years past, had stepped up.

No, the national media was between three and five or six bids for the MVC, and between two and three bids for the CAA.

"We have *never* had a year like this," Tom Yeager said at the conference's season-ending banquet. "I do know one thing. When they [announce] the selections ten days from now, we'll have more than one team."

The confusing bid scenario was actually less important than the fact that it existed in the first place. The extra credit the CAA received for UNCW's 2002 victory over Southern California under the NCAA's basketball fund would expire in two years. That meant about

$152,000 of the conference's budget—a huge number. Without a major conference-type television contract, and no possible means of garnering one on the horizon, there was not that kind of money lying around the CAA's Patterson Avenue office. It wasn't hidden in a budget line devoted to copy paper, either.

It would need to be replaced, if only to help the conference distribute more money to its member schools. This money would help avert the need, or the temptation, of more buy games and thus losses. An at-large bid would help start the cycle of success, not a cycle of mediocrity.

After all, the money was there. CBS is in the middle of its massive rights contract with the NCAA—it runs until 2013—that pays an average of $545 million per year. Because it is written to increase eight percent each year, every win in the tournament (and every team selected) soon will be worth $1 million to the winning school's conference.

It's been a lucrative, if not winding, path to this pot of gold. The first television contract for rights to program the NCAA Tournament was with NBC and grossed the NCAA roughly $1.1 million.

After the dominance of UCLA and the ebullience of Magic versus Bird in 1979, NBC re-upped in 1981 for $9.9 million. Still, games were unable to be shown during the week. *Tonight Show* host Johnny Carson, who wielded a big stick at NBC, insisted he never be pre-empted. Thus, only weekend games were available to NBC.

That's when CBS Sports President Van Gordon Sauter decided to take a shot at college basketball. Sitting in different conference rooms in a Hilton Hotel in Chicago, NBC and CBS went head-to-head for the rights to the NCAA Tournament. It was ultimately CBS's brilliant idea to show the announcement of the brackets live that carried the day. Of course, $48 million over three years wasn't exactly a tough selling point, either.

CBS has carried the tournament every year since, with the total value of the latest rights contract surpassing $6 billion. A full 80 percent of the NCAA's operating budget is generated via the revenues from this contract. With thirty-second spots selling in the $1 million neighborhood—second in cost only to the Super Bowl—it works for CBS as well.

College basketball was very different in 2006 than it was in 1979.

CHAPTER TWELVE:

POSTSEASON

"There is a real magic in enthusiasm. It spells the difference between mediocrity and accomplishment....It gives warmth and good feeling to all your personal relationships." –Norman Vincent Peale

I t's going to be huge," wrote Kyle Whelliston in his season preview article on the CAA for ESPN.com. Whelliston had no idea just how huge.

So after a rousing and controversial CAA tournament, after a gut-wrenching week awaiting its fate, and even after an NCAA Selection Show that would give new meaning to the term ramifications, the CAA got almost every wish.

It got its at-large team, the first in twenty years, in George Mason. Its conference champion, UNCW, earned a single-digit seed—ninth. Old Dominion and Hofstra would also play in the postseason NIT. There remained exasperating but national banter about this particular conference. What had the punch wrought? Did the conference, as questioned live by Billy Packer and Jim Nantz, deserve a second bid? It was truly a watershed moment.

Like moments outside of sports that are truly filled with wonder and a sense of amazement and amusement, there was a childlike aspect to March 2006. The electric smile of George Mason senior Lamar Butler was buttressed by the braces-filled smile of freshman Sammy Hernandez.

Brad Brownell and John Goldsberry, the leaders of UNCW, had their own smiles; different smiles. They were the champions and carried the swagger. There wasn't true sweating like the thirty-four at-large teams. Interestingly, the week leading up to the start of the NCAA Tournament was more businesslike in Wilmington, which mirrored the personalities of the coach and players. Though they conducted every interview and accepted each well-deserved congratulations, they had a job to do, a team to lead—and they were the champs.

It was much the same in Norfolk. Taylor got what he expected: an NIT game, though it was on the road at Colorado. He dealt with that head-scratcher and moved on. He knew the Monarchs had an opportunity to make their own statement and that would be his focus.

Pecora, however, had a different challenge. He thought they were in the NCAAs. So did his players. So did the league. But disappointment occurs. If Hofstra had been passed over by a major conference team with similar credentials it would have been understandable. After all, Pecora himself knew that this was a major conference anyway. He may not have liked it or understood it, but he could be at peace with it.

But to be snubbed by at least one, if not two, mid-majors with clearly lesser credentials defied belief. Not only would Pecora have to explain being passed over, he would have to find a way to make it gibe that the snub was indeed a snub but that they couldn't let it impact them. To lose in the first round of the NIT would justify their nonselection.

Any leader can look strong when things are going well. It is the mark of a true leader to lead in an adverse situation. This is what Pecora faced. So the Hofstra Pride went back to practice and focused. Pecora would deal his players another lesson on life.

For his part, Larranaga was everywhere, soaking up the media attention and conducting every interview asked. He answered the questions about Hofstra, the CAA, and his athletics director being on the selection committee. He didn't duck, weave, or spin.

His "cornball" routine officially kicked off, but it worked because it was genuine. He had been past this point in his career, even to the Final Four, but then he was an assistant and in the ACC at Virginia.

George Mason was his team. The CAA was his conference. It was a true accomplishment as opposed to a next step, and that is what made it special.

There was the beauty of "the run," but people who didn't become familiar with George Mason until after a victory or two or three weren't aware of what had transpired in the two weeks prior to the tourney. They had no idea just how unforeseeable this run had been, because it almost had not started. They didn't know of the incredible CAA season and its controversial tournament.

Few had done the math to realize that since ODU's Drew Williamson made his improbable, buzzer-beating three to beat George Mason on December 7, 2005, the Patriots had lost only four times: at Mississippi State, at UNCW, at Hofstra, and again to Hofstra in the CAA Tournament.

Nobody though—not even Whelliston and his fortuitous prediction—could fathom what would happen next.

———

At the end of the four days that led up to the start of the NCAA Tournament, everyone was ready for the games. The media had done its usual diligence of analyzing matchups. Off the court, fodder such as the inclusion of George Mason, the Packer comments, which major school was going to win, and every back story and side story imaginable were profiled. Finally, it was time for the actual games.

March Madness would start without a hint of the incredible magnitude of its end. Mid-majors would make their mark like no other previous year. It would not, however, look very different in the beginning.

The Friday before St. Patrick's Day, 2006, proved incredibly unlucky for UNCW. Brad Brownell's team built an eighteen-point second-half lead against ninth-seeded George Washington of the Atlantic 10. GW had raced through the regular season, nearly going unbeaten in conference play. Though the Colonials had lost in the A10 tournament to Xavier, they were considered one of the most dangerous—if not unproven—teams in the tournament.

So once UNCW took the big lead, many considered the game over. It was, after all, UNCW. An eighteen-point lead, considering their executory and plodding style, felt more like twenty-five, and that's when UNCW stopped playing like UNCW.

Once the lead reached its peak on a three-point play by Todd Hendley, 64-46 with just over eleven minutes to play, the Seahawks didn't score for the next five minutes. Complicating matters was that UNCW turned the ball over at an alarming rate, and they could not stop the GW assault. For five minutes, UNCW looked out of sorts. The Colonials scored nineteen consecutive points and led by one.

UNCW would recover, but missed free throws and missed opportunities sealed their fate.

There would be overtime.

The extra session would look remarkably like the final five minutes of the game. Beckham Wyrick hit a free throw and a three pointer and the Seahawks led 85-81 with barely two minutes remaining.

UNCW wouldn't score again and lost, 88-85.

"We lost the game because we didn't get stops," said Brad Brownell afterwards. "Down the stretch you have to get stops to win the game. That's something we've done all year and we didn't get that done tonight."

The CAA was looking very much like the CAA—another close loss on a big stage when it had a chance to win.

What became lost in the George Mason run was the rise of Hofstra. Pecora's club won twenty-six games, gaining national notoriety not only for their impressive win total, but also for the grace in which they handled the NCAA Tournament snub.

After his team had just traveled to Philadelphia and beaten St. Joseph's in the second round of the NIT on Hawk Hill, a 77-75 overtime thriller in a building that few visitors walk out of victorious ("I've seen two hundred games in this building and seen the visitors win maybe five times," said former A10 commissioner and current CAA basketball overlord Ron Bertovich), Pecora was asked the George Mason question.

"I'm thrilled," Pecora said. "It's great for our conference." Pecora was pressed about "what might have been." He replied: "I don't worry about that stuff. I've moved on. It's not life or death. It's just basketball." And that was it.

What's more is, he was right. Hofstra—after beating the Big 12's Nebraska at home and then winning at the A10's St. Joseph's—was rewarded with a home game for a chance to play in Madison Square Garden. Considering that Pecora recruits the New York area heavily, it seemed like at least a tolerable second choice.

In an incredibly ironic juxtaposition, their opponent would be none other than Taylor's Old Dominion Monarchs. Old Dominion, meanwhile, had won at Colorado (Big 12) and then won at home against Manhattan.

For Taylor, a postseason appearance at all was gratifying. Though his team was disappointed at its CAA Tournament loss, Taylor began planting NIT seeds immediately.

"An advantage we had was time to assimilate to the NIT," Taylor said, referring to the fact that the CAA Tournament was played a week before the Selection Show. "On the Friday, while everyone else was in their conference tournaments, we had a take-no-prisoners practice. I told them we're going to burn the stat sheets, burn the roles. I'm starting over."

The game itself was largely devoid of highlights. Hofstra led ODU by six at the half, but Isaiah Hunter scored nineteen second-half points to lead ODU to a 61-52 win. The game was tight, but ultimately Hofstra ran out of gas. Stokes dropped a pair of free throws to trim an ODU lead to 53-52, but Hofstra missed all six field goals the rest of the way.

The twenty-one-game home court winning streak would end, as would the careers of two of Pecora's stalwart players—Aurimas Kieza and Adrian Uter.

For Taylor, he would be back on the national stage. The NIT Final Four would pit three major conference teams: Louisville, Michigan, and South Carolina. The Monarchs would round out the field and dominate the talk.

For whatever reason, the Fates were smiling on Yeager again. He would have a representative playing in New York at the NIT Final Four, right where Drexel had begun the season in such stunning fashion.

The trip was wonderful for the ODU players, as they received an up-close tour of New York City. According to Taylor, he enjoyed the looks in their eyes when they saw the Waldorf Astoria; however, it was getting onto the court to practice at Madison Square Garden that provided the greatest thrill, and comedy.

"To get onto the floor, you have to travel up a back cage and elevator," Taylor said. "They were looking around as if 'this is no big deal.' So I told them this is how David Bowie and Liza Minnelli got there. It was a great speech except they didn't know who I was talking about!"

Old Dominion, hampered because its star Alex Loughton could barely walk, also lost Arnaud Dahi to an ACL injury. Michigan eventually wore down ODU and overwhelmed them, 66-43.

To describe the Final Four run of George Mason in game stories is a futile effort. It also cheapens what the Patriots managed to accomplish. Besides, the important part of the story surrounded the on-court action. Fewer game-action moments will be remembered in the wake of what the victories meant and the people who made them happen.

There was still the issue of actually winning basketball games. Because on the other hand, to discuss what they had accomplished without telling the story of how—the grit, determination, strategy, and big plays on the court—the players won basketball games would cheapen their efforts.

Amid the talk and questions and naysayers, Larranaga quietly focused his eleventh seeded team on its goal: victory. His approach, which would prove to be brilliant in later rounds, began in Ohio from the first time he spoke to his team.

"When you get to Dayton, have a ball," he told his players after learning they would play Michigan State. "I'm going to have as much fun as I possibly can."

All they could do was what their coach had told them. After all, they made it to the NCAA Tournament listening to the sage advice of their leader. There was no reason to think he was out of his mind now. The players would also admit that they were playing to give their senior guard, Tony Skinn, another chance to play. It was Skinn's bomb against Wichita State that would have put them on the national radar and in the tournament.

Fittingly, it began on St. Patrick's Day against the green-clad Spartans.

A tight first half saw Mason score nine consecutive points late in the half to lead 33-28, settling for a 33-30 lead. What had to be concerning for Larranaga was that his team had played well, shooting 58 percent, but only led by three. If they were unable to keep the torrid pace, he would have to alter his game plan.

He didn't have to worry. In the second half, every time Michigan State scored to tighten the game, one of Larranaga's stars would drain a three. Folarin Campbell and Lamar Butler hit back-to-back bonus shots with 10:00 to play to give Mason a seven-point bulge.

Five minutes later, the duo switched the order—first Butler then Campbell hit from deep, stretching the Mason lead back to nine. Michigan State would get the lead no closer than seven down the stretch and the game ended 75-65.

George Mason had not made 58 percent of its field goals in the second half. They hit 61 percent.

Folarin Campbell led the way, hitting all eight of his shots, and scored twenty-one points. Tony Skinn, serving his one-game suspension, cheered loudly from the bench.

In what would become a staple of celebratory George Mason fans, the "C-A-A...C-A-A" chant rose in the Dayton Arena.

"The disappointing thing is they took it at us early and kicked our butts inside," Michigan State coach Tom Izzo said afterward. Mason's Will Thomas collected fourteen rebounds and the Patriots surprisingly controlled the boards, outrebounding the bigger Spartans 40-24.

With an upset in hand and facing the defending national champions, North Carolina, it would be easy to think the Patriots would relax and savor their one NCAA upset victory. Once Mason put itself in a 16-2 hole against the Tar Heels, it looked that was going to be the case.

Grit and power and resolve, qualities that would make Taylor happy, carried the day. The Patriots didn't cave and managed to cut the deficit to a workable 27-20 by the half; they came out of the locker room flying, scoring the first eight points of the second half. Notably, Larranaga switched to a zone defense, installed specifically for this game, to slow the Tar Heels.

It would be a back-and-forth second half, with neither team able to take any kind of control or momentum. It was turning into a street fight, something that surprised the Tar Heels. After smacking George Mason, the at-large team from the lowly mid-major CAA, right in the teeth, the eleventh seed was supposed to call it a tournament.

When Tony Skinn, who didn't start the game but finished it, made three of four free throws at the end, all UNC Coach Roy Williams could do was pick up and slam down a folding chair along the Carolina bench. His team could do nothing right of late. George Mason had every answer. It was North Carolina that caved. The 65-60 final meant Mason rose from the floor to outscore North Carolina 63-46 over the final thirty-four minutes, shocking 13,000 fans in Dayton who , if they weren't wearing Carolina blue, slowly began to cheer for the Patriots.

Will Thomas and Jai Lewis pushed around the young Tar Heels, taking star center Tyler Hansbrough completely out of his game. "They sent a lot of guys after me," said Hansbrough, who scored just ten points. "That was part of their plan."

Butler, who led Mason with eighteen points, made just enough perimeter jumpers. Mason's three seniors were too much for Carolina's four freshmen. Mason had achieved the unthinkable: a Sweet 16 berth. Its opponent, ironically, would be the Wichita State Shockers.

"There's been talk about the Missouri Valley all year," said Butler after the game. "Hardly anyone has talked about the CAA. It's hard to believe we're both in the Sweet 16."

Larranaga officially kicked off the geeky coach campaign by admitting after the game, through sweat and a smile: "The last comment I made to them was, 'What color is kryptonite? They said, 'Green.' I said, 'Look at your jerseys. You have everything you need to win this game."

The media crush would grow. George Masons' players would become rock stars. The Sweet 16 appearance was especially notable in that the Patriots would play in the Verizon Center, a scant twenty miles from their Fairfax campus.

The bandwagon was bulging. Lamar Butler's smiling face made the cover of *Sports Illustrated,* the Rose Bowl of sporting achievement. Oddly, in a season full of oddities, Yeager's magic tie would see Wichita State, the team Mason played in the ESPN Bracket Busters. The victory was hailed as "the one" that got them into the tournament.

"It's not about who we play or where we play. It's how we play," said Larranaga, echoing his statements from December. Those who followed the CAA already knew what the rest of the country was discovering. Larranaga may be a cornball, but he is both intelligent and earnest. Still, the enormity of the Sweet 16, compared with a December loss, didn't elude the coach. "We are a small group that represents a larger group. We touch so many more people than just the people around us who come to the games."

Larranaga was up before 5:00 a.m. to answer emails before a day chocked full of interviews and appearances. Being close to home did carry responsibilities and a downside. He also had practice and a team to prepare.

As the George Mason players entered the Verizon Center for their Sweet 16 game, you would swear it was an early December home game. Larranaga smiled, shook a few hands, and walked gracefully but with purpose down the hallway to the team's locker room. Lamar Butler sang, out loud and particularly on key, through headphones. The team carried that kind of looseness.

There was no hint that this would be the biggest game, again, that the team had ever played.

The two hours before an NCAA Tournament basketball game, especially once you reach the Sweet 16, is incredibly anticipatory. The media gets set up and comfortable, jabbering about this and that. Television production people are working steadily on final preparations. While the fans trickle into the arena, each team begins stretching and generally getting loose. Though nothing is going on, everything is happening. It's the lure of the tournament, and the part of it nobody wants to miss. It is a college basketball moment that cannot be duplicated. Sure, there is tremendous corporate sponsorship and, of course, the NCAA is omnipotent and omnipresent, but there is a feel of sanctity to this moment—a collegiate feel.

Lamar Butler could not get the grin off of his face, and he wouldn't have to. His three pointer to open the contest was just the first blow. Folarin Campbell duplicated Butler twice.

It was a game that was far less appealing than any other in the tournament for George Mason. It certainly wasn't coming down to a final shot, like it had one month ago on the Shockers home floor.

The Patriots scored those first nine points of the contest and led 35-19 at the half. Wichita State would not get the lead below double digits until very late in the game. The final was 63-55 and it wasn't nearly that close. The Shockers made just three of twenty-four three pointers and spent the evening harassed by Mason's scramble defense, hitting just 31 percent for the game. Folarin Campbell hit his first three bonus shots and it was all downhill.

CBS beamed the game to only 14 percent of the country. In two days, George Mason would play the #1 team in the nation, the Connecticut Huskies.

"We're having a helluva lotta fun," said Larranaga afterwards. After a breath and a sip of water, Larranaga continued, perhaps taking in his own words to see how they sounded: "Moving into the Elite 8; that sounds good."

Tom Yeager, Ron Bertovich, and Tom O'Connor were like ducks— smiling on the outside and paddling like hell underneath—as they milled about the Verizon Center prior to the George Mason game against Connecticut. Nobody dared speak the words Final Four, but everybody knew. They knew what was in front of them and the opportunity it presented. They knew what that night meant and what the past two weeks had meant. There was reason for the cat-ate-the-canary smile, combined with a "what's next?" expression.

What's next was one of those basketball games that become instant classics. That a Final Four berth was on the line and that the game featured a true David versus Goliath matchup only heightened its sheer significance.

Connecticut came into the game having lost only three times all season and were bigger at every position. The Huskies looked like an NBA team when they walked onto the floor for their warmups. The Patriots were merely a college team happy to be there: Butler still smiled and the entire team jauntily bounced through their warmups. Conversely, the Huskies were all business. They were on a mission.

The Huskies began the game hot and took a seven-point lead, but could not push it further. Mason made a run to take a brief 29-28 lead before UConn awoke. A 15-2 spurt had fans wondering if this were truly the end. Mason was able to get the game back to 43-34 by the half.

The lead remained at nine, 47-38 when Mason scored the next eight points. Folarin Campbell would complete the comeback and tie the game at 49-49 with his second three pointer of the half. Though the game was tied, there remained a fleeting sense of hope. Could they keep this up? After Connecticut's Denham Brown hit a short jumper, Lamar Butler followed Campbell's three with one of his own and George Mason led 52-51.

Perhaps.

Jeff Adrian responded with a thundering dunk, one of those that serve as a signal to both teammates and opponents. Butler answered in one of the most memorable moments in the entire tournament. After spreading UConn out, Tony Skinn fed Will Thomas in the post, who whipped the ball to Butler four steps behind the three-point line with the shot clock running out. Butler's three-pointer swished, and he had also been fouled by Rasheed Anderson on the play. Butler's free throw, completing the four-point play, was the right answer to the Adrian dunk.

Though there remained more than ten minutes on the clock, it seemed George Mason had every answer, again. It had become time to believe.

The remainder of the 2006 NCAA Washington, D.C., regional basketball final was as breathtaking as basketball can muster, on any level. This game had progressed far past coaching chess matches. Players were being called upon to simply make plays, and they were up to the challenge. It was beautiful basketball. The crowd, the media, and Tom Yeager were on the edge of their seats. Verizon Center ushers openly cheered for the de facto home team.

The lead would change hands six times down the stretch and hands were wrung clean of their fingerprints. They say that tension can be so thick you could cut it with a knife. On this moment, even death's scythe wouldn't do. Butler hit two free throws with eighteen seconds to play, giving George Mason a 74-70 lead.

Then, that's when the game got exciting.

After a Marcus Williams runner with eight seconds to play swished, cutting the lead to 74-72, Connecticut was forced to foul.

In a season full of irony, it was only fitting that Tony Skinn would go to the free throw line in a one-and-one situation. Make two, and the game is likely over. Connecticut would need two possessions and there wasn't time.

Skinn missed.

Connecticut flew down the court, where Denham Brown attempted a reverse layup. The ball bounced on the rim for what seemed like

twenty minutes before dropping through the hoop. Brown had barely beaten the buzzer. In fact, the buzzer had finished sounding before
the ball settled into the net. The vacuum of exhaling fans was audible. It was an eerie moment, and it was 74-74.

Overtime.

Everybody knew that George Mason's chance had passed. They
were dead ducks. To a man, except on the George Mason bench, the
feeling was that Connecticut would run away with the game. They
had been given their second life.

Yeager said several weeks after the NCAA Tournament that noted
author John Feinstein could barely decipher the scribbles he called
notes for this game. In fairness, it must be said that "Skinn FT—
irony!" is the final note in my notebook. There is no cheering on
press row, they say, but every now and again you just have to sit back
and appreciate a wonderful college basketball game.

One man, however, was not convinced George Mason was dead.
"There's no place I'd rather be," Larranaga told his team in the huddle. "We've got to play a five-minute game. We live for games like
this!"

Will Thomas's jump hook started the overtime session, signaling
the battle to rejoin. Both teams traded baskets and body blows over
the next four minutes. With Mason holding onto an 82-80 lead,
Folarin Campbell drilled what would prove to be the ultimate dagger.
It was "the" shot that said George Mason was going to win this game.
Campbell backed down his defender and swished a tough, fade-away
ten footer with 1:13 left. After Rasheed Anderson fired up an air ball,
Jai Lewis made one of two free throws, and the Mason lead was 85-80
with forty-one seconds to play.

It was again time to believe.

The teams traded a free throw, and after Marcus Williams swished
a twenty-five footer, George Mason had the ball with an 86-84 lead.
Lewis was fouled with seven seconds to play. Same lead, nearly the
same time as in regulation when Skinn had missed. Only in this
instance, Lewis had two free throws.

Lewis missed them both.

Connecticut again hurried down the court. Brown again would take the shot. This time, though, he stepped back behind the arc. Brown wanted to end it. He did, only his bonus attempt went long, careening harmlessly off the side of the rim.

George Mason had done it. The requisite pandemonium ensued.

It was the kind of moment that is so shocking, so celebratory, so unexpected, and so spur-of-the-moment that it defies description.

Oh, there were the typical celebrations: fans with arms raised or around each other; players hugging and sprinting around the court, four fingers raised and propping the "George Mason" on their jerseys.

The media scrambled, furiously writing notes and jockeying for interview positions. Operations personnel went after ladders for the net cutting ceremony. Everybody jumped and ran and celebrated and soaked in the moment.

However, there was a subtle, unspoken difference. When Mateen Cleaves, point guard at Michigan State, brazenly said that his Spartans were going to "shock the world" and upset top-ranked Duke—and then did so—it was a great moment in college basketball. This was still a Big 10 school though, with a tradition of winning and beating an ACC school.

A mid major, one which had just pulled off two upsets and three victories, eventually was supposed to hit the wall. They were playing the top team in the country from the top conference. The David versus Goliath cliché actually fit.

This was truly, earnestly, shocking the world.

So below the usual fervor of celebration there stood the deer-in-the-headlights realizations of "what have I just witnessed." Everyone felt like there should be some sort of additional reaction; some sort of special celebration to signify the moment. The more the cheering continued and the more the result sank in, the more the utter lack of knowing how to celebrate such a moment caught hold and took root.

Ron Bertovich, the CAA's deputy commissioner of basketball, summed up the moment. Because of the postseason success of the

CAA, Bertovich's car had been sitting in the parking lot at BWI airport since Selection Sunday. It would sit for another week, as George Mason would be headed to Indianapolis and the Final Four.

All Bertovich could manage was, "Holy shit."

Though the line wasn't in Walt Disney's version of *Cinderella,* it fit perfectly.

The George Mason players laughed and smiled, while the Connecticut players walked off in silence. It was the same manner in which the teams had entered the court more than two hours ago.

"I told them right before the game that we're from a secret organization called the CAA—the Connecticut Assassins Association," said Larranaga in his now-familiar corny role. "Then, every time I said CAA in the huddle, they knew what I was talking about."

The locker room was silent just after the horn sounded, signaling George Mason's trip to the Final Four. A random amalgam of cups and chairs were strewn across the floor. One pair of shoes sat outside a locker.

When the players finally left the court, Campbell walked to the blank dry erase boards hanging in the front of the locker room and wrote: "He Guaranteed What?" This was in reference to Anderson's guaranteeing a UConn victory.

Gabe Norwood cut to the chase, reminding the world that he is a college student: "I've gotta get another haircut," he mused.

Over in a little corner of the back halls of the Verizon Center, college basketball's best, brightest, and most venerable writers huddled. They were trying to figure out when, if ever, something like this had occurred. It was little consolation that this was the first time since 1980 that there were no #1 seeds in the Final Four. The conundrum was eleventh George Mason.

———

The magic finally met its end after one of the most exciting lead-ups to a Final Four in college basketball history. The George Mason loss to eventual national champion Florida, like the Wichita State victory, was never in doubt. The Patriots trailed most of the way in the first half, but closed to 31-26 by the horn. Florida's Lee Humphrey made three straight from outside the arc in the first two minutes of the second half to run the lead to 40-28. The Gators slowly pulled away from there, leading by as many as nineteen points, and the Patriots never got any closer than nine the rest of the way. The final was 73-58.

"We came into the game feeling good about ourselves and feeling good about our chances," said Larranaga afterward. "For some reason, we were never really able to establish our rhythm, either offensively or defensively."

For the first time in a month, Larranaga didn't have the answer, but the impact of the Cinderella run was not lost on Florida coach Billy Donovan. "What they've been able to do this year is great for basketball," he said. "Most teams don't get a chance to experience what they've been able to experience. In this tournament, they were able to inspire a lot of people. There was no resentment on our team for feeling like they got all the attention or we got slighted."

There were many important and notable events that flew under the radar below George Mason's historic Final Four run.

The conference's 9-4 mark was lost in the hoopla, a tremendous improvement over its 0-4 mark the previous year. In fact, the conference had never collectively won more than four postseason games in any one season.

The additional bid and Mason victories would add another $1.2 million annually to the conference's coffers.

"We're kind of like the middle class guy with a retirement fund who wins the lottery," said Yeager. "We're revamping how we look at collectively moving everybody forward."

It would be an economic, atmospheric, and exposure boon to the conference.

Taylor's Old Dominion team went to New York. Hofstra emerged as next year's favorite after Pecora led his team to twenty-six victories.

Both defeated teams from major and mid-major conferences in the postseason. They were two CAA programs ready to stake their claim.

The NCAA Selection Committee caught all manner of hell for including George Mason and mid-majors from the Missouri Valley. The teams validated those choices and proved that the committee indeed knows what it's doing.

———

There were incredible ironies and fortuitous happenstance within the run.

- A misapplication of rules allowed Tony Skinn to play against Wichita State in the Bracket Busters event. It was Skinn's three that won the game and vaulted Mason into the NCAA Tournament. It was Skinn who would miss the first game because he had been suspended by his coach, and it would be Wichita State that Mason would draw in the Sweet 16.
- George Mason's Jai Lewis would become the first player to sign a professional contract—with the New York Giants in the NFL. Dave Gettleman, director of pro personnel for the New York Giants, was Tom Yeager's college roommate.
- Yeager would also ask George Mason AD Tom O'Connor, prior to the season, to speak to CAA fans at the conference tournament. The subject: how the committee selects the teams to the NCAA men's basketball tournament.
- Larranaga was hired by George Mason April 1, 1997. The Florida game was played nine years to the day of that signing. The Final Four that year was held in Indianapolis.
- AD Tom O'Connor's grandson was a ball boy at the Final Four. It was a Christmas present for the youth, who turned ten years old on April 1.
- George Mason President Alan Merten was once a dean at Florida.

But those were only during the closing kick. The season was chock-full of irony. Others would call it karma or destiny. Or simply inevitable.

———

Earlier in the season, the CAA had dealt with the shooting of Old Dominion guard Brandon Johnson. Though the story was replete with salacious rumor and innuendo, it had registered barely a blip on the national radar screen.

The conference also had those bothersome close losses, and a few decent wins. It wasn't until late February, however, that the national media caught on to this nice little conference based in Richmond, Virginia.

Suddenly, though, the CAA found itself splashed all over ESPN.com. Pictures and stories would detail the Tony Skinn punch and analyze its aftermath. The low blow would also be featured in most every daily newspaper, and it was repeated on SportsCenter a number of times.

The CAA had Hofstra, recognized nationally as one of the "teams with a beef."

It was clear that the CAA had entered new ground. The days of being thrilled with a full building and a narrow loss in its conference tournament final were officially over. The potential for a single NCAA upset by its lone team was now disappointing. Gone, too, were the cute days of a small conference facing the big boys. The CAA was no longer David in an industry of Goliaths. So was the comfort of knowing that outside of regional coverage, negative publicity such as the Brandon Johnson shooting could fly under the radar.

The CAA had come of age, and you could point to March 6, 2006, as to when it happened. With every SportsCenter rerun of the Tony Skinn punch, the CAA grew older and bigger. It was a defining moment, and though one neither Tom Yeager nor Tony Skinn would choose, it would be one that was darkly appropriate.

The CAA was now playing in a different world, one that was large-ly unfamiliar. The conference would need old salt NCAA people like Tom Yeager and Ron Bertovich. They at least had exposure during their long careers to the conference's new frontier. College basketball had exploded over the past twenty years and the CAA was just now seeing the positives and negatives of that. They would have to adjust.

Tom Yeager had said on the eve of the CAA final, the day after Tony Skinn's punch below the belt of Loren Stokes, that despite not having the name Kentucky or Florida or Duke, CAA schools were in that neighborhood. He was speaking specifically to the positives of high RPIs and at-large bids. Somewhere in his mind, too, he must've known that there is a negative side.

It was all new, and it all came with the new neighborhood.

CBS runs a highlight and photo montage at the conclusion of each NCAA Tournament, set to the tune "One Shining Moment." For George Mason and the CAA, the historic run was one shining moment after another.

It became a feel-good story because that's precisely what it was. It was complete with a sense of disbelief, accomplishment, recognition, togetherness, and family.

It was Lamar Butler's smile, Jim Larranaga's cornball routine, Tom O'Connor's validation, and Tony Skinn's vindication. It was fans of LSU and UCLA rooting for George Mason. It was also Old Dominion and Hofstra and the rest of the CAA.

It also served notice. This is what happens with opportunity.

CHAPTER THIRTEEN

DENOUEMENT

"I would define, in brief, the Poetry of words as the Rhythmical Creation of Beauty. Its sole arbiter is Taste." –Edgar Allan Poe

W e just had a great, exhilarating game," bubbled the coach. "Our gym was packed, everybody screaming. It was everything that basketball's about at the level of our program. For a game between two 'mid-majors,' or whatever you'd call us, it had everything you could ask for."

Surely Blaine Taylor was talking about his 2005 ODU Monarchs and their thrilling, streak-ending victory over Virginia Commonwealth. Or perhaps it was Randy Bennett after his Southern Illinois Salukis dispatched Wichita State in a late-season Missouri Valley Conference game that essentially decided the mid-major conference's regular season champion.

No, this quote was from Catholic University Coach Jack Kvancz. His team has just beaten local rival Howard University 66-61 in a late November matchup.

The year: 1977.

As I followed the fortunes of the CAA during the 2005-2006 season, and in many ways the MVC, Horizon, and West Coast conferences, I always kept in the back of my mind the singular question that hovered during this entire project: Just what *is* a mid major? It was the question I was most asked, and this caused a problem. Most of the time I had no definition, and I frequently stumbled my way through some esoteric compilation of words.

So I made it my goal to find it.

Clearly the genesis of the term *mid major* is unclear, but one of the things I found is that it matters not in the grand scheme. The important fact is that the phenomenon that has become known as "mid-major" college basketball is real and alive.

The players love the game just as much, so it matters to them. There are wins and losses, alumni, NCAA rules, coaches, study halls, girlfriends, and classes. The goals and dreams are not unlike those of J.J. Redick or Adam Morrison.

Being a mid major has nothing to do with desire or, many times, ability. It has a little to do with conference. For every SEC there is a Vanderbilt. For every WCC, there is a Gonzaga. For every Duke and Villanova (basketball) there is a Penn State and Virginia Tech (football). It has a whole heckuva lot to do with monetary resources.

The answer is still just as murky as its beginnings, rooted somewhere in between all of those factors: conference alignment, revenue generation, academic/athletic focus, television, football, and overall competitiveness.

Everyone's favorite argument starter is the Gonzaga University Bulldogs. The West Coast Conference is clearly mid major with the likes of San Francisco and Loyola Marymount in its membership. Gonzaga doesn't sponsor football, yet its basketball team is everyone's poster child for a mid major turned major.

But are they? Certainly the school is building new facilities with money generated by the on-court success of the basketball team. They win consistently and they recruit on a high level. They play major schools and are on the purchasing side of buy games. They get the ESPN and CBS games. But they are always the first team discussed when mid-majors come up. Never ask Mark Few, Gonzaga's coach, if he's clear on the matter: "It's a very poor descriptor for college basketball and has nothing to do with describing the level of a team's play and everything to do with describing the capital campaigns of the university," Few said in an interview with ESPN.com's Andy Katz.

That's not the point, however; and neither are mid-major polls and players of the year or mid-major anything. Gonzaga is the shining example that inclusion into one grouping (mid-majors) does not mean exclusion from another (majors). That provides another malleable data point for the discussion.

And that is precisely the point. Even just plain winning is used as a yardstick. Media pundits very easily write about and discuss Gonzaga no longer being a mid major because of its recent success.

But what about BCS teams that haven't been to the NCAA tournament in ten years? Kansas State and Virginia Tech have not been to the Big Dance since 1996. Michigan and Florida State: 1998. Because they are not competitive, are they now mid-majors?

Of course not.

It's really only a term of convenience. If you need a label, fit this one to your needs.

Football only exacerbates the issue. You would think that it would serve to clarify—the Big 6 BCS conferences and then everybody else. But the Big East is a huge basketball power and not so much so in football.

What's more, there is a built-in disadvantage in football that does not exist in basketball. The NCAA provides that sixty-five scholarships can be given in 1-AA football. This is twenty fewer that the allotted maximum for 1-A. This gives a clear line, one that does not exist in basketball, where everyone gets thirteen.

"I think [mid major] applies only in football," Saint Joseph's Coach Phil Martelli told the *Washington Post* in late 2004, "because we all have the opportunity to play for the championship. I think it's a silly term for college basketball."

Finally, if you are going to group schools as majors and mid-majors, that alone says that there is also a "low majors" category. Where is that line drawn?

Perhaps this explains why *mid major* is such a ubiquitous, yet impossible, term. It means so many things, yet nobody has a meaning.

It gives the media a nice way to box the grouping. It makes wonderful sports talk radio fodder, and it is money in the bank every February. To define it is impossible.

This is the exact paradox that describes why a mid major will always be defined by what it is not, rather than what it is. It occurs within the four tenets: recruiting, television, coaches moving, and scheduling.

For example, if you play in a BCS football conference, you are not a mid major. If you buy other teams to come to your gym, you are not a mid major. If you are shown more than one time on ESPN and any other national television network, you are not a mid major. Or are you? Interestingly, it always seems to come back to one thing: money.

After being completely engrained deep within mid-major college basketball for more than a year (embedded would be the term if I were covering a war), I'm no closer to the definition of a mid major than when I started.

Oh, sure. I've now gleaned an impressive list of criteria to evaluate what a mid major can be: buy games, television appearances, scheduling nonconference games, at-large bids to the NCAA Tournament, facilities, football, revenue, alumni donors, season tickets, the conference in which you play, retaining your coach after a great season, and compensation level. I could continue, but you get that point. It's in the next one that I want to be specific and clear.

The reason I cannot arrive at a precise and encompassing definition for a mid major is that the concept just doesn't exist. There is no definition. There never will be.

It will remain a nice label to give to those teams which do not participate in the BCS conferences and share in the football gold mine, thus always competing with fewer resources. It is impossible, though, to be correct in defining any singular team or situation.

It's funny. I spoke with someone at the 2006 NCAA Tournament who was telling me about the "non-BCS major." This was his way to classify the WAC, MVC, and Atlantic 10.

I tuned out quickly, because by then I realized it does not really matter. Classifications will exist as long as we have a media with the need to delineate between factions who compete with each other on unequal footing, which is fine.

Perhaps the word *classifications* is most appropriate. Kyle Whelliston and I were talking shortly before George Mason's upset of Connecticut and he said that he believed mid major was akin to minor league baseball. This makes perfect sense. The players are still professionals. Some cities have new stadiums and more attendance and bigger marketing budgets than others. They are classified into AAA, AA, and A.

What's more, AAA baseball sees a great deal of former major leaguers on its rosters, much like the BCS conference transfer to a mid-major school. In many ways, Whelliston's assertion is the most apt for the discussion.

Still, the term *mid major* doesn't lend much clarity, nor does it define anything. It's kind of like defining the "it" in the sentence "It is raining." Is "it" the clouds? The sky? The weather? You are perpetually correct, but never completely.

The criteria are there, and balance them if you must. In the end it doesn't matter, because every coach, athletic director, fan, player, media member, etc., will tell you the one thing on which they all agree: Win your games, and everything else will follow. Just ask Jim Larranaga.

EPILOGUE

UNFATHOMABLE

I t took less than two weeks for the significance of the 2005-2006 CAA season to begin to play out. National media had termed George Mason's run everything from the greatest story in NCAA Tournament history to the best sports story since the 1980 Olympic hockey team.

History will ultimately decide its place, but the words of football coach Bum Phillips ring true. Phillips was asked in the 1980s about the place of his star running back, Earl Campbell, in the history of greatest running backs ever. Phillips's response: "He may not be in a class by himself, but it sure don't take long to call roll."

The conference, on the verge of losing its second credit from the NCAA's basketball fund (generated in 2002 when UNCW defeated USC), suddenly had six teams that would stream into its coffers in the coming years. With the CAA-branded football looming in the 2007 season, long-term planning took on an entirely new meaning.

The lingering effects on the conference and its schools remained hazy. Surely there would be a bump in recruiting for George Mason, but Old Dominion had also won its way to New York. Hofstra was deep in the middle of the controversy and won twenty-six games itself. Now, everybody knew the CAA. Bruiser Flint admitted he no longer had to explain his conference when in the home of a recruit.

Importantly, Yeager would admit that he was being treated differently by everyone.

More television exposure would be discussed and ultimately contracted—more than seventy-five CAA games will hit televisions in 2006-2007. Scheduling, surely due to become even more difficult, remained a front-burner issue. George Mason scheduled a game against Duke, in Cameron Indoor, of course. Old Dominion would lure Clemson to Norfolk for an early-season tournament. (Clemson coach Oliver Purnell had also coached at ODU.)

Alan Merten, president of George Mason, would refer to the basketball season in his address to graduating seniors. Larranaga, who would speak anywhere prior to the season for free, was now able to command more than $6,000 per speaking engagement.

George Mason's enrollment, prestige, ticket sales, and annual giving would all rise. Darren Rovell of ESPN.com said that Mason received between $5 million and $10 million of like marketing.

"Basketball is our primary asset," said Tom Yeager without the slightest flinch. "I don't mean to be disrespectful to any of the other twenty sports we sponsor, but we must look at it as a business. To generate the funds to do what we do, we understand that everything runs through men's hoops."

The CAA regularly competes nationally in several other "minor" sports, but as Yeager says, "You need to pay attention to your largest asset. Like a coach once said, 'Don't win warmups.'"

Every facet of the school and of the conference would benefit, yet by how much would be years away. The main question became: What else *could* happen?

Life has a way of moving forward, so as not to keep you focused on one thing for too long. College basketball is not spared this reality. So while the nation, especially the northern Virginia and Washington, D.C., region, rejoiced and basked in the afterglow of George Mason's success, life moved on as it always has.

The conference had spring sports championships. The schools turned their attention to budgets. Coaches hit the recruiting trail; and most tumultuously, the coaching carousel would start anew.

Delaware, after several seasons of futility, fired its coach, David Henderson. The former Duke Blue Devils star had presided over a Blue Hens program that had regressed in his six seasons. The final two years Delaware had gone 11-20 and 9-21 despite having one of the league's best and most versatile players in Harding Nana.

Unfortunately, the search for a new coach was handled with little moxie. Kevin Willard, an assistant on Rick Pitino's staff at Louisville and one of the most respected young assistants in college basketball, traveled to the Delaware campus for an interview.

Willard, the son of Holy Cross's Ralph Willard, was open in his interview about a previous DUI arrest. He admitted it was a stupid mistake and that he had learned from it. With that knowledge in hand, Edgar Johnson, the AD at Delaware, offered Willard the job. Less than twenty-four hours later, though, Johnson embarrassingly took back that offer. After that, the school offered the job to Billy Taylor, the head coach at Lehigh University. Taylor turned them down.

Finally, the reins of the Delaware program were turned over to Monte Ross, who had been an assistant under John Chaney at Temple.

Drexel's Flint was connected to the Temple job, where Chaney had announced he was retiring. Ultimately the job went to Penn's Fran Dunphy. Meanwhile, Pecora signed a five-year contract extension with Hofstra and Capel (VCU) and Taylor (ODU) had two years added to their current deals, presumably to make them safe.

Pecora was the leading candidate to replace Louis Orr at Seton Hall, but negotiations never became serious. Jack Hayes struck quickly and hammered out the deal. Hayes "gets it," to use phraseology. He understands the role of athletics and how it can be successful, and Hayes has a vision for Hofstra. Pecora is a big part of that vision. So in a time span that lasted slightly more than over the weekend, Hayes locked up Pecora. He knew what was right.

"People who know me the best know that is not what I'm all about," Pecora told Tom Rock of New York's *Newsday*. "People get blind with ambition, but quality of life for someone like me is very important." Clearly, Pecora was referring to his family and their comfort with living on Long Island.

For all of the hoopla, rumor, and innuendo, and "leaks" and "right moves," Larranaga proved true to his word. Despite his constant and significant protestations, he had his name mentioned for every job except CEO of General Motors (and he likely would have landed that one). He "settled," after three weeks, for a three-year contract extension of his own with a raise of 90 percent. Collectively, northern Virginia exhaled.

With Larranaga, Pecora, Taylor, and Capel all signing extensions, Yeager knew he was averting one of the trappings of a mid major: coaching retention. The conference, however, would not escape unscathed. Hofstra would lose a coach in the weeks following the 2005-2006 season. Tom Parotta, Pecora's top assistant, landed the head job at Canisius.

Northeastern's Ron Everhart surprisingly decided to leave the Boston program to replace Danny Nee at Duquesne. Everhart had been named coach of the year in the America East in 2005, and had guided Northeastern through its transition into the CAA wonderfully, winning twelve conference games and finishing 19-11 overall. He would be leaving for the A10's bottom-feeder—Duquesne finished 1-15, 3-24 in 2005-2006. Eventually, Shawn James, the conference defensive player of the year, would follow.

Tragically, in August 2006, five Duquesne players, including Shawn James, were shot after leaving a party at the student commons. Though nobody was killed, it reinforced the fragility of life and the fact that athletes are not insulated from the good and bad of real-life experiences.

Everhart was replaced by Bill Coen, Al Skinner's top man across town at Boston College, but the major bombshells of the near-term CAA, postseason were fired by Brad Brownell and Jeff Capel. Though his team had just won the regular season and tournament championships and though he had been named coach of the year in the conference, Brownell abruptly packed his bags and left Wrightsville Beach and UNCW. After a short courtship period, Brownell signed to be the head man at Wright State of the Horizon Conference.

Those close to UNCW knew, though, that the departure hadn't been so sudden. Brownell had been privately at odds with AD Mike Capaccio, and it had gone back far past this season. Brownell was an assistant under Jerry Wainwright, who would move on to coach Richmond and then DePaul. Wainwright was a floor general and people person. Wainwright spent a good amount of time schmoozing with the media, boosters, and the community. Brownell was the x's and o's guru. Capaccio came to UNCW in 1999 and dealt mostly in development with respect to the basketball program. A chasm developed between the two when Capaccio, who many said wanted an assistant coaching position but was not offered one by Brownell, also was unhappy with Brownell's willingness to schmooze alumni and donors.

So the basketball season began and Brownell was offered a two-year contract. This did not sit well with Brownell, as the term didn't offer very much security. After a season of haggling and offers, counter offers, rumors, and innuendo, it became too much for Brownell. Capaccio's final offer, a fair one of five years according to Capaccio, wasn't enough to keep Brownell around. The CAA coach of the year left for a lesser program in a lesser conference. This was quite a departure from the CAA coaching modus operandi.

After a brutal, ugly four-week stretch, Capaccio hired Benny Moss, an assistant under Bobby Lutz at Charlotte.

Capel, however, fit nicely into the accepted model of the CAA coaching carousel. After VCU's conference championship two years ago, Capel had flirted with Auburn. When the Oklahoma Sooners called, though, looking to replace Kelvin Sampson (who had himself bolted unexpectedly for Indiana), Capel would choose to pack his bags and coach in a state that he had never visited.

That Capel had used VCU as a stepping stone was no secret. Everyone remotely associated with the university's basketball program knew his departure was a matter of when, not if.

It was the timing that caught everyone off guard. In roughly the exact time frame as Tom Pecora had signed a contract extension to remain at Hofstra, Capel had gone from recruiting for VCU to looking at real estate in Norman, Oklahoma.

Capel would make a base salary of $650,000 and coach in the Big 12. With incentives, Capel would sniff seven figures. Nobody would curse him for the move. In fact, VCU would bring Capel back for one more appearance. Two weeks after Capel became coach at Oklahoma, there was a university reception celebrating what he brought to VCU. The coach would choke up during his farewell speech.

Capel would face minor NCAA sanctions, a gift left by Sampson for extra phone calls made to recruits. Ironically, three members of the Sooners' heralded recruiting class would immediately opt to go elsewhere to play basketball.

VCU would hire Anthony Grant, Billy Donovan's top assistant at Florida, the same Gators team that solved George Mason in the national semifinals. Outgoing VCU AD Dick Sander would make it very clear that not only was Grant its first choice, but VCU's only choice. The elation and anticipation that went along with both hires was in sharp contrast to the bad taste left in the mouths at Delaware and UNCW.

That's not the lesson, however. The point is that VCU's "Villa Seven" model had once again worked to perfection; it had worked for its creator. In less than one week, VCU hired a new head coach. This would occur a few days after naming Norwood Teague its new athletics director. Both Teague and Grant had been deeply involved in Villa Seven.

In May 2006, the third Villa Seven Consortium meeting would occur on the Nike campus in Oregon. Its success was borne out in its own conference.

UNCW's Capaccio was a contributor to the Villa Seven meetings, and his new coach, Benny Moss, was on the "most wanted assistants" list. Ditto Anthony Grant and Monte Ross.

The 2006-2007 season got underway with a palpable anxiety: What would early season wins and losses mean in the big picture?

George Mason hung its Final Four banner, appropriately, prior to its home game against Wichita State. Though the Shockers gained a measure of revenge by defeating the Patriots that day was merely a mosquito bite on the tone of the day. There was reason to celebrate, and the Patriots did so in an appropriate fashion: no big speeches, just an appreciation of the accomplishments of a special team.

Though Old Dominion would travel to Washington, D.C., and knock off the eighth-ranked Georgetown Hoyas, the signature wins were escaping the conference. Likewise, bad losses were creeping up on them. Hofstra lost its first two games of the season to also shed its darling status. Drexel would drop a pair of winnable early-season contests.

It created an interesting perspective. One year ago, if the CAA could tout a road victory over the number eight team in the country and a victory over a Big 12 winner, as UNCW had accomplished over Colorado, people would be happy. There would be a refrain of "Boy, it would have been nice to get a win in those close losses," but nobody would panic.

However, in the aftermath of George Mason, Old Dominion, and Hofstra, it meant something different. Nobody yet knew what, but they knew there was a significance this season.

As for the players, they scattered far and wide. Mid-major stars increasingly find a professional career and riches playing in the fast-growing European leagues. The crop of players in the 2005-2006 CAA season were no different. In fact, they were the poster children of this growing phenomenon.

Most notably, George Mason's burly big man, Jai Lewis, would sign a contract with the New York Giants. Lewis has remarkably soft hands and agility that belies his frame—the combination made him a physically perfect tight end. After trying to make a go of it, Lewis eventually left camp and signed a contract to play basketball in Israel.

Lamar Butler took his sweet shooting stroke and memorable smile to play in Poland, and Tony Skinn signed in France.

John Goldsberry, the gritty playmaker and leader of the conference champs, UNCW, packed his bags for Germany. Nick George, VCU's bouncy front man from Manchester, England, headed to Italy. Aussie Alex Loughton, a four-year mainstay in Norfolk for Taylor, signed to play in Spain. Northeastern's Jose Juan Barea would sign with the Dallas Mavericks, and then make the team as a free agent.

Hofstra's star trio didn't go far—home. Loren Stokes, Antoine Agudio, and Carlos Rivera were all underclassmen and returned to Hempstead for the 2006-2007 season. Stokes was named the conference preseason player of the year, and Agudio also was named to its first team.

Seven CAA mainstays would be playing professionally in seven different countries, including the NBA. It was a tribute to the talent level and depth of the CAA. That Stokes, Agudio, and company would return only added to the story.

The conference moved on like time—it was business as usual. Old Dominion was having a banner season in baseball; the VCU women's tennis team was undefeated; and there were track and golf championships to be held. All needed appropriate attention and time, for all are part of the brand—even the gorilla called football, which was set to begin play in 2007.

The impact of George Mason's run to the final four, if it is even quantifiable, remains unclear. It may be years before the true impact of a Final Four run by a CAA school can be fully vetted.

Perhaps Yeager is correct. Though the conference's check from the NCAA basketball fund would nearly double, to $2.1 million, "the biggest thing," he says, "is that it provided credibility to the fan base of this league. For all of those fans that love their team but in the back of their mind wonder...it translates into a better belief." And that's the start.

Until true meaning could be gleaned, however, "moving on and moving up" would be the mantra. Although the conversations would be somewhat different, April of 2006 would look remarkably like April of 2005. Though the conference meetings would play out in Myrtle Beach and not Baltimore, they would talk about the same things. Coaches, old and new, would recruit. Players would work out. Ron Bertovich had a schedule to create. There was an opening in the Preseason NIT tournament next November and the committee was interested in a CAA team. (Ultimately UNCW got the invite.)

Though there remained a sense of anticipation, the tumult of 2005-2006 in the CAA was done. It was an odd paradox.

While those associated with the CAA could and should and did enjoy the moment, they also had a job to do. They faced a responsibility: George Mason, and really Old Dominion and Hofstra as well, proved that these are the kinds of things that happen when you take the time to build an athletics program properly. VCU was the model of how athletics departments should be run.

Unfathomable not only captures the amazing run of George Mason, but it also describes a season in the Colonial Athletic Association. Nearly two months after the conclusion of the amazing, exhilarating run, Yeager still became a tad misty-eyed when recalling the stories.

"There was nothing phony about them," said Yeager, shaking his head and staring into space, oddly using the very same word Taylor had used a year earlier in describing mediocre major conference teams. "Nobody stays in downtown [Indianapolis] during the Final Four. They did. Lamar Butler asked for his name card after an interview. Everybody jumped into it because it was such a magical story."

The CAA media day in October 2006 would come off magically. Media interest was exponential. For many reporters used to having their choice of coaches, it was culture shock to wait in line. The *USA Today* and *Washington Post* had reporters there. The buzz in the ESPN Zone in Washington, D.C., was palpable and positive.

Everyone knew the carrot was out there—what would 2006-2007 bring? The step forward for the conference was a giant step and a huge footprint. Everybody knew, though, that the "yesterday's news" syndrome loomed. Everybody also heeded the lesson: This is the pay-off. This is also merely step one.

Index

Acknowledgments

J ohn Feinstein, whose work I deeply admire, summed up these pages perfectly in his wonderful book about one season in the ACC, *A March to Madness*. Feinstein noted that he loved the acknowledgments, because "they give me the chance to remember the people I spent time with on a project, and to become nostalgic about a book that isn't even in bookstores yet."

How very true.

I'll never forget Tom Pecora offering me his own shoes so that this slob author would be appropriately dressed during a visit; or Jim Larranaga coming over to me and shaking my hand and saying hello as his Patriots entered the Verizon Center and prepared to play Wichita State in the Sweet 16; or Blaine Taylor's inability to hide near giddy excitement when we talked minutes before Old Dominion's very first practice of the season; or sitting in the stands at VCU's Siegel Center talking to Jeff Capel about what it's like being a young, African-American coach.

I can't even begin to describe the moments immediately following the buzzer ending in the George Mason/Connecticut game and being with Tom Yeager, Ron Bertovich, and Rob Washburn. There are so many moments, I could fill another book with those personal stories. It's that nostalgia Feinstein writes about and I feel this day. It makes me wonder what sitting at a 2006-2007 CAA game will be like.

For me, though, I most want to thank the people who believed in the project from its origin:

Dr. Richard Sander, the former athletics director at VCU, who didn't

laugh me out of his office when I presented him with this idea nearly two years prior to writing this section. It's no coincidence Dr.
Sander is listed first. When you talk of visionary leaders, he is near the
top of that list.

Rob Washburn from the CAA and Jeremy Kniffin from Hofstra, both
of whom took a chance based on one phone call and a Google search.

Matt Smith, a go-to guy in every respect.

All my friends and family, especially my sisters Kelly and Kimber
and my brother Robb, who, even if they didn't fully understand or
agree with what I was doing, supported me.

Mike Ellis, who I still count on for perspective and opinion. There
is a reason everybody who comes into contact with Mike both likes
and respects him.

There is no way I could write about mid-major basketball and not
thank Kyle Whelliston, especially for his, uh, input. This is really your
show, Kyle. Park in the garage next time. Ken Pomeroy was another
wonderful source of data and conversation.

The athletic directors, beyond Dr. Sander: Jack Hayes, Dr. Jim Jarrett,
Dr. Wayne Edwards (you're undefeated at home with me there),
Norwood Teague, and Tom O'Connor (you still need to mow my lawn).

The sports information folks, who also believed, beyond Jeremy
Kniffin: Phil Stanton, Carol Hudson, Richard Coco, Maureen Nasser,
Mike Tuberosa, Peter Schlehr, Mark Kwolek, Mark Harris, and Tina Price.

Folks at the CAA: Tom Yeager, Ron Bertovich, Rob Washburn (so
good he gets two mentions), Robert Goodman, and Tripp Sheppard. I
don't know if there is enough thanks to cover how good they were to
me in this entire process. It's beyond ridiculous.

All the folks at Villa Seven that didn't know me but were willing to
talk. The beat reporters who didn't shun the strange face and voice,
especially Rich Radford. While I was spending time thinking of the
perfect questions they were asking the necessary questions.

Major players: Jay Bilas, Craig Littlepaige, Dick Vitale, Seth Davis,
Joe Cantafio, Gregg Doyel, and Chris Dortsch.

The assistant coaches, always willing to tell me good times and bad times: Kevin Brooks, Rob Wilkes, Tom Parotta (good luck on a well-deserved new challenge), and David Duke. Assist to the Hofstra family (John Corso, Tim Paul, Mike Kelly) and VCU family (Andrew Hartley, B.J. Burton, John Slaughter).

Those who may not know it: Olive Thomas, Jerry Peters, John Feinstein, Larry Canale, Frank Finn, Ira Berkow, Skip Lindsay, Anto-NEE-o Jainez, Shelton King, Fred Jeter, Tom Comi, Dave Pierpont, Chris Metsala, Josh Holman, Mex Carey, Steve Rodeffer, Rick Childers, Bill Heffelfinger, Jonathan Williams, Gary Welch, Dale Duncan, Matt Josephs, Mitchell Bradley, Yoni Cohen, Gina Panettieri, J.D. Griff, Sam Albano, and Scott Lazear.

Those who know it but prefer to remain anonymous, and those whom I've shamefully omitted for no other reason than my memory is fading.

Special mention to the participants in Whitey Cup XIII and XIV, especially the executive committee of Kevin Rotty and Bart Nasta. The Oregon Hill Funk All-Stars and John Coltrane provided the mood for editing. Thai Garden and the Gold Ram get assists for helping the idea brew in my head.

Special thanks to the folks who directed traffic as best as possible. I know I wasn't the easiest: Dianne Long, Bev Hopcroft, Clarice Smith, Michele Cruey, and Ann Donohoe.

My editor, Peter Lynch, and the heroes at Sourcebooks. Thanks, Michael Ryder, Stephanie Wheatley, Tony Viardo, Heather Moore, and Anne Landa.

Finally my deepest and most heartfelt respect, thanks, and appreciation goes out to the coaches. This could not have happened without the incredible support and giving of time from these guys. Absolutely unreal. I learned that they put up with far more than anyone would believe, and I tried to respect that fact. Hopefully I was successful.

Here's to you Tom Pecora, Blaine Taylor, Jeff Capel, Jim Larranaga, Pat Kennedy, and Bruiser Flint. I wish all of you success in everything you do.

About the Author

Photo by Kathleen Baber

Michael Litos spent the first eight years of his career as a magazine writer and editor for several sports and sports memorabilia titles with Landmark Communications. He has interviewed sports celebrities from Mickey Mantle to Alex Rodriguez to Brett Favre. He's been quoted on multiple occasions in *USA Today* and once received a personal letter of appreciation from Chris Berman of ESPN. He lives in Richmond, Virginia.

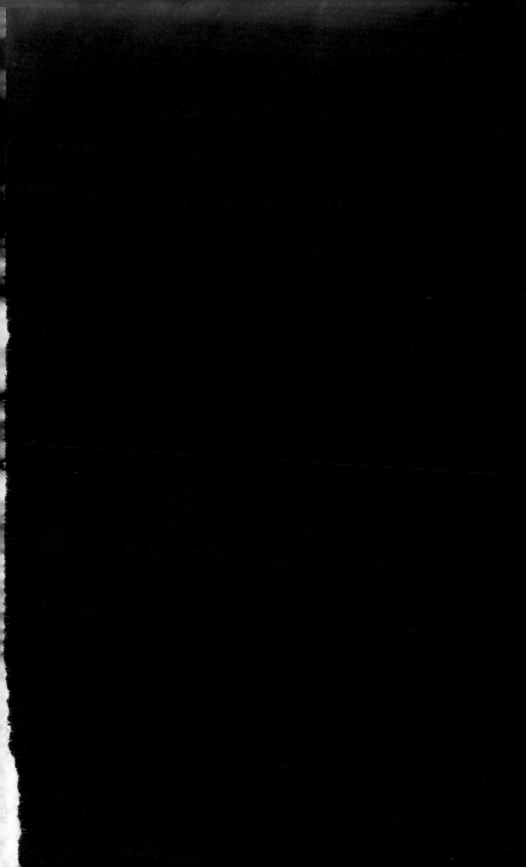